FUNDAMENTALS OF EXTENSION EDUCATION AND MANAGEMENT IN EXTENSION

About the Author

Dr. K.A. Jalihal (born on 3rd April 1927), B.Sc.(Agri.)., M.S. (USA), Ph.D. (USA), started his career as a Lecturer in Agronomy, Agricultural College, Dharwad in 1947 and has subsequently worked as (a) Superintendent of Agricultural School, (b) Assistant Professor of Agronomy in Pune Agricultural College, (c) Head of the Tobacco Research Station at Nippani, Belgaum district, and (d) Professor of Agronomy & Extension in the Hebbal Agricultural College. He was the first Registrar of UAS, Bangalore in 1965 and then worked as a Professor and Head, Department of Agricultural Extension from 1966 to 1975. For a period of 12 years, he worked as Director of Extension. He has published more than 100 research papers and book entitled, "Pragmatic Rural Development for Poverty Alleviation" published in 2003 by the Concept Publishing Company, New Delhi.

After retirement, he has worked as Evaluation Committee Member of the Indian Council of Agricultural Research, New Delhi for reviewing the work of Watershed Development Programmes in the entire country. He was one of the members of the Government of India Team on Bhutan to develop an agricultural development programme for that country. He also worked as the Consultant for the National Council of Applied Economic Research.

Dr. V. Veerabhadraiah (born on the 5th May 1945) has served in various capacities in the UAS, Bangalore as Instructor, Assistant Professor, Associate Professor, Professor, Regional Co-ordinator of National Demonstration Project of ICAR, Head of the Department in Agricultural Extension and Director of Extension. He is currently serving as the Emeritus Scientist in Agricultural Extension of the ICAR at UAS, Bangalore. Dr. Veerabhadraiah has published 200 papers and three books. He is a fellow of the Indian Society of Extension Education and recipient of O.P. Dahama Memorial Award for excellent achievement in extension teaching and training and also recipient of G.S. Vidyarthi Award for excellence in field of extension work. Also, he was a member of the Scientific Panel on Extension of the ICAR.

Fundamentals of Extension Education and Management in Extension

Dr. K.A. Jalihal
Former Director of Extension and Dean, UAS, Bangalore

Dr. V. Veerabhadraiah
Emeritus Scientist (Agril. Extension) of ICAR
and
Ex-Director of Extension, UAS, Bangalore

CONCEPT PUBLISHING COMPANY, NEW DELHI-110059

Cataloging in Publication Data—DK
Courtesy: D.K. Agencies (P) Ltd. <docinfo@dkagencies.com>

Jalihal, K. A., 1927-
Fundamentals of extension education and management in extension/ K.A. Jalihal, V. Veerabhadraiah.
p. cm.
Includes bibliographical references.
Includes index.
ISBN 8180693481

1. Agricultural extension work—India. 2. Rural extension—India—Management. I. Veerabhadraiah, V., 1945-, joint author. II. Title.

DDC 630.715 095 4 22

ISBN: 81-8069-348-1 (HB)

First Published 2007

Published and Printed by
Ashok Kumar Mittal
Concept Publishing Company,
A/15-16, Commercial Block, Mohan Garden,
New Delhi-110059 (INDIA)

Phones : 25351460, 25351794
Fax : 091-11-25357103
Email : publishing@conceptpub.com

Preface

Extension Education is not merely providing out of school education to people to help them to develop but also to take the systems from the field of extension management to strengthen the effectiveness of extension work. This is particularly so in implementing agricultural programmes in the rural areas.

The general thinking in the country is that agriculture has not developed in particular areas because of lack of resources, namely men and materials. However, mere provision of these resources will not automatically lead to progress in agriculture. The most important missing link is the vital management input which has not received attention all these years. In USA, agricultural development was rapidly achieved because of investment in management inputs.

Another component needed for improvement in implementing agricultural programmes is to find out practical approaches which are possible and feasible without involving too much additional money investments. The available empirical data on these aspects needs to be studied and suitable recommendations are included in the literature.

While writing this book, the above mentioned points have been given due attention. Accordingly this book is slightly different from the traditional books on Extension Education. The book has been written mostly by using information already written by both the authors during last 30-40 years. Various organizations who sponsored the writings of both the authors are mentioned below.

The Extension Education Department and the Agricultural Education Department of the University of Tennessee, Knoxville, USA provided opportunities to the senior Author when he was a student for M. S. degree in 1959-60 to write term papers on selected topics related to extension education, adult education, extension programme planning and role of extension subject matter specialists. Most of the material of these term papers have been used in writing the first part of this book. When the senior author was a Ph.D. student at the University of Wisconsin, Madison, USA during 1967-68, he contributed term papers on Local Leaders' Role in extension, Leadership qualities and extension training". These term papers helped in writing Chapters 2, 8 and 10 of the book. When Dr. Jalihal was a Ph.D. student for two years at the Division of Agricultural Extension, IARI, New Delhi during 1968-70, he contributed term paper on the concept of extension which helped to write the chapter 1 of this book. A special paper on "Motivating Rural Communities for Action" was prepared by the senior author on a request made by Indian Social Sciences Research Council, New Delhi in 1973 which material was used in writing chapter 3.

The senior author also attended an International Seminar organized by the Food Institute, East-West Centre, Hawaii, USA on "Implementing Public Programmes in Agriculture", which was held in May 1976. He contributed a paper on "Block Demonstrations" to the seminar group. Very useful seminar class materials were supplied to all participants. The information from these materials came handy to write chapter 11, which topic is included for the first time in extension literature.

In writing chapter 7 on "Functions of Management in Extension" contributed by second author Dr. V. Veerabhadraiah, the State Department of Agriculture assisted him by giving special assignment to deliver series of lectures and also to bring out a special booklet on the topics covered during the lectures.

It is, therefore, necessary for the authors of this book to express sincere gratitude to all the above mentioned organizations for providing initiative, support and technical guidance which enabled the authors to undertake intensive library research in preparing these papers.

The authors are grateful to many extension scientists—Dr. A.G. Sawant, former Vice-Chancellor, BSKKV, Dapoli, Maharashtra and former member, ASRB, ICAR, New Delhi; Dr. B.S. Hansra, Joint Director of Extension, IARI, New Delhi and former Assistant Director General (Extension), ICAR, New Delhi and Dr. G. Eswarappa, In-charge Director of Extension, UAS, Bangalore for their interest and encouragement in the preparation of the book. The authors profusely thank Sri. Ranganath Mangalvedkar, Associate Professor, Dr. K.N. Ramanna, Professor, Dr. T.N. Anand, Editor, Sri N. Rajanna, Associate Professor, Sri B.R. Chandrashekar,

Personal Secretary and Smt. K. Nagamani, Senior Assistant, Directorate of Extension, UAS, Bangalore and Smt. K.R. Dinamani, Retd. Personal Secretary, UAS, GKVK for extending various types of assistance in the preparation of the book.

The authors express their gratitude to M/s. Concept Publishing Company, New Delhi, who made frequent enquiries at the time of preparation of the manuscript and for neatly publishing the book.

Bangalore
15th August, 2005

K. A. Jalihal
V. Veerabhadraiah

Contents

PART – II
MANAGEMENT IN EXTENSION

PART – I
FUNDAMENTALS OF EXTENSION EDUCATION

1

Extension, Agricultural Extension and Adult Education

1.1 ORIGIN OF EXTENSION

The term, "Extension Education" was used for the first time in England in 1873, when it was referred to teaching activities of the universities outside their campuses. It was, therefore, of "Extension" of the University – Extension of its teaching functions away from its campus locations. Further, the same university staff who taught at the campuses served as Extension teachers outside the campus. When it was started, Extension not only dealt with agriculture but any subject matter, like science, health etc. Thus, the University Extension went to people where they lived and worked.

In USA, the term Agricultural Extension was first used in 1894 by E.B. Vorhees of New Jersey, who presented this subject as "The attitude of the college towards University Extension". He described what he said they were calling agricultural extension work which began in New Jersey in year or two previously and which consisted of lectures on (1) soils and crops, (2) feeding plants, (3) animal nutrition etc. Short courses were held in seven different towns in the state and such was the beginning of organized work with the name that was later to become a special department of every land grant college of USA.

In 1905, Kenyon L. Butterfield recommended to the standing committee on Extension work be appointed in association of Agricultural Colleges. This standing committee submitted a report to the Country Life Commission urging the need for organized attack on the educational problem in the country. This report concluded as follows:

> "To accomplish these ends we suggest the establishment of a nation-wide extension work. The first or original work of the agricultural branches of the land grant colleges was academic, in the old sense; later there was added the great field of experiment and research; there now should be added the third coordinate branch comprising extension work, without which no college of agriculture can adequately serve its state. It is to the extension department of these colleges that we must now look for the most effective rousing of the people of the land."

Another development as part of extension work, beginning was seen by establishing Seed Corn Trains organized by Prof. Holden in Iowa State of USA which was one of the first effort to reach large number of farmers for the two years 1904 and 1905, the seed corn Trains made it possible for the college to present the message of better seed at 1235 meetings reaching 145,363 people in 10,000 miles of travel. Around 200,000 copies of Bulletin 77 of the Iowa College on the selection and care of seed corn were distributed (Bliss *et al.*, 1952).

In 1903, Dr. Seaman A. Knapp of Lousiana State proposed to establish a demonstration farm under the Department of Agriculture in farmers' fields provided community would select a suitable place and raised sufficient amount to cover any losses that might be sustained by the owner and operate around the farm by reason of following directions of the department in the matter of planting and cultivation. This was the beginning of the farmers' co-operative demonstration work (Bliss *et al.*, 1952).

Dr. Knapp's philosophy was, agricultural conditions can be changed by demonstrations and not by simply talking.

In the USA, extension work in agriculture took its firm roots in 1914 with the passage of Smith-Lever Act which established Co-operative Agricultural Extension work in Land Grant institutes and the Act provided the following (Knapp, S.A., 1952):

> "In order to aid in diffusing among the people of the United States useful and practical information on subjects relating to agriculture and home economics, and to encourage the application of the same, there may be continued or inaugurated in connection with the college or colleges in each

State, Territory, or Possession, now receiving or which may hereafter receive, the benefits of the Morrill Land Grant College Act of 1862 and of the Morrill College Endowment Act of 1890, agricultural extension work which shall be carried on in cooperation with the United States Department of Agriculture.

Cooperative agricultural extension work shall consist of giving of the instruction and practical demonstrations in agriculture and home economics and subjects relating there to persons not attending or resident in said colleges in the several communities, and imparting information on said subjects through demonstrations, publications, and otherwise, and for the necessary printing and distribution of information in connection with the foregoing; and this work shall be carried on in such a manner as may be mutually agreed upon by the Secretary of Agriculture and the State Agricultural College or Colleges receiving the benefits of this Act."

The basic fields of work were agriculture and home economics, in which men, women, boys and girls participate.

Origin of Extension Work in India

It was Mahatma Gandhi in the 1920s, who promoted the concept of Village Development by what he called establishment of Rama Rajya (Mukherjee, 1962). He initiated what he called as constructive programme "Rebuild the life of countryside" on which he laid too much stress and which he made an integral part of his philosophy of non-violence – struggle for freedom. The principal plans of this programme were (1) Communal unity, (2) Removal of untouchability, (3) Prohibition of liquor, (4) Use of Khadi, (5) Promotion of village industries, (6) Uplift of under-privileged classes and women, (7) Full development and utilization of local resources, (8) Promotion of economic equality, (9) Self-sufficient village economy, (10) Self-reliant village community.

Gandhi's ideas were well perceived by Rabindranath Tagore, later called, what is known as "Sriniketan Experience". He was inspired by Gandhiji's ideals and started village reconstruction work in selected villages. It was at the time when nobody bothered about the villages and villagers. Tagore's ideas were always to illustrate a few basic principles by giving a confidence of a few villages at first. Once villagers found that they could stand on their own feet, once they had confidence and followed to progress, they were more able to say, when they needed professional back up even though we were not always equipped to give it.

During the same period when Rabindranath Tagore carried out village work in Sriniketan, two more extension projects were in operation, one in Kerala located at Marthandam in old Cochin State popularly known as Marthandam Project. The second work was in Gurgaon district in Punjab popularly called as Gurgaon Project which was headed by Mr. Brayne who was the District Collector at that time.

The Marthandam Project was headed by Dr. Spencer Hatch and associated with local YMCA. The important lesson drawn from Marthandam Project was that demonstrations should be conducted by farmers on their own fields, if they have to learn new ideas. The development work which was taken up under the programme, covered (1) Institutional work, (2) Rural sanitation, (3) Agricultural development, (4) Education, (5) Cooperation, (6) Social reforms, (7) Coordination and Publicity.

During 1930s and 1940s, some more exploratory extension projects were taken up in the then states of Baroda, Madras and Uttar Pradesh. Based upon their experience, the pattern of extension service was primarily based on the work of Ittawah, Pilot Project of Uttar Pradesh. During the First Five-Year Plan Period, a pioneering National Extension Service (NES) was initiated in 1953. The Pilot projects were taken up, which were later expanded on a nationwide basis. The Community Development Programme included multi-subject matter extension work in the fields of agricultural science, home sciences, social education, industries, panchayats, co-operation, animal husbandry etc. with evolution of community development programme in India in 1952.

1.2 THE CONCEPT OF EXTENSION

The meaning of the term, Extension as used in this book, is not the same as the literal meaning of this term as commonly given in the Dictionary. Our view of the concept of extension is a system of education for development. Even with this connotation, the term extension is in usage for over 150 years in the world and over 50 years in India. It is, however, curious to know that even today the meaning of extension still continues to be understood in different ways. Recently the term "extension education" is also being used primarily to refer to developmental education while the term "extension" is many times used more or less synonymous to the term development. Since this will create confusion regarding meaning of extension, it is better to use extension only as related to developmental education. Hence, from this point of view, it is desirable not to make any distinction between the term extension or extension education. It is also necessary to use the term development for the wider process that also includes extension as one of its components. The other components that are involved in the process of development can be broadly stated as (1) Supplies, (2) Services, (3) Credit, and (4) Organization.

Based on this consideration, the distinction between extension and development can be diagrammatically shown as follows:

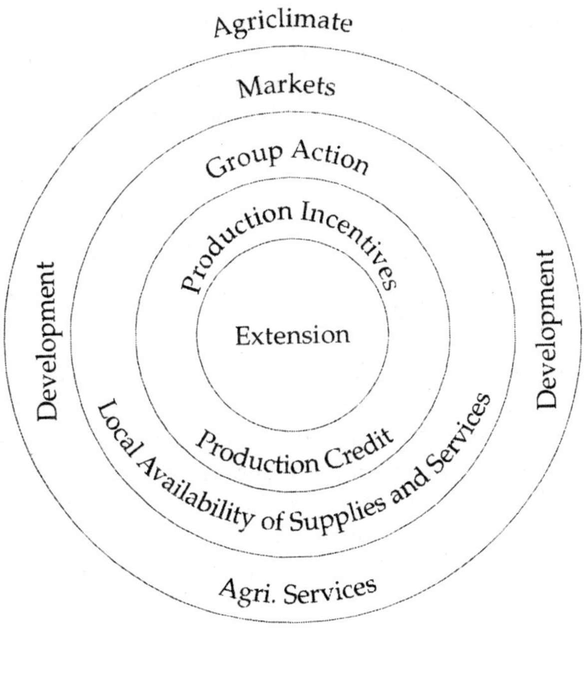

Relation of Extension to Development

The terms, 'Extension' and 'Development' are not really one and the same since they carry distinct meanings. In spite of this, many a time people wrongly understand them as the same. Development of any area or people must be recognized as a wider concept, which makes use of extension as one of its many components. In other words, development requires more than merely an educational programme although extension has to play a pivotal educational role in development. Besides extension, there are other equally important components, which are needed for development.

This relationship of extension to development has been brought out clearly by the UNESCO while discussing the role of community development in the following words:

> "In relation to the people, community development is essentially both an educational and an organizational process. It is organizational as it involves group action on the parts of people in the pursuit of common interest and also it brings about revival of existing institutions and creation of new ones. Secondly, various forms of assistance are required. These include the technical advice, technical assistance, help with equipment, organization of supplies, and provision of credit or grants in aid."

For the present times the words "community development" mentioned above can be replaced by rural development.

Components of Extension

The concept of extension should be understood in relation to its two components, namely (1) The Essence, and (2) The Form. To study the Forms of extension without understanding its Essence, generally leads to confusion. The essential feature of the extension process and its other essential components together constitutes what is called the Essence of Extension.

The Form of Extension refers to the way in which the extension system operates, i.e. how its different components are organized.

The Essence of Extension

There are four aspects of Essence of Extension as stated by Mosher. These are: (1) Essential features, (2) Specialized educational process, (3) Supporting activity, and (4) Creed.

1. Essential Features

These describe how extension differs from other kinds of education like regular school education and adult education. Some basic ideas which describe the essential feature of extension can be listed as under:

(a) *Extension is solely an educational process*: There is no difference of opinion on this idea, although in India we many a time use other developmental activities like supplies, services, credit, etc. as a part of extension. Two statements from noted authorities need careful attention in this regard. These are:

(i) "Extension is simply a word we use to indicate the whole complex of activities that enter into a programme that is educational in its philosophy, its focus, its objectives and its methods."
—Edmund Des Brunner (1945)

(ii) "The Extension process is one of the education. Any method or activity which is not education is not part of the extension process, no matter how essential it may be and even though it may be carried on within what is called an extension service, perhaps even by the same personnel."
—A.T. Mosher (1958)

(b) *Extension has to be taken to the people*: In regular or formal school type education, the people who are to be educated generally go to school, colleges, or teaching institutions and enroll and get educated. However, in extension by and large people who are to be educated cannot go to places like schools etc. for getting education. It is the extension which has to go to the people wherever they are to be educated. This idea can be illustrated by the following simple line drawing.

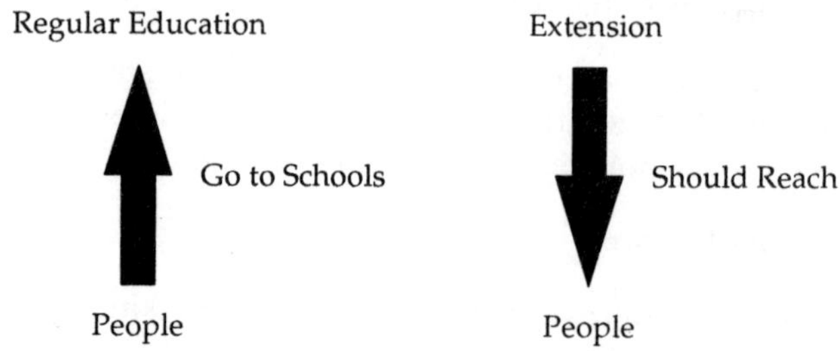

All characteristics we generally talk about extension like informal, voluntary, out of school, large clienteles, problem-oriented etc. can be deduced from this basic idea. Two statements are relevant in this regard:

(i) "A unique fact about it (extension) is that it was the nation's first organized system of education designed and operated to teach people where they live and work, how to do a better job of what they are doing".

—P.O. Davis (1952)

(ii) "This is extension work by which is meant all kinds of educational efforts, directly with people, both old and young, at their homes, and on their farms; it comprises all educational work that is conducted away from the institution and for those who cannot go to schools and colleges".

—Country Life Commission, USA

(c) *Extension has specially established organization*: This means that only that part of out of school system of education carried out by a specially created agency to do is called extension. Legans pleads in this connection by stating:

"Institutions for promoting change have to be established and operated effectively to activate the dormant powers of people and to guide their aroused desires towards social and economic improvements".

The extension organisation may be established by Government or by a University or even by any private association or agency.

(d) Extension is a part of adult education as well as different from it.

This idea can be pictorially shown as follows:

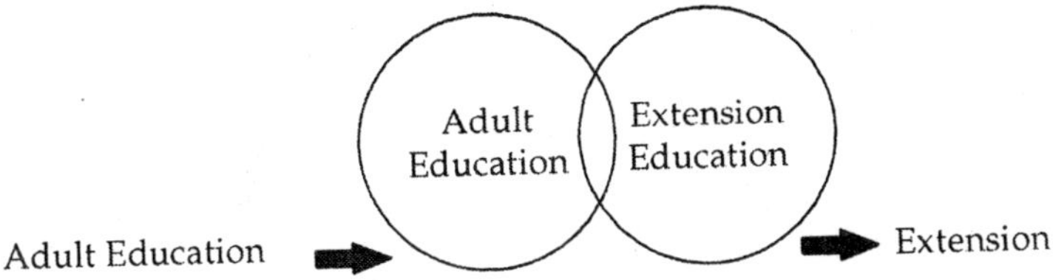

Adult education also known as continuing education has objectives similar to extension. Adult education, however as the name implies, is primarily concerned with adults, while extension clientele also includes youth. Another major distinction between adult education and extension is that, extension is invariably a specified agency sponsored programme as discussed earlier. Adult education, on the other hand, is concerned of several organizations and institutions both government and private including business and industry.

(e) Extension is interested in changing actions of people. Even regular school type education is interested in bringing about changes in the behaviour of people like knowledge, skills and attitudes. In extension, besides bringing about changes in the behaviour of people, we are equally interested in bringing about changes in actions of people. This phenomenon necessitates distinct approach to the formulation of extension principles and use of extension methods and technique which are again special to extension.

2. *Specialized Educational Process*

Since extension involves the establishment of relationship for learning between an extension worker and people primarily in out of school situations, the ways in which these relationships are established become important. According to Rogers and Shoemaker, diffusion which is the central theme of extension is in essence a special kind of communication interested not only in bringing about changes of knowledge, skills and attitudes but also a further change of overt behaviour. For this to happen it is necessary that the combinations of teaching methods and techniques to be used in extension must be woven around the basal methods and techniques which provide confidence building situation.

3. Supporting Operations

There are five activities which may be called supporting operations to extension. These are (1) provision of subject matter specialists, (2) preparation of a work plan. (3) preparation of calendar of events, (4) planning for in-service training, and (5) planning for evaluation.

These supporting operations get more formal as extension programme gets bigger and older but they are present atleast informally or even unconsciously in the extension process at all the times. No doubt these supporting operations if properly carried out increase the efficiency of the teaching activities by extension workers but they are no substitute for them. They must remain behind the scene. A word more about specialist role is necessary. Research tested subject matter is extension's food.

Extension workers are required to possess some research knowledge before they join the extension service through pre-service training. They gain some more by some induction training before they start working. But that is not the end of the story. New knowledge continues to develop through research. How can this new knowledge be made available to extension workers. Research people themselves can contribute in this connection but their direct contribution will not be adequate. There is a need of specialized people to bridge the gap between research and extension. These are the subject matter specialists. So provision of subject matter specialists is a part of the essence of extension. How they are provided is not important as long as they perform their functions satisfactorily.

4. Creed

Extension is a profession. One of the distinguishing characteristics of any profession is the zeal, enthusiasm and the readiness to serve the individual community at large. Albert Mayer (1949) calls this as the morale. While the Allahabad Extension Workers term it as Creed. Confidence in the ability and judgment of people on the part of extension workers is a part of Essence of extension. Where this confidence does not exist it must be earned by extension workers through integrity and devoted service.

The Form of Extension

As already defined, this term is used in this discussion to mean organization. One point to be recognized in relation to this dimension is that, "In every country where extension work is in progress, its various aspects demonstrate the value and necessity of adapting methods and structure to local conditions."

Three major aspects which account for the variation in different forms of Extension work can be listed as:

(1) The kind of agency doing Extension work,
(2) Subject matter areas handled by the agency, and
(3) The kind of worker system. These are discussed as follows:

1. Form as Related to the Kind of Agency

We are here concerned with the type of agency doing extension work. According to D. Franco, an international seminar group has concluded that there are four major types of agencies doing extension work:

(a) Educational Institutions or universities, e.g. U.S.A. and Scotland.
(b) Straightline administration from one government ministry, e.g. Japan, U.K., Germany, Netherlands.
(c) Cooperative approach through participation of more than one ministry of government, India's Community Development Extension Work till Agricultural Universities were established.
(d) Extension through non-governmental societies – e.g. Denmark

There are also many variations to the types quoted above. The form now emerging in India after the establishment of Agricultural Universities is a variant of these types as under the new type both the government departments and the university will be cooperating. The main concern relating to the agency is not whether one type is superior to the other but as Sanders says, "its form of organization is important only as it expedites or hinders achievement of educational objectives."

2. Form Based on Subject Matter Areas Handled

According to subject matter areas handled by Extension agencies, five major patterns are seen: (a) Agricultural Extension, (b) Extension work in agriculture, Home Economics and Youth work, (c) General Extension, (d) Multi-subject matter extension, and (e) The new university extension. Some detailed description of these forms is given as under:

(a) *Agricultural Extension*: Here the extension service is only interested to promote educational programme in the field of Agriculture, e.g. Agricultural Advisory Services of the European countries.

(b) *Extension Work in Agriculture, Home Economics and Youth Work*: The attention here is on three broad areas, e.g. Coop. Extension Service of the USA. Agricultural Extension service of Japan and Extension Work in Scandinavian countries.

(c) *General Extension*: The term refers to the Extension work mostly in non-agricultural subject matter areas handled by universities. This is also known as the 'Extra mural· programme'. It is in this form that Extension took its birth as a distinct educational system associated with a specific organization when the term Extension was first coined by the Oxford Commission in 1850. According to Allen, "General Extension is the instrument by which education in fields other than Agriculture and Home Economics is brought to adults by Land Grant or any other type of University". This general extension differs from other forms in that as Reber says, "for many years since its beginning this general extension work was carried on without any distinct organisation for its operation". Almost all universities in India have some kind of this general Extension work.

(d) *Multi-subject matter Extension*: Under this form, many subject matter area including Agriculture are handled by the same Extension agency, e.g. Community Development Extension work in most of the underdeveloped countries. The philosophy behind this approach is spelled out by the Indian Grow-More-Food

Enquiry Committee Report of 1952 in the following words:

> "The economic aspects of village life cannot be detached from the broader social aspects; and agricultural improvement is inextricably linked up with a whole set of social problems. That all aspects of rural life are inter-related and that no lasting results can be achieved if individual aspects of it are dealt with in isolation."

Taylor *et al.* state that giving priority to the most important subject matter area is an accepted philosophy under this multi-subject matter approach.

(e) *The New-university Extension*: This is the latest in Extension's subject matter approach and can be called multi-subject matter approach. This form has taken shape very recently in some of the U.S. Universities of California and Wisconsin. This form is meant to handle all conceivable subject matter areas that a well-developed university of the American Land Grant type is dealing. It combines the General Extension and Extension work in Agriculture, Home Economics and youth work together with the communication media like Radio and T.V. under one unified Extension organization of the university. The philosophy behind this joint programme is explained as follows:

> "University as an educational institute has a variety of resources and authoritative personnel and a wealth of technical knowledge and this expertness can influence the social, economic and educational status of people in a society. These educational resources should not be limited to the process of educating only the young in a traditional way but should be extended beyond the boundary of the University to the entire State. Educational Institutions must occupy a very dynamic place in the society and must play an active role in the efforts of the society in analyzing problems that exist and in providing solutions to these problems, Educational institution are not isolated from the society."

3. Form as Related to the Extension Worker System

This describes the number of workers, distribution of clientele area and the subject-matter they deal with. Two main forms are identified under this heading: (a) Specialized Extension worker system, and (b) Multi-purpose worker system.

(a) *Specialized Extension Worker System*: In this worker system, one Extension worker is generally not required to handle educational work in many areas, e.g. In the U.S. Coop. Extension service, there are separate Extension Agents for Agriculture, Home Economics, Youth work etc. In this system the clientele area per worker will be usually large. According to Kelse and Hearne, "the expansion or maintenance of various types of work or the use of specialized country worker is a matter of state policy, available finances and administrative procedure." Sanders states that "the continued strengthening of subject matter oriented programmes in this specialized arrangement provided the framework for developing a segmented clientele."

(b) *Multipurpose Worker System*: In this system, a single Extension worker is required to be responsible for educational work in different subject matter areas like Agriculture, Animal husbandry, Rural industry, Public health, Social education etc. This system was an innovation introduced by the Etawah Pilot Project, India. In explaining this concept, Mayer (1949) says:

> "At the village level, advice and help in agriculture, animal husbandry and public health are not very technical. It has been found that one worker backed up by available personnel at a higher technical level can do agricultural demonstrations, animal husbandry inoculations and human vaccinations, help with insect control and anti-malaria work and help to organize simple public works by the people. Being multipurpose, he needs to cover fewer villages. In other words, he visits and works in the villages of his circle frequently enough so that he becomes well known and well recognized and well received."

According to Mosher (1958), the multipurpose system requires many more Extension agents within a given geographical area and much more frequent personal contact among people. He further explains that this multipurpose concept should not be literally understood as tackling all educational activities in different subject matter areas at one and the same time. Taylor (1967) *et al.* explain this idea by saying, "Each V.L.W. was to be a multipurpose worker; giving more attention to agriculture than any other special field, but neglecting no technical aid programme which any self-help organized group in any one of the 15 pilot project areas might request."

To sum up we can define extension as follows:

> "Extension is purely an educational profession undertaken largely in out of school situation and aimed at teaching people both adults and young in their own location by a specialized agency having field workers and specialists working in cooperation; this teaching is further dependent on extension's own educational process which is organized and operated in a planned way in order to promote desirable changes in the lives of people by diffusing the scientific knowledge and encouraging its application by people's action.

1.3 WHAT IS AGRICULTURAL EXTENSION?

There are various views about the meaning of agricultural extension. Some people plead that because agricultural extension organization has got experts to deal with agricultural extension, organizations should plan programme for farmers to utilize this expertise. Many others have the feeling that because agricultural extension organization is highly competitive one, there is no harm if agricultural extension organization can dictate the farmers what should be done to improve agriculture. Another view is that because agricultural development requires a number of services, the job of field extension workers should include providing all of these services at the field level. They, however, agree that 75-80 per cent of the time of the field agricultural extension workers should be devoted to educate farmers on agriculture.

In view of these above-mentioned interpretations of agricultural extension job, it is necessary to analyze these viewpoints and arrive at the correct meaning of the term agricultural extension.

Those pleading that agricultural extension organization should plan programmes for the farmers and leave only to carry out these plans by the farmers should first ask for themselves the following questions.

1. Have not all of us in our earlier years been untrained and uneducated?
2. We believe to dictate plans to the farmers without giving them a chance to know better technological methods and give them an opportunity of doing what they themselves think as the best?

Do we deny the fact that farmers who have cultivated agriculture over a period of years know more about the requirements of agriculture as compared to the so called experts who are located in offices away from the rural areas? Then again, who is more capable of developing a sufficiently flexible programme that would take care of the different conditions found on different farms such as the rainfall received, facilities available for irrigation, market changes encountered and the varying requirements of operating capital as well as variations in the acreage of farming managed by different farmers. When we consider all these questions, we will agree that farmers themselves are the most competent persons to prepare their own plans, of course with the assistance of the field extension workers of the agricultural extension service.

Regarding the second viewpoint that agricultural extension organization should dictate farmers what should be done by them is it in line with the democratic philosophy, which has been accepted in our country in preference to the authoritarian angle. In a democratic set up it is the farmers who are masters of the land and what should be done by them to develop the agriculture instead of some outsiders like agricultural extension workers who have no share in the form of property to tell them what they should do.

The other point suggested that agricultural extension workers should provide all services required by farmers by the agricultural extension organizations, have not imagined how these added responsibilities come in the way of performing these primary tasks of educating farmers about developing agriculture by using new technologies. Is it, therefore, not logical to delegate different responsibilities to different organizations to provide these various services required by farmers? In this connection, we might agree that since all of these seem to be equally important, the agricultural extension workers besides shouldering the main responsibility of educating farmers as their legitimate function can act as nodal persons to help farmers to get other services needed by contacting the other organizations entrusted with those responsibilities. This is what is called as "Rural Vacuum" theory in extension work (Mosher, 1978).

In the ultimate analysis we will then agree that the primary function of agricultural extension in all democratic countries of the world is to educate farmers to help themselves.

Differences between Extension Education and Regular School Type Education

1. In extension education extension educators have to go to the people wherever they are located. In the regular education, however, the schools are functioning and the students have to enroll in the schools and go to the schools for getting education.
2. In extension education it is the farmer who is the master of the situation and is free to decide whether or not he should benefit from the education that has been given by the field extension workers. This, we call it as voluntary type of education.
3. In extension teaching the focus has to be given on problem solving to help farmers to get rid of those problems. The extension education has to be problem oriented and not any prescribed curricular oriented.
4. In extension education there is no place for teaching the theoretical aspects relating to a practice but what is important is to help the people in understanding practical methods and procedures to solve these problems. For example, farmer's crops are infested with disease or insects want knowledge of specific information as to what they should do to kill the insects or combat the disease and also know how to carry out these remedial practices. The relevant theoretical know-how can be given later on to the farmers when they are not so busy with their crops.

5. In extension education, felt needs of farmers have to be tackled first by ascertaining those felt needs by extension workers. There might be some more problems as perceived by the extension workers but these have to wait till they become felt needs of the farmers. In extension teaching successful completion of the project taken on hand is very important to develop security on the part of farmers. Thus the old proverb "nothing succeeds like success" is more relevant in extension education.
6. In extension education, learning by the rural people will have to be horizontal as compared to the vertical type of learning observed in school type education where it is primarily the teacher who hands over information to the students. Farmers who participate in extension education also learn from one another and experience is the best teacher. It should be 'farmer teaches farmer' and extension worker has only to play the role as a catalytic agent.
7. In extension we cannot apply yesterday's methods today and be in business tomorrow. As we solve old problems, new problems will appear which require a revision of our methods. This will necessitate that extension worker should be in constant touch with the agricultural educational institutes and the research stations to know up to date methods to solve various problems of farmers. Thus, there will be two-way channel to establish in extension: (i) to take the solutions to solve the problems already worked out, and (ii) to communicate new problems of farmers to be communicated to research staff for further solutions. In this task, the extension field workers should be encouraged to consult their former professors/scientists concerning any problem, which they do not know how to solve. Frequent contacts of the extension workers with other colleagues and with the college and research stations should become a regular practice with them. In turn, the colleges and research stations should pay immediate attention to the problems brought to them by the extension workers from the field. Thus, the field extension workers bring the current problems of the farmers to be considered for solution

and carry back the latest findings from Agricultural research for the benefit of farmers.

8. Agricultural extension cannot be a success unless voluntary leaders are involved in the process of extension education. It should be clearly understood that there would never be adequate number of field extension workers for carrying out effective extension work with the farmers. Extension work can be multiplied several fold when local leaders are identified, trained and used in extension work. The number of local leaders to be used varies depending upon the particular stage of the extension and also how well the leaders are trained and how much time they can devote for the welfare of the farmers in the community.

Extension Workers Training

The key to the progress of agricultural extension organization in India depends on how the extension workers are satisfactorily trained and also on the earnest and conscientious work devoted by them. The field extension workers can be trained by the Agricultural College Staff/University staff who in turn should be in close contact with the research stations. Training in extension methods though important cannot be the only pedagogical aim since a good field extension worker must be a well rounded individual who should be familiar with the various aspects of agricultural sciences which should include different subject matter areas like plant and soil sciences, animal husbandry, agricultural economics including co-operation and marketing, agricultural engineering, insect and pest control as well as a fundamental knowledge of related basic sciences such as chemistry, botany, plant pathology, entomology etc. Agricultural extension programme has been established in India because it is necessary to increase the yield of crops and livestock as well as to help farmers in developing knowledge of proper marketing and to show them how they can use co-operative work to their advantage so as to assist in increasing their income. Ultimately the desired end should aim at improving the standards of living for farmers and their families. If this is not reflected, then the main objective of extension work has not been fulfilled.

The greatest job of field extension workers in agriculture is not to teach the people what to think but instead how to think. In a democratic country, it is necessary to see that farmers are trained to think for themselves and to become sufficiently independent to able to solve their important problems. In training extension workers, the teachers must have their own scope broadened. They should not limit their thinking to the four walls of the college classroom. He will read widely, become familiar with important current issues, regional problems, national trends and even international developments. A good extension teacher should be a frequent visitor to the villages. In this connection, we should remember what Gandhiji said, namely "to know India, we must know the villages".

Lastly, a good teacher or extension worker should remember that change is the basis for growth. As conditions change, the material for teaching extension should likewise be revised so as to include up to date information. Good teaching should reflect on active process of learning. It should never be static. It can only survive through new thoughts, new illustrative material, new approaches and new challenging questions put before the learners. It should not be taught as a memory course but as one that teaches the learners to think. This should remain as the real purpose of education. It should be remembered that learners retain only few of the facts they learn through education. The real objective of teaching is to help the learners in acquiring principles and ideas that will remain stable in the mind through the years.

In sum, we should remember what Karl Pearson expressed several years ago which is as follows:

> "I have no recollection of atleast 90 per cent of the facts that were taught in school but the nations which are derived remain in my mind as the really valuable part of my school equipment for life."

1.4 ADULT EDUCATION: OBJECTIVES AND PURPOSES

Why adult education? This is a common question posed by many persons. The following three statements have tried to answer this question.

Thorndike (1935) rightly makes out a case for adult education in the following words: "For thousands of years, it was an avowed or tacit assumption of human education that learning belonged primarily to infancy and childhood. People did and should learn then most of the facts, principles, habits and skills, which they used in later years. The young were supposed to amass a stave of information and ability, the income from which supported them through life. This assumption, though questioned occasionally by thinkers, persisted as an accepted and acceptable basis of orthodox theory and practice until recently. It is now seriously challenged under present conditions if it were true, and that it is in fact, false. It would now be unfortunate if learning was restricted chiefly to childhood and youth, first, because the world is changing so fast that what one learns from 5 to 20 years is often not useful from 35 to 60 years, second, because men and women have now so much leisure time that they could, if they had the ability, to keep up with the changing world; third, because the diffusion of power from the few to the many makes it desirable that the many learn more than they do or can learn in childhood. Other justifications could well be added. Well informed and intelligent students of human affairs will agree that trustworthy knowledge of possibilities of learning in adult years should replace proverbs and taboos on determining educational policy and action."

Bryson (1936) explains the importance of the adult education in the chapter "Why so a learning?" "A society like our own is undergoing rapid change in industrial and social processes with a constant acceleration and complication. The primary task of handing down the social heritage becomes increasingly difficult. That education is no longer so simple or so static is evident to any one who will compare what he himself learned in high school with what the present generation of high school students are undertaking to learn. And, it is because there is so much to be learned from anyone who wishes to be at home in the modern world and because so little of it can be counted on to have validity over a long period of time that education can no longer be considered a terminal phase of life."

The very simple notion of getting an education and then going out into the world to use it, no longer suffices. Learning becomes a necessary element in the life process, continuing as long as life continues. The conscious organization of adult education, that is, the provision of opportunities for continuing intellectual betterment, has become not merely desirable but necessary.

Modern civilization cannot be given over to new generations of children and safely entrusted to them if they continue to work only with what they can learn in their first intense educational experience.

Lorge (1947) in his thought provoking article "Never too old to learn" explains his theme by stating "Since the population is growing older, formal schooling must either last for a longer span of life or it must be supplemented."

Objectives and Purposes of Adult Education

On going through the literature on adult education, it is observed that differences in point of view or of emphasis are perhaps fundamental in this particular area of objectives or purposes.

The first broad statement of objectives is taken from the Handbook on Adult Education in California.

"Adult education embraces the learning achieved by adults during their mature years. It is new learning not just a continuation of learning. The major purposes of adult education are first to make adults in the community aware of individual and community needs and second to give such education as will enable them to meet problems that exist now. Adult education stems directly from the people. The curriculum is based on present needs and problems.

Adult education tends to give the understanding and skills that promote effective democratic living to those who have the responsibility now of solving the problems of democratic society. Adult education also develops and enriches their lives and the community in which they live. Such a programme can be a major factor in the better adjustment of personal, social and economic needs and obligations. More specifically stated, the objectives of adult education are the following:

1. To make adults aware of their civic responsibilities to one another and to the community, the nation, and the world.
2. To make them economically more efficient.
3. To develop a sense of responsibility and a knowledge of how to proceed in making personal adjustments to home life and family relationships.
4. To promote health and physical fitness.

5. To provide the means for encouraging cultural development and an appreciation of arts.
6. To supplement and broaden educational background.
7. To provide for the development of educational interests through opportunity for self-expression.

Ralph E. Crow (1949) has prepared the second statement of purposes, which read as below:

> "Adult education aims to extend opportunities for improved living to all people of all ages regardless of class, creed or colour. It is for everybody, regardless of how limited or how extended his formal schooling."

It aims to capture the interests of the "teenagers", who have just left day school and to give these young people a chance to progress along normal educational lines with the rest of their fellowmen. It gives some who left school several years ago, the chance to regain the opportunities which they foolishly, or through force of circumstances, gave up when they were young. It gives them, as well as those who may have had extended formal schooling, an opportunity to keep on growing, and to become better parents, technicians and citizens. It helps adults to discover their talent abilities and encourages them to develop their potentialities. Adult education aims to prepare for upgrading those regularly employed, thereby increasing the efficiency of the workers on the job and preparing them for the next level of employment. It aims also to assist in preparing workers for employment in new fields.

Many adult education activities serve as tension release. This is particularly true in activities in which an opportunity is provided to create things. Adult classes bring together groups of people with similar interests and tend to satisfy the feeling of belonging.

Adult education programmes should contribute to the development of individuals and groups, fitting them to do intelligent, unbiased thinking so necessary in attempting to solve the ever-increasing political, economic and social problems which confront people everywhere today.

Paul H. Sheats and others, who have discussed the chapter on scope and purposes of adult education state that, for appearance, all of these purposes listed above appear to be worth while and have a contribution to make toward the enrichment of adult learning; but only when the situation demands to take up adult education work we will be forced to select few objectives.

They further state that out of all these purposes four selections indicate some of the various positions, which have been taken as to the fundamental purposes. They quote one statement of purpose as given by Sir Richard Livingston. "The aim of education is to know the first rate in any subject that we study with a view to achieving it as nearly as our powers allow. We should have brought order into our education by realizing its true aim and we should have deepened in our minds through practice, the sense that a worthy purpose in life is the desire for excellence, the pursuit of the first rate – the most obvious field is our job in life, our vocation in the usual sense of the word."

For the second statement of purposes these authors quote the report of the cooperative study at the Lincoln schools. According to this, basic purpose of adult education programme is to help the individual adult develop his abilities in such a way that his life becomes more satisfying to himself and his community is enriched by his increased knowledge or skill. For the third statement of goal, these authors quote the policy committee of the Canadian Association for Adult Education, which states in the following words:

> "The primary tasks of adult education, therefore, are to awaken people to the possibilities and dangers of modern life, to help them with knowledge and leadership, and to provide channels of communication between different cultural, occupational and social groups so that the solution of human problems may be sought against the broadest background and in the interest of all. In short, the task is the imaginative training for citizenship."

These authors have taken the fourth and final interpretation of fundamental purpose from the article by Willard S. Townsend. "The primary purpose of the adult education movement is to serve as a channel whereby adults learn to understand, live with, tolerate each other, bringing a new dignity and wellbeing to all. Adult education must be functional and not an ornamental mantelpiece in the field of democratic education."

If we study these above quoted four important purposes of adult education, we find that the difference of opinion exists as to whether the major emphasis of adult education should be on individual or social needs.

If a continuum can be drawn with both of these at two extremes, few adult educators will be found in these extremes, while the great majority will be located somewhere in between points.

The Adult Education Association of the U.S.A. states – "the fundamental goal of adult education is to enable adults to deal intelligently, democratically and peacefully with the problems posed for individuals and communities by the pervasive fact of change."

Bryson (1936) discusses the functions of adult education in terms of agency or subject matter. He divides adult education according to functions in five types: (1) Remedial, (2) Occupational, (3) Relational, (4) Liberal, and (5) Political.

1.5 EXTENSION WORK FOR THE RURAL YOUTH

Why Youth Work in Extension?

Extension is out of School Education for all rural people, whether young or old. Development programme of India, which has accepted Extension as its main method has, therefore, definite responsibility for youth work. Where is the need to bother about the youth and take up Youth work in Extension? This question could be answered partly by the Great Chinese Proverb which states, "If you want to plan for a year – plant a seed. If you want to plan for ten years, plant a tree. If you want to plan for hundred years – plant men."

How can men be planted? A child is the father of man. Men can only be planted if provided youths are trained to develop as good citizens. Hence, the future of any country depends on the development of its young people. Youths are, therefore, our precious assets who can play an important part in reshaping the destiny of any nation. India's future and the future of its Research and Development Programme, thus, depends to a large degree on the development of its young people.

Part Played by the Youth

What part does these young men and women play in the development of a country? Youth has become an important issue in our country, as almost 1/5th of our population comprises young men and women. This is especially so because we do not know what to do about them or for them. A large number of these youths themselves are not aware of their vital role in building their country. Luther Evens, Former Director General, UNESCO, expressed this idea some years before when he said, "young people in many parts of the world have long been wondering how they might help to improve living conditions in the so-called under-developed areas which exist in every continent. How young people can join hands in fighting the great battle of our times, the battle against hunger, disease and ignorance." It should be remembered that it is the present day youth to whom it is committed the trusteeship for the future. Their vision, unselfishness and well directed efforts are going to determine what their future will be. The role of rural youth is still more vital especially for our country. India, an agricultural country, is going to remain so for many years to come. Hence, the future of rural India rests upon the development of the present day village youth. The rural youth will also influence the city thinking. We know the great industrial revolution is taking place in our country as a result of planned economy. These industries not only take away large areas of cultivated land but also will absorb large number of youth coming from rural areas. This is but natural in a predominantly agricultural country like ours. Infact, this has been even considered as one of the serious problems as far as village leadership is considered. This is because many of the rural boys who go to schools and colleges never come back to villages. It is this rural youth who will generally set the ideals and dominate the thinking of the entire nation. This means that rural youth must be the best schooled and the best trained youth in the nation.

Objectives of Youth Work in Extension

Extension work with the young people is not aimed at replacing their formal education. However, it intends to carryout an out of school type education with them to utilize their leisure time properly. The objective of youth work in extension is generally expressed as the development of boys and girls through self-help programmes and the improvement of farm, home and neighbourhood practices in such a way that the youth are brought in touch with the best in each environment and helped to make of themselves, efficient, public spirited and useful citizens.

In more specific terms, the objectives may be listed as follows:

1. To help the rural youth in developing desirable ideals and standards for farming, home making, community life and citizenship.
2. To give technical instructions in farming and home making so as to develop their outlook.
3. To provide an opportunity to learn by doing through individual and group projects.
4. To instill in the minds of rural youth an intelligent understanding and appreciation of nature and their environment.
5. To teach rural boys and girls the value of research and make them scientific minded.
6. To train them in cooperative and self-help action.
7. To develop habits of healthful living like dignity of labour, the intelligent use of leisure and desire to continue to learn.

The line of approach for assisting the youth to attain these objectives is educating them to develop their four important faculties—4 Hs – Head, Heart, Hand and Health by a judicious combination of work and play in their programmes. This development of 4 Hs is explained by a pledge, which is taken by each youth member joining the youth organization called 4 H clubs in the U.S.A. which reads as follows:

"My Head to clearer thinking
My Heart to greater loyalty,
My Hands to larger service, and
My Health to better living for
my club, my community and my country."

Contribution from Youth Work

Rural youth work in extension also can be expected to make the following important contribution to the development of extension work.

1. **Youth can teach adults:** It is an accepted psychological principle that young people take less time to understand and to be conditioned by the old culture. They are also imaginative and delight in adventure, easy to work with them and encourage them to accept new ideas and practices than with the adults. The youth can thus serve as effective transmitters to their parents and other village elders of improved practices.
2. **Youth work will solve the problems of working with future adults:** We are finding difficulty with the present day adults because we did not work with them when they were young. If we could get hold of the present day youth and train them properly, the success of working with the villagers in future would be more or less assured. This is so as by that time the youth of today would have become the men of tomorrow.

Specific Advantages

Experiences gained in many countries support this viewpoint. Extension work with the youth has played a vital role in the agrarian advancement and rural prosperity in those countries. The young farmers' clubs of England, the Folk Schools of Denmark, 4 H-clubs and Future farmers and home makers of the United States of America have all been praised for the meritorious work done in rural reconstruction and advancement of extension education. The contribution made by the extension youth work in the U.S.A. is given below to serve as an example. According to the report of the U.S.D.A, the 4 H-club work in the U.S.A. has:

(a) trained young men and women for leadership,
(b) improved farmers and rural communities through Agricultural extension and Home making practices,
(c) increased attendance of rural people at colleges,
(d) revived Community, Country and State affairs, .
(e) encouraged co-operative and community consciousness and efforts,
(f) implanted the concept of citizenship in Young people, and
(g) kept the right type of boys and girls on farms.

Our Task in India

The time has come when we in India should realize the importance of youth especially the rural youth and develop sound extension work for them. In the initial stages of our Community Development Programme, enough attention was not focused on developing India's greatest potential human resource in its youth. Fortunately, the administrators have now realized this lacuna. Let us keep tempo and establish a useful youth work in extension to create in the youth a progressive attitude, the habit of learning by doing and earning while learning, willingness for co-operative working and desire to serve the community at large.

1.6 ROLE OF EXTENSION IN MODERNIZING AGRICULTURE

Agriculture in India is still a way of life. The greatest task of planning in India after independence has been to modernize agriculture. This process of modernizing or development of Indian agriculture depends on the influence of many factors according to Mosher (1966), an authority on agricultural development. These are: (1) Markets, (2) Constantly changing technology, (3) Local availability of sophisticated equipment, (4) Providing incentives for farmers, (5) Transportation, (6) Education for development, (7) Providing credit, (8) Group action by farmers, (9) Improving and expanding agricultural land, and (10) National planning for agricultural development. All these factors can be compared to links of one chain and thus the strength of this chain depends on the strength of each of these links. It is also now being recognized that education for development is one of the most important factors promoting agricultural development and without its influence the impact of other factors involved in the process of agricultural development will not be felt.

There are various forms of educational systems in a society – primary, secondary, college, basic, vocational, extension and professional. They are having different objectives, content, quantity and quality. Of all these, extension education is more close to developmental education, which is a must for accelerating modernization of agriculture. The key element in the process of agricultural development is the human factor – the interest, ability and willingness to change on the part of millions of farmers around the world. Leagans (1961) puts this idea in a strong way by stating:

> "Rural development in a democratic society is not a matter only of plans and statistics, targets and budgets, technology and method, material aid and professional staff or agencies and organizations to administer them; rather it is an effective use of these mechanisms as educational means for changing the mind and actions of people in such ways that they 'help themselves' attain economic and social improvements."

Extension Education is another name for educating people in order to have education for development. It is a specialized form of broader concept of adult education or continuing education and is designed both for adults and young people but mostly for adults and attempts to educate them in out of school situations. Thus, through extension, education is taken to the people wherever they are. Extension education aims to help people in their life setting to improve its physical, biological, economic and social qualities. Programmes of extension education can have substantial positive effect on the production incentives of farmers once-other influencing factors listed above have already been provided. Extension education is not only meant for taking research results to farmers by giving them the needed knowledge and skill as generally thought of, but also acts as a motive force which can substitute new procedures for old traditions and values, overcome reservations about the risk and uncertainties involved in new practice, accelerate the transition of farmers from a subsistence level of living to business-like farming, stimulate the development of auxiliary services and generally make agricultural planning more realistic and practical.

Institutions are instruments created by society to help in fixing the confines and impose from upon the activities of human beings in achieving their objectives. Farmers like others view themselves as parts of the system in which they live. Hence, attempts to change their patterns of behaviour without creating, modifying and developing an institutional system conducive to progressive change may not only be difficult but perhaps impossible. An organized extension education system is an institution and like other institutions the adequacy of its development, technological resources, administrative support and utilization determines the quality and quantity of its impact on the change process. The central question is, therefore, not only to create and maintain an institution for carrying out extension work which India has already done so far, but to develop the same to required levels of quality and to channelise its impact in order to maximize its contribution to agricultural development and social and economic growth.

The Community Development Programme, which was started in 1952, was designed to have extension education as a key process around which all other community development processes had to be built. While conceiving this idea, the function of extension education was combined with other community development process not only at the organizational level but also at the same time to carryout other related community development functions like supplies, services, regulatory and organizational activities. Mosher (1958) had stated that although it is possible to combine extension education with other processes of community development, one of the likely dangers is the possible destruction of the power of extension education through unwise combination with other community development activities.

It is generally agreed that even after 50 years of working of the extension education system as part of Community Development and Rural Development Programmes in India, the average farmer at the village level remains more or less uneducated in the field of scientific farming. Many people attribute this to the non-suitability of the village level worker (*Gramasevak*) to educate farmers in technical agriculture. There is, however, no empirical evidence to support this contention. On the other hand, all the available research results indicate that so far whatever change has taken place in rural areas is primarily due to the efforts put forth by *Gramasevaks*. As Johnson (1971) has identified "The VLWs do most of the agricultural extension work. It is they who popularize co-operative credit societies. There is also nothing wrong with the educational competence of the *Gramasevaks*. After all as Johnson states "VLW has education, he has been given intense training". The extension workers in Netherlands are more or less of the same educational level as Indian *Gramasevaks*. When these extension workers in Netherlands have been able to educate farmers in their country satisfactorily, why not the Indian *Gramasevaks*? The real problem is not the competence of the *Gramasevak per se* but rather the inflexible system in which he operates.

The three major problems which arise as a result of this inflexible system can be stated as: (1) multipurpose role of *Gramasevak*, (2) lack of real in-service training, and (3) absence of new approaches in the use of extension methods.

In order to enable the *Gramasevaks* to carryout their educational work in an effective way, it is necessary that their multi-purpose role that is combining extension education with supplies, services etc., has to be done away with. It is, therefore, necessary that educational work needs to be separated from other non-educational work by making non-educational work the entire responsibility of other *Gramasevaks* in the same block. At least some pilots study to test the performance of this type of approach are immediately needed.

If the quality of extension work is to improve, it is necessary that the persons employed as extension workers particularly the *Gramasevaks* be trained properly for the job to be done. In our country we have so far mostly depended on pre-service training of *Gramasevaks* for their effective work. Although some in-service training programmes have been started it could be said that they are only marginal. A report on Modernizing of Indian Agriculture (1969) has to say the following in respect of *Gramasevaks* training. "Unfortunately in recent years most of them (VLWs) have tended to become demoralized and relatively ineffective for lack of proper training.... The country simply cannot afford to let this important man power asset to waste.... It is essential that this man power should be improved and motivated to better development work but also be equipped for undertaking the more demanding field work required for the modernizing of agriculture."

In-service training, in order to be effective, has to be taken to the field. Such type of training has to be organized around demonstration plots in the villages by agencies like Agricultural Universities so that realistic and problem oriented training can be taken up in all the blocks and it should be possible to reach all *Gramasevaks* at the same time. With the introduction of the Training and Visit system sponsored by the World Bank in 1970s, the problems of multipurpose extension worker has been taken care of and the training aspect has now been emphasized and to some extent over emphasized.

However, the T & V system did not recognize the need for multi subject matter extension approach needed in rural areas. The system only concentrated its attention to the Department of Agriculture. In village work, it is necessary to educate farmers in all agricultural sciences like crop production, horticulture, animal husbandry, sericulture, fisheries etc. Ignoring this aspect has been one of the major deficiencies of the T & V system.

Regarding in-service training, the T & V system rather overemphasized this aspect by prescribing a fortnightly training for the village workers. Within a very short time, this over emphasizing of training was revealed and now the in-service training has been scheduled once in two months. The other aspect of providing field oriented training on demonstration plots using the first stage or frontline demonstrations for training has not been promoted in the required way.

New approaches in using extension methods and techniques are also needed to educate farmers in a more effective way. One such new approach is what is known as Whole Farm Demonstration. In this method the effectiveness of education imparted to extension worker will be treated in a more realistic way since under this programme he will have the responsibility to prove that whatever he teaches will be reflected in the increased profit or income to the farmers. In the whole farm demonstration, planning of farm is important in order to help the farmer to maximize his net income over a period of years. This method, therefore, calls for constant educational efforts with selected farmers as the planning and implementation requires identification of the potential for development, needs and interests of the farmer and availability of resources and training in farm management techniques and such whole farms, developed in a particular area, become the centre of agricultural development in the local areas so that other farmers will be able to use new agricultural knowledge leading to modernization of agriculture in that village.

1.7 SOME BASIC CHARACTERISTICS OF LEARNING AND TEACHING AND THEIR IMPLICATIONS FOR AGRICULTURAL EXTENSION

The maximum effectiveness in Extension Education results from the skillful creation of opportunities or situations in which people gain the abilities necessary for successfully meeting their needs and interests in a way that it gives the results. This is, in essence, the primary task with which Extension workers are confronted.

There are a number of basic truths that have proven to be helpful in this undertaking when well understood by the Extension worker. Some of the fundamental ones are the following:

1. **Learning is growth-like and continuous**
   (a) Begin where the learner is.
   (b) The new must be related to the old.
   (c) The pace must be adjusted to the learner's capacity.
   (d) The idea must be brought to the attention of the learner repeatedly.
   (e) Over time (follow up).
2. **Learning is purposeful**
   (a) The learning must make sense to the learners—per cent of retention falls very rapidly when no opportunity to practice; the best time to learn something is at the time it is needed.
   (b) Progress must be constantly appraised and redirected, Evaluation.
   (c) Objectives must be clear to the learner and to the instructor, and kept in Sharp focus.
3. **Learning involves appropriate activity by the learners that engage a maximum number of senses: seeing, hearing, feeling, tasting, smelling**
   (a) Learning results through self-activity: it is an active process on the part of the learner.
   (b) Activities appropriate to the specific learning situation must be used.
4. **Learning must be challenging and satisfying**
   (a) Teacher motivation of the student is essential in making learning more challenging.
   (b) Appropriate and timely recognition should be given to student's achievement.
   (c) Standards demanded of lèarners should be given to student's achievement.
   (d) The instructor should focus all teaching material and effort on building in the mind of the learner a mental

picture of himself in a new situation that has satisfaction and value to him.

(e) There should be a friendly atmosphere.

(f) Subject matter content must be significant for the learner and useful to him.

5. **Learning must result in functional understanding**

   (a) Memorization alone is temporary unless reviewed or put to use in a practical situation.

   (b) Programme content should be organized into meaningful units.

   (c) Activities that stimulate use situations are most effective.

   (d) Content – subject matter – is useful only as it contributes to the chosen objective.

   (e) Effective learning requires that learners not only acquire knowledge but also the meaning of knowledge.

6. **Learning is affected by the physical and social environment**

   (a) The general physical environment should be suitable to the kind of learning taking place and to the activities selected for the learning situation.

   (b) Specific physical factors should be suitable to the kind of learning taking place and the activities selected for the learning situation-humidity, lighting, ventilation.

   (c) The teacher should recognize and utilize the effects of the social environment on learning. Use all people.

7. **Learning ability varies widely among individuals**
   The level of communication and the level of difficulty of content must be in line with the learner's ability

8. **Learning, in general is a gradual process usually requiring several exposures over time before extensive change results**
   The use of several different methods over time should be planned for most teaching units: (i) To review content and process. (ii) To show relationship between what has been learned and what is being taught.

9. **Learning capacity starting at about age 6 increases rapidly until about age 20, then it tends to level off remaining generally so until about 50 years of age and possibly longer. Rate of learning declines after about 35 years.**

Reasons

(i) Less acute vision—(ii) Less acute hearing, (iii) Slower reaction time adults correlate ideas a little slower, (iv) Greater reluctance to learn and increased fear of failure, and (v) Decline in learning exercise.

Conclusion

The learning capacity of adults probably decline very little with age when attempts to learn are continued, but rate of learning does decline after 35 years of age – about 1 per cent per year.

Implication

Arrange and use equipment that will enable all the audience to see clearly what is going on: use sharp contrast of colours and large charts, diagrams, pictures, writing etc. adults comprehend spoken word better than written word.

1.8 PRINCIPLES OF ADULT TEACHING

How can one identify good teaching? What are the characteristics of the good learning situation? An analysis of many experiences in which learning has taken place reveals certain condition that they have in common. They are stated here as principles of adult teaching:

1. **The adult learners should understand and subscribe to the purpose of the course.** If the students are to work efficiently they must know the general goal of the course, they must be able to see the picture as a whole and have a clear sense of direction. It is important, therefore, in describing the course, to state these goals explicitly and for the instructor to interpret them at the first meeting.

If the learners are, in addition to work enthusiastically, they must have apart in setting the specific goals of the course. They must have assurance that the instruction will be directed towards their problems. An informal discussion of problems at the first meeting will help to make the specific goals of the course meaningful to the students.

2. **The adult learners should want to learn.** In adult education, it is assumed that most rural people come with a desire to learn, since they usually, come voluntarily. It is not uncommon, however, for the teacher of adults to be faced with the problem of having to encourage a student to want to learn. The desire to learn generally springs from a feeling of inadequacy because of the gap between where one now is and where one would like to be. A learner is likely to loose his desire to learn if this gap seems too insurmountable. An understanding teacher can help a learner analyze his goals and abilities realistically so that he is stimulated to want to achieve what he can.

3. **It is necessary to create an informal climate in the learning situation.** Since the interaction among members of the group is an important source of learning, the teacher has a responsibility for establishing the kind of atmosphere that will facilitate group discussion. His own attitude of understanding, acceptance and respect for personality will tend to spread to other members of the acquainted with one another at the first meeting by having them introduce themselves and give a brief statement about their experience and interests. If the instructor looks upon his role as that of leader and learner rather than that of schoolmaster, he will be more successful in establishing the type of social situation that is most conducive to adult learning.

4. **There should be favourable physical conditions.** The arrangement of chairs, tables and equipment should take into consideration the comfort of the students and the desired type of relationship among them. For example, if the relationship is to be one of free exchange, then the

chairs should be sensitive to temperature, ventilation, lighting and outside noises and distractions.

5. **The adult learners should participate and should accept some responsibility for the learning process.** The best way to learn is by doing. When a person does something or says something in his own words it is much more likely to become a part of him than if he watches someone else to do it or hears someone else to say it. In general, the more active the learners are in a learning situation, the more they will learn. They will also learn more if they feel some personal responsibility towards the group process. For this reason, it is wise for the teacher to have many of the decisions about group activity made by the group. The group that is largely self-managing will produce better learning experiences than the group that is dependent upon the teacher. Furthermore, active participation and a sense of responsibility increase the adult learner's enjoyment of the process.
6. **Learning should be related to and should make use of the learner's experience.** The presentation of ideas and knowledge, if it is to be meaningful to the learners, should be adapted to their level of experience. This does not mean talking down to some and up to others. It means relating and applying the generalizations being taught to the kinds of experiences represented in the group. Adults learn by associating a new experience to a past experience – by relating the unknown to the known. In teaching a course in retailing to a group of department store executives, one would use quite a different set of illustrations from those he would use in teaching the same course to a group of rural feed salesmen. The experience of the students also enters into the learning situation as a rich source of knowledge. The members of any adult class will possess a quantity of varied experiences that can be used for the common benefit of the entire class.
7. **The extension worker should know his subject matter.** We must not minimize the importance of subject matter. If the teacher is to be effective in guiding the student into worth-while learning experience he must possess expert knowledge of the subject being taught. The

extension worker must know the **literature of the field** well enough to select materials intelligently and to suggest sources to which learners may go for information. He must know the subject matter well enough to organize it in proper sequence, and to serve as on-the-spot resource for information.

8. **The extension worker should be enthusiastic about his subject and teaching it.** Enthusiasm is contagious. An extension worker, who obviously likes what he is teaching and derives personal satisfaction from teaching, will soon have a class of enthusiasts. Enthusiasm is the best motivation to learning.
9. **Adult learners should be able to learn at their own pace.** In every adult class there is a wide range of experience, education, aptitudes, interests and abilities. Provision should be made for these individual differences. Learners who learn rapidly can be encouraged to do more advanced work or to pursue individual projects. Slower learners should be assured that in adult education they are not competing with others, but only with themselves.
10. **The adult learners should be aware of his own progress and should have a sense of accomplishment.** Each learner enters a course with certain objectives. If his interest is to be maintained he must have a sense of progressing towards those objectives. The wise teacher will plan cautiously for periodic demonstrations, exhibits, personal interviews, recitations, and other means whereby the students can measure their progress. There are many opportunities in the classroom for the teacher to point out individual and group accomplishments. It is an accepted principle of educational psychology that reward is a more effective stimulus to learning than punishment.
11. **The methods of instruction should be varied.** In any given learning situation, the extension worker will probably have a choice of several methods of instruction. For example, if the problem is to learn about housing in a certain community, the extension worker would have a choice of learning, showing a motion

picture, examining wall charts, or taking the group on a field trip. A good extension worker is skillful in using all teaching methods, varying them according to the requirements of the situation and the needs of the students. This helps to maintain interest, stimulate learner participation, and meet individual differences.

12. **The extension worker should have a sense of growth.** It is important to the extension worker's own attitude that he should consider the teaching experience as an opportunity for his own personal development. If the teacher is a fellow learner, his interaction with the students is bound to be more stimulating than if he has the attitude that he knows all that is to know and is in the group merely to pass along his knowledge. The attitude of the teacher is the strongest force in determining the climate of the group and the attitudes of the students.

13. **The extension worker should have a flexible plan for the course.** It will help both the extension worker and the student to have a clear idea of what they are doing and where they are going if the plan for the course is flexible, based on the objectives agreed upon by the group. In certain types of courses, such as science or mathematics, in which the learning of facts is relatively more important than the development of attitudes, skills, or appreciation, this plan may be quite detailed and rigid. In most courses concerned with adult problems, however, the process is likely to be more subjective and the plan will have to be more general and fluid. The plan may be merely a rough outline, or it may be a series of carefully worked-out lessons, projects, or laboratory experiments. In any case, the plan should be formulated in such a way that the learning sequence is from simple to complex, from known to unknown; that the aims of each unit are connected with the aims of the course as a whole; and the need for illustrative materials is predictable in order that they will be available when needed. A characteristic common to most of these principles is what might be called "ego-involvement". Ego-involvement is the condition in which a person completely identifies himself – his goals,

his values, and his interests – with whatever he and his fellow students are doing it. This condition is probably the ultimate goal of educational methodology, for when a person "loses" himself in the learning process, he learns most effectively.

1.9 ROLE OF EXTENSION EDUCATION IN THE DEVELOPMENT OF THE RURAL POOR FOR THE 21ST CENTURY

1. Development and Extension

Development is a wider concept as compared to extension. Besides extension education, which is a central component of development, there are other important components in the development process. The process of Agricultural Development has the following components, namely (1) Agri-support, (2) Agri-climate (3) Local Planning, and (4) Local leaders and local people (Mosher, 1966). The diagram below, explains this concept. Thus, extension education alone cannot deliver the goods in development. Similarly, Development cannot take place without the support of extension education.

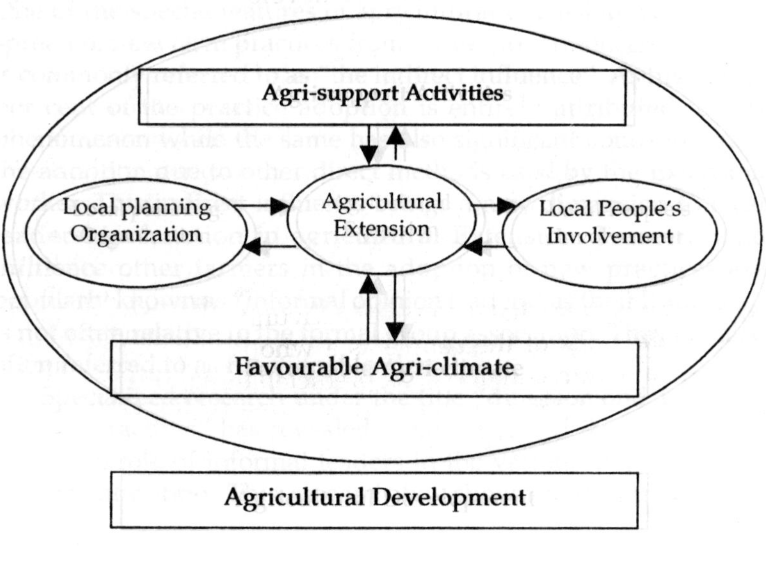

2. Objectives of Rural Development Programme and Responsibilities of Extension Education

The operative objectives of rural development extend beyond any particular sector. They encompass improved productivity, increased employment and thus greater income for the masses as well as minimum acceptable standards of food, shelter, education and health as per norms prescribed. Therefore, a national programme of rural development should include a combination or mix of activities including projects to raise agricultural production, create increased employment, improve health and education and provide safety nets for rural poor, develop communication and improve housing. The identification of specific target groups for which programme objectives must give attention since sizable number of farm families of the rural pours headed by women, special attention needs to be given for their active involvement to speed up the progress of development. There is need to create employment opportunities for the rural unemployment and underemployed at their doors. This can be done by developing cottage and village industries and supporting enterprises. Similarly, asset development and asset availability are two more objectives in the rural development programme. Fifteen important objectives can be stated for this purpose. It is necessary for the extension education to clearly understand their responsibilities in respect of these objectives, the type of responsibility as the case may be. An attempt is made to prepare a chart indicating this aspect which should be understood by the extension education agencies. In this connection, the rural vacuum theory mentioned by Mosher (1978) requires more attention. The T & V system of Extension has described and prescribed. The role relating to supplies and services of education workers without specifying it as nodal function. While implementing extension programmes, if extension observes certain deficiencies in social system it has to play its part in solving the problems due to this deficiency. This can be done by taking up nodal responsibility. The enclosed table indicates the specific responsibilities of extension workers for each objective.

Table: Objectives of Rural Development

Sl. No.	*Objectives*	*Type of Responsibility for Extension*		
		Legitimate	*Nodal*	*No responsibility*
1.	Identification of Beneficiaries	✓	✓	—
2.	Using the existing resources available	✓	—	—
3.	Increasing agricultural production	✓	—	—
4.	Encouraging rural poor to take up nonfood-grain agriculture and subsidiary enterprises and cottage industries to increase their income	✓	—	—
5.	Generation of employment in the rural areas to provide jobs for unemployed and under employed	—	✓	—
6.	Promoting small industries in the rural areas to generate employment for the rural poor	—	✓	—
7.	Undertaking rural works programme		✓	—
8.	Intensive social welfare programme to provide improved infrastructure consisting of cheap food, clothing, shelter, health and educational facilities	—	✓	—
9.	Creating infrastructure to improve communication, transport, marketing and other facilities	—	—	✓
10.	Assisting rural poor to get access to services	—	✓	—
11.	Creating an effective organization for administering rural development programme	—	✓	—
12.	Providing safety nets to rural poor	—	✓	—
13.	Undertaking programmes for development of rural women and youth	✓	—	—
14.	Promoting people's participation	✓	—	—
15.	Encouraging non-governmental organizations and local institutes to participate in the programme of rural development	✓	—	—

3. Development of Programme Areas for the Objectives of Rural Development

Listing detailed programme objectives is only the first essential step, which helps to formulate more specifically stated working objectives or what may be called as programme areas for action to be taken in implementing the rural development programme. This action oriented programme areas are required to be enunciated for each programme objective after looking to the urgent needs of the particular local region, taluk or village. In the present day work of rural development, this aspect of developing programme areas is completely ignored and therefore, it is necessary to consider this aspect seriously. Some examples of developmental programme areas for few objectives are indicated in Annexure I.

4. Strategies Required in Implementing Rural Development Programme

By strategies we mean the ways in which actions have to be initiated to fulfill the objectives of the programme speedily and effectively. Experience of handling rural development programme has suggested a number of useful strategies. A list of 20 important strategies is furnished in Annexure II.

5. Methods and Techniques Needed to Educate the Rural Poor

The problem of the rural poverty can be handled more effectively than before, provided a pragmatic and practical methodology is followed in the place of one that is now being practiced in India. The present day top down subsidy oriented approach with a wrong belief that people cannot know what is best for them should be changed to education oriented method highlighting empowerment of the people aided by loans and safety nets. According to Nobel Laureate Amartya Sen (1998), the programme should be people oriented and not commodity oriented. It is necessary to use the following requirements while using methods and techniques.

(a) It is necessary to understand and use some important guidelines drawn from the good work done in some rural areas. A list of 32 such guidelines is made available in the book by Jalihal and Shivamurthy entitled

"Pragmatic rural development for poverty alleviation—A pioneering paradigm".

(b) To start with, intensive work should be done with a few selected rural poor families in every village and get them lifted above the poverty line so that they will become examples for other rural poor to follow. This method is seldom undertaken.

(c) Discussion sessions should be held with the rural poor to help them to select the programme. In these sessions, experiences of some rural poor who have come above the poverty line are to be presented by those farmers themselves to motivate the intended beneficiaries.

(d) These discussion meetings should be held only during the spare time of the rural poor. Night meetings are ideal for this purpose.

In order to enable the poor to attend field trips organized outside the village, it is necessary to pay not only the cost of travel, but also to pay compensation for the loss of their daily wages, which they have to forego during the field trip days.

While educating the rural poor, a new method known as technology systems approach should be used, which treats each rural family as a separate unit for guiding on the required technology for each family to enable it to cross over the poverty line. While selecting technologies, cost effective and sustainable technologies should be given preference. Technology to be recommended should be thoroughly tested locally before recommending the same.

6. Development of Rural Poor is Not a One-shot Affair, but Requires Systematic Work Over a Period of Years

What is required, is continuous guidance and assistance to the family for a period of 3-5 years till the family becomes self sustainable to increase its income level.

7. Assisting the Rural Poor to Get Access to Services

It is necessary to provide what are known as management services which include detailed operational activities to get the benefit of the various kinds of services like training, credit, supplies, services, marketing etc., at village level. Involvement of NGOs is necessary for providing the assistance.

8. Group Efforts are Needed to Help the Unorganized Rural Poor

The purpose of this method is to help the rural poor in organizing themselves into small (10-15 persons), informal socially and economically homogenous groups around common income generating activity, so that they can benefit from the larger scale of operating. There is no need that these cooperative groups should be registered under the Cooperative Society Act. Informal groups have several advantages over registered societies.

9. Enlisting the Participation of Rural People and the Basic Village Institutions is a Must

Local leaders' contribution to rural development is invaluable. There will be no cost to the government to utilize local leaders who will multiply the efforts. Of paid government workers many times. In the community development days, the three basic Village Institutions, viz. the Panchayats, the Village School and Village Cooperatives were assigned some specific functions in the promotion of village programmes. However, since the start of the rural development programming these institutions have remained in the background and are not actively involved. The publication, "Three Basic Institutions" brought out by the Government of India in 1959 had prescribed the role of these Institutions in the development programmes which need to be re-considered for implementations.

10. Sustainable Empowerment of Rural Poor Women in Agriculture is a Must

Although women's empowerment programme has been initiated with the World Bank assistance through 'DWCRA '—Development of Women and Children in Rural Areas which was initiated in 1982, it will take 74 years to cover every village in India. Hence, the programme of this kind has inherent weakness in not reaching a majority of rural women. Subsidiary oriented programme like this, are not useful in the long range and what is needed is to develop new programme inspiring voluntary efforts by group leaders.

ANNEXURE I

1. **Programme areas for the objective No. 3:.** Increasing agricultural production
   (a) Increasing agricultural production to the potential available.
   (b) Increasing agricultural production of small farmers.
2. **Programme areas for the objective No.4:** Encouraging the rural poor to take up non-food grain agriculture and subsidiary enterprise and cottage industries to increase their income.
   (a) Developing entrepreneurship of the rural poor for taking up income generating projects.
   (b) Providing proper technical guidance both for initiating and for competing income generating projects.
   (c) Providing working capital for completing the projects.
   (d) Creating marketing infrastructure and facilities for the success of income generating projects.
   (e) Providing safety nets for the projects to cover the risks
3. **Programme areas for the objective No.12:** Providing safety nets to the rural poor
   (a) Insurance support for rural poor to take care of unexpected losses due to vagaries of seasons, insect pests and diseases.
   (b) Providing credit on terms which reduce risk and uncertainty.
   (c) Research emphasis to reduce risk and uncertainty.
   (d) Improve marketing and processing facilities to reduce price fluctuations and risks.
   (e) In the PDA system, coarse grains should be stocked.
   (f) Village grain banks should be established for the benefit rural poor

4. **Programme area for objective No.13:** Undertaking programmes for development of rural women and youth.
   (a) Improve women's access, especially of those belonging to poor category to vocational training, science and technology and development education in all villages on priority basis.
   (b) Availability of credit for rural women for project work.
   (c) Programmes to liberate rural poor women, from constant fear, illness and premature are necessary.
   (d) Supporting the empowerment programme of rural women by targeting the young women.

ANNEXURE II

Strategies for Accelerating Rural Poverty Alleviation

- Balanced approach for development
- The programme for rural development should include a wide range of activities
- The programme must aim at sustainable development and equity in the growth of the rural poor
- Local planning should focus for a successful strategy
- New type of de-centralization is necessary for a good strategy of rural development
- A sound strategy of rural development demands due focus on agricultural development
- Development of rural growth centres
- Stop subsidy schemes
- Stage-wise development of the area to be planned
- Enlist the support of the Basic Village Institutions in rural development work.
- Use other categories of rural people to generate employment to rural poor
- Develop suitable organizations for implementing rural development programme at local levels
- Provision of safety nets to the rural poor is a must for any good strategy
- Institution meant for providing services to the rural poor must themselves reach the poor.
- Coordination at all levels is important.
- Assistance to rural poor to get access to services is a must
- Identification of rural poor and preparing area maps
- Introduce transparency in government supported, projects
- Empowerment of women in rural development.

REFERENCES

Allan, H.R. (1962), *Open door to learning,* Univ. of Urbana Press, Urbana.

Anonymous, (1960), Class Outline (mimeo) prepared for Agril. Extension Course, Dept. of Extension, College of Agriculture, Hebbal.

Anonymous, (1960) *Some Basic Characteristics of Learning and Teaching and their Implications for Extension.* Unpublished mimeo issued by the U.S.D. (1) A Federal Extension Service and (2) Course outline prepared for the course Ag. Extn. 513, Agril. College, Hebbal in 1960.

Anonymous, (1963), Evolution of Community Development Programme in India, Ministry of Community Development, Panchayath Raj and Co-operation, Government of India, New Delhi.

Anonymous, (1969), Modernizing Indian Agriculture – A Report on the Intensive Agricultural District Programme (1960-68), Vol. I, Expert Committee on Assessment and Evaluation, Ministry of Community Development, Panchayath Raj and Co-operation, Govrnment of India, New Delhi.

Anonymous, (1952), "Excerpts from report of Country Life Commission." In Land Grant College Committee on Extension Work appointed in 1905 in R.K. Bliss *et al.* (eds), *The Spirit and Philosophy of Extension Work.*

Benor, D. and Baxter, M. (1984) *Training and Visit System of Extension.* World Bank, Washington D.C. USA.

Brunner, Edmund des, (1945). "Summary of the conference in conference report on the co-ordination of extension methods and techniques towards rehabilitation of War Torn countries, U.S.D.A. Extn. Service,

Bryson, Layman (1936)., *Adult Education* (New York).

California State Department of Education. *Handbook on Adult Education in California* XVIII. Bul. No. 4, May 1949.

Clyde, M. Hill and S.M. Brownell, Directors of study Section XI, Adult Education. 1945-46 Board of Education of the school district of Lincoln, Neb. Report of the Cooperative study of the Lincoln Schools.

Davis, P.O. (1952), Extn. Work – Past, present and future in R.K. Bliss (ed.) *The Spirit and Philosophy of Extension work,* U.S.D.A. Washington D.C,

Jalihal, K.A. and Shivamurthy M., (2003), *Pragmatic Rural Development for Poverty Alleviation.* Concept Publishing Co., New Delhi.

Johnson, A.A. (1971) "Extension Agencies" in Waheeduddin Khan (ed.), Papers and proceedings of the Workshop-cum-Seminar on Rural Institutions and Agricultural Development, National Institute of Community Development Hyderabad.

Kidd, J.R. (ed.) 1950.Adult Education in Canada. Toronto – Canadian Association for Adult Education.

Knowles, M.S., (1953), *Informal Adult Education*. Association Press, New York.

Krishnamachari, V.T. (Chairman), (1951), Report of Indian Grow More Food Enquiry Committee.

Knapp. S.A. (1952), The place demonstrations should have in extension work in R.K.Bliss *et al.*(ed). *The Spirit and Philosophy of Extension Work. op. cit.*

Kelsey, L.D. and Hearne. C.C. (1966), *Co-operative Extension Work* (3rd Edition). Comstock Publishing Associates, Ithaca, New York, U.S.A.

Large, Irving. Never Too Old to Learn. Baltimore, *Bulletin of Education*. Vol. 33.

Leagens, J.P. (1968), Paper presented to the conference—Strategies for behaviourial change in International Agricultural Development, Cornell Univ., Jan. 15-19.

Leagens, J.P. (1961), Extension Education for Community Development in *Extension Education in Community Development*, Directorate of Extension, Ministry of Agriculture and Co-operation, Government, of India, New Delhi.

Livingston, Sir Richard (1952), *The Essentials of Education*. The Atlantic Monthly CCIX No.1.

Lloyd. W.A. (1952), Development of the Extension Ideal in the Association of Land Grant Colleges and Universities in R.K. Bliss *et al.* (editors). *The Spirit and Philosophy of Extension Work. op. cit.*

Mayer Albert (1948), *Pilot project India*, Univ. of California Press.

Maunders, A.H. (1972), *Agricultural Extension—A Reference Manual*. FAO, Rome

Mc. Neil, D.R. (1967), University Extension Makes a Difference in Wisconsin University The University of Wisconsin.

Mosher, A.T. (1966). *Getting Agriculture Moving*. Agricultural Development Council., New York.

Mosher A.T. (1978). *Rural Vacuum Theory in Introduction to Agricultural Extension*. Agril. Dev. Council., New York.

Mosher, A.T. (1958), *Varieties of Extension Education and Community Development* Comp. of Extn. Pub. No. 2 Cornell University,

Mukerjee, B. (1961), *Community Development in India*. (First Edition), Orient Longmans, Bombay.

Ralph, E. Crew. (1949), *Handbook for Adult Education Teachers* Cleveland: Cleveland Public Schools.

Reber, Lowis E. (1915), The Scope of University Extension and its organizations and subdivisions. N.U.E.A. proceedings, Madison, Wisconsin.

Rogers, E. M. and Shoemaker, F. F. (1969), *Communication of Innovations – A Cross Cultural Approach*. The Free Press, New York.

Sanders, H.C (ed.) (1966), *Co-operative Extension Service.* Prentice Hall Inc. New York, U.S.A.

Sen, Amartya (1998). *Rural Development withoutsafety Nets has no Meaning.* Statement made at the first press conference after getting his Nobel Prize. *Economic Times.*

Sheats Paul H. *et al. Adult Education in the Community Approach* The Dryden Press, New York.

Smith, C.B. & Wilson, M.C. (1930). *The Agricultural Extension System of the United States.* John Wiley & Sons, Inc. New York.

Taylor, C.C. *et al.* (1967), *India's Roots of Democracy.* Orient Longmans, Bombay.

Thorndike (1935). *Adult Interests.* The McMillan Co., New York.

2

Role of Local Leaders in Agricultural Extension

2.1 WHY LOCAL LEADERS IN EXTENSION WORK?

Extension's fundamental objective is 'development of people'. Extension aims to achieve this through informal educational work. It should be remembered that Extension's clientele is always large. Reaching this large number of people with the informal educational task, therefore, requires a systematic approach. The Extension organizations need to establish some communication channel or channels to carry out this educational task.

> "An overall appraisal of this process of communication reveals that each culture has two systems of channels and techniques; one developed and utilized by the scientific, technical and administrative authorities, the other developed and utilized by the rural communities. Each of these is deep rooted and firmly established among its supporters, with its peculiar equipment, material facilities, institutions, behaviour patterns and emotional content... One of the primary tasks of Extension is to recognize and understand these differences and then to work at bringing the two systems of communication closer until they are geared effectively."

Each communication channel both official and local operates through the group structure formal and/or informal. The Leader, by virtue of his central position in the group must play a part in this communication process.

Leadership in an Extension educational programme has, therefore, two dimensions: (1) The professional leadership, and (2) Local or lay leadership.

Professional leaders are the Extension personnel employed by the Extension service and the local or lay leaders are the local people who assist in the Extension educational work voluntarily without expecting any monetary reward. Local leader in Extension work may, therefore, be defined as "an identified person chosen by some methods to represent a group in one or more of planning, organizational or subject matter activities of concern or interest to the group". Mere knowledge about the existence of these two components of leadership is not enough for Extension administrators and Extension workers.

Smith observed 75 years ago that the importance of local leaders in Extension work is generally assumed by one and all but their real value in reaching large number of farmers is seldom understood and utilized by Extension workers. Although this statement may not apply now to the U.S. Extension workers, it reflects the situation now in India.

Local leadership has many implications for Extension work. Fifteen important reasons for using local leaders can be listed as follows:

1. Local leaders are the only adopted leaders by the village groups.
2. Local leaders are indispensable for any activity by local groups.
3. Local leaders speak in the language of local people.
4. Local leaders give anchor to alien Extension work and facilitate its growth.
5. Local leaders know the inside knowledge of the community.
6. Local leaders keep the professional leader in touch with the local problems.
7. Local leaders set the example for others to follow on new ideas and methods.
8. Local leaders make the work of professional leader to be of permanent value to the group.
9. Local leaders are also teachers.
10. Local leaders multiply Extension efforts many fold.

11. Local leaders add strength to the Extension programme.
12. Local leaders keep Extension work moving even in the absence of professional leaders.
13. Local leaders help Extension service perform its job at low cost.
14. Local leaders in Extension develop ability to face new problems in other fields.
15. Local leaders facilitate Extension service reach its fundamental objective of helping people to help themselves.

2.2 INSTITUTIONAL LEADERS AND AGRICULTURAL EXTENSION

The leadership objective of India's Community Development Programme was to "assist each village first in having effective *Panchayats*, cooperatives and schools and through these village institutions plan and carryout integrated multiphase family, village, block and district plans". This objective naturally aimed at emphasizing the role of the leaders of formal institutions even to the extent of ignoring the role of other kinds of leaders. As discussed earlier, this approach has not succeeded in reaching the expectations. People may argue that the leaders chosen by these institutions were not effective and probably selection of good institution leaders will produce the results. However, there is something more basic underlying this question. These various formal institutions and working with their leaders do provide a situation more or less in line with the functional theory of leadership in as much as different group situations are involved. But the question is, do these formal institutions satisfy all the group situations in a village in which farmers are involved? The answer will be yes if, and only if, certain sociological situations exist.

As Desai (1961) and Dube read, this philosophy implicitly accepts the following two major sociological assumptions:

1. That the individuals, sections, groups and strata forming the village community have a large number of common interests, sufficiently strong to bind them together through formal institutions.
2. That the power structure in the village is concentrated in the so called rural elite elected to the formal institutions

and that all village people including farmers look to them as real leaders in all of their activities.

A detailed analysis relative to these two assumptions is necessary.

A large number of sociological and socio-anthropological studies conducted in India in recent years clearly indicate that the informal group relations based on caste and other strata are more important in village life than formalized group structures and it will be helpful to recognize them. Even where vigorous attempts are made to activate formal institutions, the informal group life has its say. A large number of formal organizations as Desai (1961), comments "are operating more as paper organizations" without touching the social aspects of rural life.

Even more important is the possible future trend these scientists are able to visualise which is decidedly in the other direction than thought by the Government. There is widely in Indian villages today, a process of social change from the traditional forms and others is taking place. The newer forms may not be those proposed by legislators and planners.

Regarding the second assumption of the power structure concentration, the present pattern is such that there is no overlapping between the power structure of the formal institutional groups and those of the other informal groups.

A detailed analysis of the power structure is made by Dube (1962). His observations are worth quoting:

> "A closer study of group dynamics in village communities reveals several different levels of leadership, each with somewhat specialized functions. Many persons commonly described as leaders as suggested earlier, gained this position because of their contact and influence with the officials and regional politicians. Some of them have adopted this role semi-professionally. Their role and functions in village life are fairly well defined and specialized. However, their influence in other spheres is almost negligible. An excellent village politician is rarely a model farmer; the latter is generally an obscure and a political person who minds his own business. In adopting agricultural practices, people are more likely to follow his example, rather than that of the local politicians."

And lastly, what are the trends of the power structure concentration in future? Ronald Powers has summarized the research findings on the power structure pattern of groups. In more stratified groups, the research indicates the power structure taking the pattern of a "power pool". "The power pool has 10-25 persons who are the power actors of the community. Within this more or less loosely knit group, there may be specialization or structures to suit different issue areas". The most important finding of the power structure theory relative to the point under consideration is that the top power actors do not usually hold positions of formal authority within the community. An inverse relationship exists between the current social power and position of authority. It is thus unlikely that even in future the power structure is likely to concentrate in few institutional leaders.

The above discussion makes it clear that informal leadership is also important in promoting agricultural projects along with formal institutionalized leadership. Let it not, however, be concluded that institutional leaders have no role to play. Neither can both of these leaders perform their functions without the help and assistance of other kinds of leaders.

2.3 INFORMAL OPINION LEADERS IN AGRICULTURAL EXTENSION

One of the special features of agricultural Extension work is the spread of new farm practices from farmer to farmer. This is what is commonly referred to as "the indirect influence". As high as 20 per cent of the practice adoption is entirely attributed to this phenomenon while the same has also significant contribution in the adoption due to other direct methods used by the Extension worker. This indirect influence brings a new dimension to local leadership function in agricultural Extension. Farmers who influence other farmers in the adoption of new practices are popularly known as "informal opinion leaders "as their leadership is not often relative to the formal group association. They are also often referred to as functional leaders.

Specialized research under the title "diffusion and adoption of farm practices" has revealed many basic and important facts about the role of informal leaders in the various stages of farm practice adoption. This research has shown that "mass media sources, such as farm magazine, newspapers and radio and television are most important at the awareness and interest stages. Neighbours and friends are more important than mass media at the evaluation and trial stages. When farmers use a new practice on a small scale, agricultural agencies generally are secondary in importance to neighbours and friends". Research work in India has also shown that neighbour to neighbour communication is of great importance in the diffusion and adoption of farm practices than any other communication channel.

This informal leader influence has several implications for Extension work. First, it helps the Extension service to reach large numbers of farmers without Extension workers themselves being required to reach them all. Second, it might also make the Extension work little hard because unless these informal leaders are first identified and are sold the new practices, the adoption process may not spread. It is particularly so as the effective informal leaders seldom proclaim that they are leaders and also because there is little overlapping among the different types of opinion leaders.

Research in the field of diffusion and adoption has, however, uncovered some valuable information. If all Extension workers know, understand and use this information, the seemingly difficult job of identifying and using informal leaders can be transformed into a systematic and simple one. A brief interpreted summary, relevant to the use of these leaders is presented below.

The five categories of adopters located on the time scale of adoption from first to last are: (1) innovators, (2) early adopters, (3) early majority, (4) late majority, and (5) laggards or late adopters. The characteristics of these categories are also identified. However, the first three categories only have potential as informal leaders. It is now clear that all these three categories are not equally effective in their influence on the large scale adoption by other farmers.

The innovators are the leaders who adopt the practice very first but their leadership activity may at the most motivate the early adopter category. The informal leaders who are real adoption leaders are the early adopters and early majority in communities that have progressive farming while in underdeveloped countries with traditional farming; only early majority can do that job.

Innovators are likely to be active in formal organizations both in the community and outside, while early adopters are generally active in the community organizations, the early majority will only have informal contacts within the community.

Another contribution from this research is that the leadership activities of these three types of informal leaders are inter-related. Successful trials by innovators are generally necessary to motivate early adopters. Early majority will look to the results of early adopters before they adopt the practice.

And lastly, innovators are most likely to commit mistakes as they start trying the practice without even the knowledge of Extension worker and as such proper help and guidance may not be available to them. Although early adopters may often cooperate with the Extension workers, their cooperation may often be due to factors like prestige and obligation rather than the real interest about the practice. Hence, there are more chances of their failure too. It is, thus, not very easy to involve early majority group unless Extension workers guide the innovators and early adopters successfully.

Before concluding it is necessary to recognize that use of other kinds of village leaders is required to identify and work with informal opinion leaders as it takes multifarious organizational activities to locate, motivate and work with them.

2.4 KINDS OF LOCAL LEADERS FOR AGRICULTURAL EXTENSION IN INDIA

Discussion so far was mainly concerned with the detailed analysis of the relative roles of the institutional leaders and informal opinion leaders. Let it be again made quite clear that although these two kinds of leaders are most important, India's rural development cannot effectively use them without the assistance of other kinds of local leaders. It is quite necessary to develop a new philosophy as Saville has stated, "Leadership in villages is of various kinds and promoting agricultural programme requires the use of all these various types of leaders."

Innumerable case studies are being reported to show how an Extension programme failed because it did not use a particular kind of leader. It is not the intention of this discussion to go further into the details of such case studies as a new philosophy that all kinds of local leaders are necessary has already been enunciated.

Suggestions, however, are often made that new patterns of local leadership should be developed and used in Agricultural Extension work. This philosophy more or less ignores the importance of the existing local leaders. The leadership objectives stated by the Community Development Programme of India more or less subscribes to this philosophy. As the present discussion has already shown such a philosophy does more harm than good.

What the Extension worker needs today is nothing more than a theoretically sound, culturally compatible and practically feasible, simple work guide for his assistance to enable him to use the various kinds of leaders effectively.

The main concern here is to identify the various kinds of locally available potential local leaders and see what type of leadership function as indicated in the definition of the term local leader can best be performed by each.

The following approach is used to develop this discussion. Some of the commonly performed functions local leaders in the US Extension work are reviewed first in order to know what types of leadership functions can be spelled out relating to the definition of the term local leader. Secondly, the types of local leader potential that is now available in India's villages will be listed. And finally, a sample suggestive guide will be developed for the use of Extension workers.

Local Leaders' Functions in the US Extension Work

The Federal Extension Service of the US classifies the local leaders employed in Extension work into three broad groups according to their function:

1. **Organizational leaders:** Persons whose job is to give leadership to certain Extension projects or programmes and to teach or put in lessons in these projects.
2. **Project or Teaching leaders:** Persons whose job is to give leadership to certain Extension projects or programmes and to teach or put in lessons in these projects.
3. **Informal or Indirect leaders:** Persons who have influenced but which may not be in an official position.

Trend describes the local leadership into two broad types:

1. **Action leaders:** Those actively involved in planning, executing and/or evaluating the Extension programme. They are further subdivided into 4 sub-categories:
   (a) *Organizational leaders* – Persons involved in the administration and operation of organizations.
   (b) *Subject matter leaders* – Persons assisting in teaching subject matter.
   (c) *Activity leaders* – Persons required to assist while doing special activities and events.
   (d) *Programme planners* – Persons responsible for advising and assisting in development of programmes at various levels.
2. **Opinion leaders:** Persons who by virtue of their social position, age, education, family, reputation, wealth, prestige or political contacts influence opinions in most action programmes.

According to Niederfrank, six forms of local leaders operate in Extension:

1. Formal-organizational, official
2. Project-teaching
3. Informal-indirect influence
4. Opinion, sanction, power leadership
5. Action programme leadership
6. Information leadership

A combined list of these various listed functions after eliminating the over lappings will give us the following types of local leader functions:

1. Programme planners
2. Opinion, sanction or power leaders
3. Information leaders
4. Organizational, formal or official leaders
5. Project, teaching or subject matter leaders
6. Activity leaders
7. Informal or indirect influence leaders.

One more can be added to suit India's extension development work.

8. Supplies and services leaders

These above listed functions will be used as the basis for developing the simple guide, which is as follows:

Programme Planners

1. Traditional leaders
2. The sectional leaders
3. Political leaders residing in the village
4. Leaders of informal groups
5. Special interest leaders
6. New emergent leaders
7. Village headman
8. 'Talati' or village 'Shanbog'
9. Village school teachers
10. Directors of cooperative societies
11. Secretaries of cooperatives societies
12. Office bearers of youth club
13. Office bearers of 'Mahila Samaj' office bearers of taluka farmers forum residing in the village
14. Village traders and businessmen
15. Secretary of 'Panchayat'

Opinion, Sanction or Power Leaders

1. Traditional leaders
2. The sectional leaders
3. Special interest leaders
4. Political leaders residing in the village
5. Leaders of informal groups
6. Members of elders' committee
7. Trustees of the formal caste councils
8. Trustees of temple committees
9. Office bearers of 'Mahila Samaj'
10. Informal opinion leaders
11. Village headman.

Information Leaders

1. Village headman
2. 'Talati' or village 'Shanbog'

3. Secretaries of the cooperatives
4. Village school teachers
5. Special interest leaders
6. New emergent leaders
7. Informal opinion leaders in agriculture
8. Innovator farmers
9. Secretary of 'Panchayat'

Organizational, Formal or Official Leaders

1. Panchayat members
2. Directors of cooperatives
3. Secretaries of cooperatives
4. Office bearers of youth clubs
5. Office bearers of 'Mahila Samaj'
6. Leaders of village volunteer force
7. Secretary of 'Panchayat'

Project, Teaching or Subject Matter Leaders

1. Innovator farmers
2. Informal opinion leaders
3. Village teachers
4. New emergent leaders
5. Special interest leaders
6. Leaders of village volunteer force
7. Office bearers of youth clubs

Activity Leaders

1. Traditional leaders
2. The sectional leaders
3. Political leaders
4. Leaders of informal groups
5. Trustees of the formal caste council
6. Trustees of temple committees
7. Village headman
8. 'Talati' or village 'Shanbog'
9. Office bearers of youth clubs
10. Village school teachers

11. Office bearers of 'Mahila Samaj'
12. Leaders of village volunteer force
13. Special interest leaders
14. New emergent leaders
15. Secretaries of cooperatives
16. Secretary of 'Panchayat'
17. Innovator farmers
18. Informal opinion leaders in agriculture

Informal or Indirect Influence Leaders

1. Innovator farmers
2. Informal opinion leaders in agriculture
3. Special interest leaders

Supplies and Services Leaders

1. Directors of cooperatives
2. Secretaries of cooperatives
3. Political leaders
4. Secretary of 'Panchayat'
5. Village traders and businessman

This guide is prepared in the hope that if local leadership promotion activities are accordingly started, group dynamics will start operating and many potential leaders will become active leaders and a cooperative attitude towards agricultural programmes will develop and even new leadership patterns may arise. Leader training activities should also start simultaneously for those local leaders who volunteer to participate in these various types of functions.

2.5 TYPES OF LOCAL LEADERS IN INDIAN VILLAGES

The following types of local leaders are available in Indian villages, who can be used as local leaders in Extension work:

1. The village leaders – Persons who are generally regarded as leaders of the entire community or at least a dominant part of it.

   (a) Traditional leaders – Leadership due to their status, wealth and traditional position.
   (b) New emergent leaders – Persons achieving their position by acquiring special qualifications or by distinguished service, e.g., highly educated person or distinguished retired official.
2. The sectional leaders – Persons not having general acceptance but whose influence extends only to particular sections of the community like castes, factions, territorial units of the village and that of splinter political groups.
3. Special interest leaders – Persons whose influence is largely focused on their individual specialities.
4. Political leaders – This includes the members of the village 'Panchayat', Taluk Panchayats, Zilla Panchayats and the members of the state legislatives if resident of the village.
5. Directors of the cooperative societies.
6. Secretary of the 'Panchayat'.
7. Secretaries of the cooperative societies.
8. Office bearers of youth clubs.
9. Office bearers of 'Mahila Samaj' (Mahila Samaj is a women's club).
10. Trustees of the formal caste councils.
11. Members of the elders' committee.
12. Office bearers of taluka farmers' forum if resident of the village.
13. Leaders of village volunteer force.
14. Trustees of temple committees.
15. Village headman or the 'Patel'. He is the hereditary village official entrusted with the task of maintaining peace and collecting land revenue. He has 2 to 3 messengers to assist.
16. "Talati" or village "Shanbog". He is the official village record keeper.
17. Village traders and businessmen.
18. Village school teachers.
19. Leaders of informal groups.
20. Innovator farmers – farmers always interested in trying something new.

21. Informal opinion leaders in agriculture. Average size farmers who by their sound judgement and practice serve as models to other farmers.

These categories are not entirely mutually exclusive as overlapping do take place. The role and functions of these different types of leaders in the village life are fairly well defined and specialized in particular fields mostly non-agricultural. All the same, these local leaders have some role to play in the promotion of agricultural projects by just extending their present role and functions. It will be sheer folly to ignore such a vast potential.

REFERENCES

Anonymous., (1956), "Volunteer Leadership". U.S.D.A. Federal Extension Service Mimeo, A.E.P. – 110 (6-56).

Anonymous, (1949), Experience with Human Factors in Agricultural Areas of the World. Extension Service and Office of the Foreign Agricultural Relations, U.S.D.A. Washington D.C.P.20 (Mimeo).

Anonymous, (1961). Evaluation of Gramasahayak Programme. Programme Evaluation Organization, Planning Commission, Government of India, New Delhi, pp. 10-11.

Batten, T.R. (1965), *Human Factors in Community Development Work.* Oxford University Press, London, pp. 110-120.

Clarence King (1958), *Working with People in Small Communities.* Harper and Brothers, New York Chapters 1,4 and 8.

Desai, A.R. (1961), *Rural India in Transition.* Popular Book Depot, Bombay, Chapter V.

Dubey, S.C. (1962), *India's Changing Villages.* Chapter IV.

Edward H. Spicer (ed.) (1952), *Human Problems in Technological Change,* Russel Sage Foundation, New York, Parts I and II.

Ellen K. Garber, (1961), "Leadership as it relates to Extension" in G.L. Carter and R.Clark (ed.) *Selective Readings and References in 4-H club work.* National Agricultural Extension Centre for Advanced Study. Madison, Wisconsin; p. 92.

Murray Ross and Charles Henry, (1966), *New Understanding of Leadership.* Association Press, New York. p. 79.

Rogers, E.M. (1962), *Diffusion of Innovations,* Free Press of Glencoe, New York, p. 209.

Ronald Powers, (1965), Identifying the Community Power Structure, Ames Iowa, Co-operative Extension Service, Iowa State University of Science and Technology.

Saville, A.H. (1965). *Extension in Rural Community*. Oxford University Press, London.

Smith, C.B. (1932), "The Problems of Reaching More People", *Extension Service Review*. 3 (6): 89-93.

3

Problems, Needs and Motivation

3.1 FIELD PROBLEMS

What are Field Problems in Agriculture?

They are unsatisfactory aspects of the agricultural situation in different localities.

Types of Field Problems

1. Field problems which can be solved with the complete research – These become extension problems.
2. Field problems which need attention by the future research.
3. Field problems with newly developed innovations or poorly tested research results—which are called second generation problems.

The first step in agricultural development programme should be initiation of a highly integrated research programmes directly connecting to farm problems at one end and to basic research at the other.

How the Field Problems Could be Identified?

1. By travelling in rural areas.
2. Participation in discussions with farmers.
3. Developing a systematic programme of adaptive research.
4. Maintaining contact with extension workers.
5. Analyzing the practices thoroughly.

Dynamics of Agricultural Technology

1. Scientific agricultural technology goes on developing till it finds final application in the field. This is the process of adaptation or application.
2. Knowledge of field problems assumes importance during this process of application.

3.2 NEEDS

A basic characteristic of innovations which is related to their acceptability is whether or not they satisfy existing needs in the local communities. Almost all past change programmes, except those in community development, have been selected and introduced on the basis of technical and economic considerations by the planners. And if the innovation recipients did not have the powers of rejection, this policy must be satisfactory. However, it largely ignores the crucial problem of motivation. If there is no need for a new practice, and if change programme is to succeed, there will be a necessity to generate needs – a relatively difficult task. On the other hand, if the projects of technical and economic improvement can be selected for which positive motivation already exists, the problem is greatly simplified.

Needs which influence local level change projects can be subdivided into three categories as below (Niehoff, 1965):

Demonstrated Felt Needs – a need which the project recipients are aware of to the extent that they solicit assistance from the change agent or local authorities for its fulfillment.

Ascertained Felt Need – a need which although already existing is only latent in the awareness of the recipients and is clarified through consultation with the change agent.

Generated Need – a need, which is created through deliberate efforts of the change agent.

Demonstrated felt needs are those through which the local people have attempted to solve their own problems, would seem to have the strongest motivational influence. In general, where such needs occur, it is probable that little more than technical know-how is necessary for acceptance. One of the best illustrations of the positive force of such a need is reported from village India. The local farmers lived near a river, which had been flooding each year, and washing away some of their agricultural land. They had tried to construct dikes to prevent such erosion but these were washed away each year. The change agents provided engineering expertise to assist them in making strong dikes capable of withstanding the river's force. Cooperation came quickly and the dikes were constructed through self-help (Mayer, 1949).

Probably the most common type of felt need, which occurs in village level project is, that is based on solicitation. The local people hear of a change agency operating in the area and go to them for the solution to their problem. Although this seems to provide a sound basis on which to build a technical change project, there is the difficulty that the solicitation may be as much for the expected rewards or subsidies as for the technical know-how, which the agency may provide. Most change agencies have the dual function of providing assistance funds and technical advice to local communities. It is probable that the second role is paramount in the minds of many villagers in developing countries; thus, solicitation may primarily be for the expected rewards. An excellent example where a solicited felt need was utilized without providing subsidization is described in a development project in Uganda. The local people approached the district officer who was passing through the area and requested that drilling rigs be sent to their villages to make wells. He informed them that the rigs were not scheduled for that area but that he would assist them in constructing self-help dams; but they would have to do all the work. Enthusiasm was seen abed at first but picked up again and eventually the whole idea caught the imagination of the villagers. For one dam 3,000 people are reported to have turned out for the first day's digging. Within several months three dams were finished another dam due to be finished shortly, though one was faltering through lack of participation.

Ascertained felt needs are decided upon through mutual consultation of the change agent and the potential recipients, and not through physical surveys done by the change agents. Needs decided upon by the basis of such surveys would be those of the change agent and though they might be significant, they would not necessarily be agreed upon by the potential recipients and consequently would lack positive motivational force. An example of the utilization of ascertained felt needs is described in a rat control project on Ghana. The change agent was primarily concerned with lowering intestinal parasitism. However, on the basis of grain loss through rat degradations, he then initiated a rat control project, knowing that rat elimination would also help health conditions. The local people co-operated fully (Cowper, 1958).

Though generated needs provide a less sound motivational basis for innovation, they can also produce innovation, particularly if the new practices are demonstrated to be beneficial. Thus, it is reported that an agricultural improvement project in India, the local farmers claimed to be satisfied with their existing varieties. However, new seeds were accepted by some anyway and the advantages observed were sufficient to convince them to continue growing the new varieties (Mayer, 1949).

It is hypothesized that projects based on existing or felt needs will be adopted more quickly than those based on the generation of needs, since a positive motivational force already exists. Further more, it is believed that demonstrated felt needs are most significant for change, while solicited and ascertained felt needs follow in that order of significance.

3.3 HOW TO MOTIVATE FARMERS?

People are motivated to learn if they can satisfy a basic need through learning. Basic needs, wants, desires, motives, incentives or urges have been classified in a variety of ways. The following categories are reasonably adequate for extension teaching purposes:

1. The desire for security – economic, social, psychological, and spiritual security.
2. The desire for new experience – adventure, new interests, new ideas, new friends, and new ways of doing things.
3. The desire for affection or response – companionship, gregariousness, and social – mindedness; the need for a feeling of belonging.
4. The desire for recognition—status, prestige, achievement, and being looked up.

These are all powerful motivating forces stated in a general way.

A more specific classification of the incentives for adult learning has been given by Irving Lorge (1947) as quoted by Wilson & Gallup (1954).

1. People Want to Gain

(a) Health
(b) Time
(c) Money
(d) Popularity
(e) Improved appearance
(f) Security in old age
(g) Praise from others
(h) Comfort
(i) Leisure
(j) Pride of accomplishment
(k) Advancement; business, social
(l) Increased enjoyment
(m) Self-confidence
(n) Personal prestige

2. They Want to Be

(a) Good parents
(b) Sociable and hospitable
(c) Up-to-date
(d) Creative
(e) Proud of their possessions
(f) Influential over others
(g) Gregarious
(h) Efficient
(i) "First" in things
(j) Recognized as authorities

3. They Want to

(a) Express their personalities
(b) Resist domination by others
(c) Satisfy their curiosity
(d) Emulate the admirable
(e) Appreciate beauty
(f) Acquire or, collect things
(g) Win others' affection
(h) Improve themselves generally

4. They Want to Save

(a) Time
(b) Money
(c) Work
(d) Discomfort
(e) Worry
(f) Doubts
(g) Risks
(h) Personal embarrassment

It becomes the job of the extension worker to understand the basic wants or incentives of the people with whom he is working. He should show the learner how to satisfy these basic wants by learning new things. The extension worker finds the personal goals of the learner and tie in his teaching with these goals. Interest in better health for herself and family may stimulate the home maker to learn better food selection and preparation. The need for a higher income may be the incentive to the farmer to learn how milk can be produced more profitably by feeding dairy cows according to milk production.

When people are shown how learning a subject will enable them to satisfy a desire or realize a need, they are being motivated to learn. A great impetus is given to leaning when the learner can see that what he learns will be of immediate value to him in making his own life more satisfying. A desire or a want, therefore, is the most definite and dynamic of motives, from the educational point of view.

Essentials in Adult Learning

Of the many requirements in adult learning, four have important application to Extension.

1. Adults learn best (most rapidly) when they have a strong desire to learn: Many people come to the Extension wanting information and assistance on definite problems. They already have a desire to learn, and the stronger their desire, the more intensive will be the mental and physical effort which they will put forth. These are the people easiest to teach. Many others (and these include a group which Extension has not been reaching effectively because of limited staff) have but a faint and confused desire to learn. With them this desire must be aroused. They are the people most difficult to teach.

2. Adults learn best when they have clear goals: No one, either as an individual or as a member of a group, can act to the purpose until he has definitely decided what he wants to do. When the learner realizes what he needs to learn in order to accomplish what he wants, he is well on the way in the learning process. When the learner decides to act, energy is released which can be put into action. Only a limited number of attainable goals should be undertaken at one time. It is much better for the learner to decide on a few easy goals that can each be mastered in turn, than to fail because he set up too many or too difficult goals. Where the learner does not have worthy goals the extension worker may well gradually direct the teaching toward better goals. Success or failure is significant only with reference to one's goal. In the absence of a goal or objective one response is no more significant than another and no evaluation of progress can be made.

3. Adults learn best when they put forth an effort to learn: A third requirement in the learning process is to put forth effort.

Each person must do his own learning because no one else can learn from him. Learning is an individual matter. People develop skills, habits, and the ability to solve problems through practice, a step-by-step process. What is practiced is learned.

Continued practice is necessary for the prevention of learning and for the development of habits. A farmer has not necessarily learned to follow a recommended practice because he tried it. He has learned it if he continues the practice.

The extension worker needs to get the learner to do whatever is to be learned with increasing expertness and with a better and better quality of action is repeated that determines the rate of learning, but the intensity or effort which the learners puts into each repetition. One vivid, intense action may be enough to learn, whereas a score of half-hearted repetitions may be relatively fruitless of learning.

4. Adults learn best when they receive satisfaction from what they have learned: It is now well established that learners seek success in what they want to do and what they tend to avoid situations which frustrate them. They learn best when there is some reward for learning, in terms of needs satisfied or a general feeling of accomplishment. Things learned which produce satisfying action tend to be repeated. The farmer who obtains a larger yield of corn by planting hybrid seed is likely to continue this practice. Satisfaction from one learning experience stimulates interest in other improvements. It is frequently necessary for the extension worker to help the learner to see that he is moving towards the desired goal and to help him recognize and appreciate the progress that he is making.

All four factors in the learning process are interrelated and together make a true learning situation. A strong desire to learn needs to the establishment of a learning goal. Knowing what one wants to do encourages purposeful action. Meaningful repetition of that action strengthens learning. The satisfaction derived from the successful attainment of a worthwhile objective stimulates desire to continue learning towards other related goals.

Motivating Factors

There are several factors which motivate farmers to take up new practices including new crops. These are classified into two categories, viz. initiating motivating factors and principal motivating factors. These are indicated as follows (Niehoff, 1968):

Initiating Motivating Factors	**Principal Motivating Factors**
1. New experience	1. Security
2. Affection	2. Recognition
3. Competitive situation	3. Economic gain
4. Obligations of friendship	4. Other gains
5. Curiosity	5. Sense of achievement
6. Authority	
7. Hope	

Only the principal motivation factors ultimately influence farmers towards perceived practical benefit which will continue to motivate farmers to take up fruit cultivation in areas where it is not grown at present.

3.4 PROBLEMS OF TRANSFER OF AGRICULTURAL TECHNOLOGY AND HOW TO MOTIVATE COMMUNITY ACTION

The task of transfer of agricultural technology is considered effective only when it results in increased agricultural production at an expected rate. From this point of view during the nine completed Five Year Plans, the transfer of agricultural technology has been only marginal. Agricuitural production in India has been no doubt steadily increasing since independence. From 50 million tonnes of food grain production in 1950, to 212 million tonnes in 2004. As pointed out by Swaminathan, this increase, by and large, has taken place through an expansion in total as well as irrigated areas rather than through substantial per acre increased production. During this period, the per acre yields of agricultural crops have remained awfully low except in case of wheat.

Recent statistics of food production indicates the immense potential of transfer of agricultural technology since the average yields of crops in the country today are only 1/3 to 1/6th of the yields which can be easily obtained by using new agricultural technology as shown by the results of National Demonstrations. Thus, India has faced with a stupendous task of transfer of agricultural technology. The very slow progress achieved in increasing per hectare yields even under the planned development is clear evidence that the problem of transfer of technology is a complicated process. Looking from this point of view, the target of increasing agricultural production in the Tenth Plan period at the rate of 5-6 per cent per year is the most crucial and complex issue facing agricultural leaders of the country. Promoting planned change in this regard is a challenging process of skillfully combining the effects of many critical factors including custom and tradition, ideology and technology, risk and resources, supplies and services and education and a sense of purpose. Crucial in this great task is of course the education of the farmer and farm leaders. However, by educating the farmer alone, it has not been possible to transfer the agricultural technology. Too little attention has been given to improve his environment of incentives, technology and facilities, which would encourage and enable him to respond. To accelerate the process of transfer of agricultural technology policy and strategy must also deal with all sections of the total system and its sub-system, which affect the producer (Loomis, 1971).

Problems of Transfer of Agricultural Technology

1. *Transfer of Technology Requires Improvement in the Total System Not Only in the Technology in its Dissemination*

The real transfer of technology takes place when majority of farmers residing in a locality makes use of that technology. Agricultural scientists, by and large, believe that this can be achieved by developing the needed technology and disseminating its knowledge among farmers. No doubt this is an essential condition for the transfer of technology, but definitely not a sufficient condition. It is the total 'gestalt' or pattern of the society, which plays its role in the transfer of technology. Social scientists like Schultz (1964) and Mosher (1966) have tried to focus on the need to understand this aspect of the problem of transfer of technology. Mosher has spelled out three broad categories of activities which form this totality of the target system viz., (1) Factors related to farmers themselves, (2) Agri-support facilities, and (3) Favourable agri-climate. Transfer of agricultural technology can be accelerated once the agri-support operations and agri-climate are made to function effectively. Attempts to change farmers' behaviour without creating, modifying and developing an institutional system conducive to transfer of technology may not only be difficult, but perhaps impossible. There are several empirical evidences to support this hypothesis. Hodgdon and Harpel Singh (1964) reported that farmers of Madhya Pradesh did not adopt new agricultural practices because of unfavourable conditions, under which inputs were made available to farmers. Very recently, it is reported that farmers of Punjab are switching from cultivation of high yielding varieties of wheat to Bengal gram due to increase in the fertilizer cost. The first author of this book visited a village in Raichur district of Karnataka where he was told that 200 acres of paddy land previously under high yielding varieties has now been reverted to non-high yielding varieties due to lack of availability of adequate quantities of fertilizers in time.

This problem has been duly recognized in India by the administrators and planners. However, much more efforts are needed to provide adequate agri-support facilities and to create a favourable agri-climate than are being made at present.

2. Technology Adapted to Different Environments is Needed

There is a general feeling in the country that there exists an extensive backlog of accumulated research knowledge waiting to be used by farmers. This assumption leads to the conclusion that either farmer is not sufficiently educated about the new agricultural technology or adequate agri-support facilities and favourable agri-climate are not available. This can be accepted only in respect of such technology, which has been found adapted to a particular environment but still not transferred on large scale. There is enough evidence, however, that in many localities the increase above the very low prevailing yields forthcoming from the application of the presently recommended new technology may give insufficiently attractive economic returns. In other words the new technology recommended actually may not be applicable to those localities. For example, in spite of its rapid spread in India from 200 acres in 1964-65 to 9,600,000 acres in 1969-70, the IR-8 variety of rice and the package of cultural practices do not fit all situations (Cummings, 1971). The same thing can be said for new varieties like the IET-1991. This is particularly so when rice is grown under different agro-climatic conditions. For example, in Karnataka this variety cannot be profitably grown in coastal areas, hilly areas and drill sown areas as well in other areas where monsoon paddy planting is generally delayed till August-September. Thus there is a need to establish what Cummings (1971) calls a "firm technological base for innovation" before a high probability of success can be expected. This is one of the main problems hindering the transfer of agricultural technology.

3. *Risks of Innovation Must be Covered Through Crop Insurance in Drought Prone Areas*

Developmental policy to promote quick transfer of agricultural technology must be truly National and that this requires concentration on modernization in the subsistence sector. Institutional innovation is, however, basic to such modernization of subsistence agriculture. One of such institutional innovations is a system to cover the risks of innovation. Schultz (1964), who is considered as an authority on transfer of technology in traditional cultures, has made this point clear as early as in 1964 by stating "some form of crop insurance should be provided for farming areas dependent upon crops for most of their income and, whenever, by nature of the area yields fluctuate widely". Millikan and Hapgood (1967) in their recent book "No Easy Harvest" emphasize the need for innovation insurance particularly insurance against loss following the use of new inputs requiring substantial additional outlay. They assert that farmers who have little capital to fall back on are reluctant to incur this cost. Japan and Mexico have shown considerable progress in the transfer of technology in recent years. In both of these countries, crop insurance has helped farmers to accept innovations. In India crop insurance assumes importance since 80 per cent of farming is still rainfed and of this, major portion is subjected to uncertain rainfall. One of the main technological innovations in dry farming areas is the use of artificial fertilizers. Without the use of this fertilizer technology it is almost impossible to increase agricultural production of dry land crops. Use of fertilizers in these dry farming areas, however, carries some risk factors especially in years of drought. A case study of the promotional programme on dry land Ragi fertilization in Karnataka state conducted from 1961-65 has revealed that in spite of a very intensive educational programme coupled with all agri-support facilities, majority of small farmers have been found reluctant to use of fertilizers on dry land Ragi. This is because favourable agri-climate has not been created by way of starting crop insurance to cover the risk involved in using fertilizers on dry lands. This question assumes more importance today with the increase in the cost of fertilizers. Unless there is some public undertaking of such risk, transfer of fertilizer technology in drought prone areas will not be possible. Karl Deutsch (1971) therefore focuses attention on "risks of innovation", as an important aspect of transfer of agricultural technology.

4. *Priorities Should be Determined to Accelerate Transfer of Agricultural Technology*

Present approach in promoting transfer of agricultural technology generally consists in developing state-wide programmes on selected technological innovations, which are then communicated to districts and blocks for implementation. This centralized type of planning often ignores specific needs of local areas (Rudramurthy, 1965). Radhakrishna Shetty (1973) reports that only in 3.63 per cent of Gramsevak circles, demonstration programmes were available for all the important crops of the area studied.

As a result of such types of situation, many innovations not suited to particular areas are being promoted and many areas are not having any promotional programmes for transfer of agricultural technology. A new strategy is, therefore, needed which focuses attention on local planning, in order to accelerate the transfer of agricultural technology. Mosher (1969) has developed a new concept relevant to this aspect which he calls "determining place priority". According to this concept, it is necessary to classify farming areas based on the inherent capacity of each area for agricultural production with an estimate of the immediacy of this potential for agricultural growth. From this point of view, each region could be classified either as area of immediate growth potential (IGP area) or area of future growth potential (FGP area). In areas of immediate growth potential, completed research has already produced technology that has been proved to provide the basis for substantial agricultural growth with respect to at least one major crop of the region for which there is an adequate market demand. In such regions a rapid diffusion of known agricultural technology is the most urgent need and all other efforts made to transfer that technology are likely to produce quick results. In the second region, viz. FGP areas, research to develop pertinent high production technology is presently lacking, and here, the most urgent need is to engage in the research to find out suitable technology which will convert the region into one of immediate high potential. In order to accelerate the transfer of agricultural technology, the following important steps suggested by Mosher (1969) requires to be followed after identifying the potential of the area: (a) Cover each IGP area with fully equipped and functioning farming districts of optimum sizes. (b) Design the procedure of all local agri-support activities in IGP areas particularly to improve the need of operators of smaller farms and less responsive farms no matter what the size of their farms. (c) Get started with long term investments needed to turn the future potential of FGP area into an immediate potential particularly focusing attention on the needed research and adaptive trials.

5. *Transfer of Agricultural Technology Should be Recognized as a Planned Social Change Involving Social Action*

One of the main reasons for the slow transfer of agricultural technology in India can be said to be the lack of clear understanding of this process from the sociological point of view. Several studies as reported by Mendras (1958), Ramsey and others (1959), Green (1961) and Jones and others (1965) have clearly indicated that more emphasis on educating individual farmers on new technical information has been found to be insufficient for a quick transfer of agricultural technology unless due regard is also given to social relationships and social action. Loomis (1971), therefore, makes out a strong plea that transfer of agricultural technology must be recognized as a process of planned social change in which the concept of social relationship is part and parcel of any attempt to bring about the development of a specific society. The planned social change always requires a programme which must be carried out by local people and Extension workers in various capacities in social relation to each other both regarding its formulation and its implementation and shall seek to assign roles to incumbents of various positions. The social action model of Extension programme planning as advocated by Beal and others (1966) spells out this sociological approach in more specific terms. According to this model, 4 important social action phases are involved in transferring any agricultural technology, viz., (1) Initiation, (2) Legitimization, (3) Diffusion, and (4) Organization for action. This means that transfer of agricultural technology in a particular area requires programmes to promote these different kinds of social action covering a period of time and this cannot simply be achieved by isolated activities to be conducted in one season or by launching an ambitious programme to reach all people at one time. There is utter ignorance about this aspect among the professional leaders who are required to promote the transfer of agricultural technology.

6. *Empathy and Not Ethnocentrism will Help in the Quick Transfer of Agricultural Technology*

Years of experience with Extension work have revealed that change-agents and agencies promoting transfer of technology are often quite ethnocentric. They often tend to think that what practice they recommend is always superior to the practice hitherto followed by farmers and fail to see the clear cut results which are available. An example of this kind of ethnocentrism can be seen the promotion of high yielding rice variety programme in monsoon in the IADP district of Mandya of Karnataka state. Right from the beginning of the HYV programme in 1965-66, attempts were made to popularize coarse IR varieties (IR-8 and Jaya) of paddy in the district. Results of trials in the early years of the programme indicated that although these new IR varieties produced more yields, the net income derived was not very attractive in kharif since the price obtained by these coarse high yielding varieties was almost 30-35 per cent less than the price of fine varieties grown by farmers earlier. In summer, however, the picture was different since no fine varieties were grown by farmers in that season. This simple economic fact was not recognized by the Extension agencies who continued to force the programme to popularize IR-8 and Jaya varieties in kharif even till 1971-72 with practically no success. It was only after the medium fine variety of IR-20 came into the scene that the high yielding variety programme started having its impact on the kharif paddy crop of Mandya district. Research by Jalihal and others (1974) indicated that IR-20 a medium fine variety although introduced as late as 1971 had spread faster than the coarse varieties of IR-8 and Jaya which were being popularized since 1965-66. The rapid popularity of the newly introduced fine variety of IET-1991 has further supported this viewpoint.

The change agents and the agencies promoting change must, therefore, develop 'empathy', i.e. they must be able to understand facts from the point of view of farmers. The advantages of a change agent with a high degree of empathy are that he will be better able to see needs beyond the clientele's felt needs and goals, create settings which enable clients to evaluate the reality of their perceptions of themselves and give clients help in discovering new ways of action based on the need for new skills. As Leagans (1971) has pointed out "the empathetic gap between farmers and government officials is often of such magnitude that essential programme content is not transferred through education from paper plans to the minds and actions of farmers".

7. *New Directions to Improve the Quality of Extension Systems are Needed to Speedup the Transfer of Agricultural Technology*

A nation-wide Extension system under the Community Development Programme has been built up in India since 1952 for accelerating the transfer of agricultural technology. Many efforts have been made especially since 1960 to focus attention on selected areas and to improve the quality of this Extension system. Notable among these efforts can be listed the IADP approach and the IAA programmes. The central question, which is relevant in this context, is whether these efforts have helped to develop the Extension organization to he required level of quality and to bring about speedy transfer of agricultural technology in the selected areas.

Non-official evaluation reports have not observed any appreciable advantage of the IADP approach in this regard. According to Dorris (1971), the achievement of cultivators in the IADP areas were not better than the progress made by farmers in the non-IADP areas. His observations indicated that the IADP's use of a crop plan for each participating cultivator, supported by intensive educational actions, adequate crop credits and production supplies although designed to achieve a rapid increase in the use of additional fertilizer, improved seed and plant protection materials, did not produce significance difference than the less intensive and less expensive methods used in the Community Development Districts. Dorris has therefore concluded that 'factors other than the doubled Extension and cooperative department staff, the crop plan and the added service facilities placed in the IADP districts, were more important in influencing change".

A recent report on the assessment of the IADP work by Desai (1972) has also pointed out that "the strategy of intensification of efforts – administrative, technical and financial on an area basis has not achieved the objective of a rapid increase in the levels of agricultural production".

In order to improve the quality of Extension organization of India for speedy transfer of agricultural technology, the following new directions are necessary which have been also suggested by Leagans (1971) as variables associated with the quality of Extension systems.

1. Multipurpose role of Gramasevak should be done away with by removing unwise combination of Extension education work with supplies, services, etc., in the same person. This can be done by reallocating work distribution among VLWs and AEOs so that there will be separate VLWs and AEOs for carrying out Extension education and other CD activities. This has been done in the country after the start of T & V system in 1970s.
2. Organizing new type of short duration field oriented training for all Gramasevaks during each season in order to take training to the field as recommended by Batten (1962). This is necessary since the report on Modernization of Indian Agriculture (1969) has focused attention on Gramasevaks' training when it said "unfortunately in recent years most of them (VLWs) have tended to become demoralized and relatively ineffective for lack of proper training". This can be done by setting up training teams at various levels as recommended by the National Commission on Agriculture in India (1971). The training imparted should, however, be on specific items of technology, which are to be promoted during that season in that area. This problem has been solved after the commencement of the T & V programme in 1970s.

Motivating Community Action

1. Motivational Approach

Transfer of agricultural technology requires voluntary participation of farmers in adopting new farm practices. There are two motivational approaches, which may be used to create interest among farmers regarding new agricultural technology, viz. (1) Intrinsic motivation, and (2) Extrinsic motivation. In intrinsic motivation, the person is encouraged to do something for its own sake. Here the drive is desire for the activity in question. It is possible to develop this approach by using some strategy so that large number of farmers in a particular area gets motivated. In the other motivational approach i.e., extrinsic approach, the individual is encouraged to do something not entirely for its own sake but also as a means of obtaining some external desirable goal, which is specially, related to the activity. Extrinsic motivation, therefore, does not arise entirely from something inherent in the person or the situation confronted by him, but is a consequence of an artificially introduced incentive. Using subsidies for demonstrations in order to encourage the transfer of agricultural technology belongs to this type of extrinsic approach.

One of the main obstacles coming in the way of motivating community action has been the use of such extrinsic motivation in our developmental programmes particularly for demonstrations. There are two major deficiencies in using this approach. The first one is that it will not always ensure the people to perceive the practical benefit of the new practice. Even a practice, which may not be really beneficial to farmers, can be promoted for some time with the help of subsidies. When such thing happens it will soon lead people into frustrate situation and as a result, time, efforts and money spent on motivating people will not be rewarded. Further, in many situations, as pointed out by Foster (1961), people interpret free things as something without value. Foster has also quoted many case studies to show that acceptance of promotional programmes based on free things has been negligible. The second deficiency is that it will limit the promotional work to the extent of budget available and under our economic condition; there will always be limited budget.

Use of intrinsic motivational approach on the other hand will avoid these drawbacks. This approach could be developed by following three stages in our work of transfer of technology of any new practice, viz. (1) Test demonstrations or trials, (2) Early demonstrations, and (3) Late demonstrations. All of these stages could be implemented without the use of subsidies. In the test demonstrations or trials, it is necessary to verify the local applicability of recommended practices and to modify the recommendations if needed to suit local conditions based on testing. What is required in this stage as recommended by Dandekar (1964) is some arrangement by means of which atleast a small number of progressive and intelligent farmers in each district or smaller area may participate actively on their own in the testing work and a forum where they may regularly report the findings of their experiences in a scientific manner. This stage would, therefore, ensure the success of the practice under local conditions. The second stage of early demonstrations consists of conducting some demonstrations by each Extension worker in farmers' fields at their own cost. If these results show large net returns for the money and work expended, the Extension worker may want to motivate farmers on community level, by undertaking the last stage, viz. late demonstration stage by making vigorous efforts to persuade large number of farmers to have demonstrations in their fields. It is, therefore, necessary to take steps every year to see that agricultural extension programmes are developed at the local level. This is a must before considering the programmes handed down from top.

2. *Motivating for Action Through Group Discussion*

Extension workers often meet farmers individually and try to cause interest in them to adopt new practices. A research study by Jalihal and others (1973a) has shown that most of the time of Gramasevak is utilized in this way. Research in the field of Social Psychology has, however, indicated that discussion-group method is superior to lecture or straight talk method in motivating individuals for action. Kurt Lewin's study (1952) during the Second World War is a classic example in this regard. Experiences using the group discussion approach have produced effective results in the transfer of agricultural technology by motivating community for action even under Indian conditions. The recently launched coordinated programme on the economic use of fertilizers in Karnataka state has provided empirical validity for this approach. In the summer of 1974, group meetings were organized in 5 villages for encouraging farmers to use fertilizers economically. In four out of these five villages, the method proved effective and large number of farmers joined together to have "block demonstrations" to see the advantage of the new method of using fertilizers economically.

3. *Promoting Achievement Motivation*

Quick transfer of agricultural technology is directly related to the innovative behaviour among farmers. Those farmers who are more innovative are likely to test new technology first. Research conducted in recent years has revealed that high achievement motivation is related to innovative behaviour among farmers (Rogers and Svenning, 1959). There is also enough evidence to show that achievement motivation is related to (a) the amount of exposure to mass media, (b) the amount of political knowledge, (c) the degree of cosmopoliteness, (d) the level of literacy, (e) the years of formal schooling, (f) the educational aspirations, (g) the occupational aspirations, and (h) a positive attitude towards credit. It is, therefore, necessary to focus attention on encouraging some of these variables among farmers in order to increase their achievement motivation. McClelland (1971) reports the results of an experiment conducted in Kakinada of Andhra Pradesh where educational work with businessmen assisted to increase their achievement motivation.

So programmes to accelerate the transfer of agricultural technology should also focus attention on increasing the achievement motivation of farmers.

REFERENCES

Anonymous, (1969), Modernization in Indian Agriculture – A report on the Intensive Agricultural District Programme (1960-68) Vol. I. Ministry of Food and Agriculture, Government of India, New Delhi.

Anonymous, (1971), Interim Report of the National Commission on Agriculture on some aspects of agricultural research, extension and training, Government of India, Ministry of Agriculture, New Delhi.

Batten, T.R. (1962), *Training for Community Development.* Oxford University Press, London.

Beal and others, (1966), *Social Action and Interaction in Programme Planning.* Iowa State University Press, Ames, IOWA, USA.

Cowper, Laurence T. (1958), *Rural Health Education in Community Development Bulletin*, London.

Cummings, Ralph W. (1971), Agricultural Research and Technology", Leagans and Loomis (eds.) *Behavioural Change in Agriculture – Concepts and Strategies for Influencing Transition*, Cornell Univ. Press, Ithaca.

Dandekar, V.M. (1964), "Motivating farmers to increase Agricultural production", VII F.A.O. Regional Conference for Asia and the far East, Manila.

Desai, D.K. (1972), "Intensive Agricultural District Programme – Analysis of Results in Pramit Chaudhary (ed.)," *Readings in Indian Agricultural Development.* George Allen and Unwin Ltd., London pp. 140-154.

Dorris, Brown, D. (1971), *Agricultural Development in India's Districts.* Harward University Press, Cambridge.

Foster, G.M. (1961), *Traditional Cultures and the Impact of Technological Change.* Harper and Row, New York.

Green, James, W. (1961), "Success and Failure in Technical Assistance – A case study", *Human Organizations*, Vol. 20, pp. 2-16.

Irving Lorge, (1947), Effective Methods in Adult Education, Report of Southern Regional Workshop for Agricultural Extension Specialists pp. 23-38, North Carolina State Col.

Jones and others, (1965), *Some Human Factors in Woods Burning: A Study of Charge in Beliefs in Louisiana.* Bulletin No.601, Louisiana State University.

Jalihal, K.A. *et al.* (1973), "Some aspects of adoption of high yielding varieties of paddy in Mandya District with particular reference to small farmers", *Mysore J. of Agric. Sciences*, Vol. 7. pp. 608-615.

Jalihal, K.A. *et al.* (1973a), "A study on how Gramasevaks spend their time", *Mysore J. of Agric. Sciences*, Vol. 7, pp. 603-607.

Lewin, Kurt, (1961), "Group decision and social change" *Readings in Social Psychology*, (3rd Edition), Maccoby E. E *et al.* (eds). Rinehart, New York.

Leagans, J. Paul, (1971), "Extension Education and Modernization in Leagans and Loom's (eds.)," *Behavioural Change in Agriculture – Concepts and Strategies for Influencing Transition.* Cornell Univ. Press. Ithaca pp. 101-143.

Mayer Albert, (1948), Pilot Project India, University of California, Berkeley.

Millikan and David Hapsood (1966), *No Easy Harvest*. The dilemma of Agriculture in underdeveloped countries: Little Brown, Boston, USA.

Mosher, A.T. (1969), *Creating a Progressive and Rural Structure*. Agricultural Development Council, New York.

Mendras, H.C. (1958), Les Paysons *et al*. Modernization de 1 agriculture, Paris: Centre National de la Recherche Scientifique.

Neihoff Arthur, (1965), Diffusion of technology; A Mimeo. George Washington University, Human Resource Research Office, Alaxanderia, Virginia.

Radhakrishna Setty, (1973), "Knowledge of Grama Sevaks about Extension Programme planning and the nature of Agricultural Extension Programme development at the Gramasevaks' Circle level". Unpublished M.Sc. Thesis, UAS, Bangalore.

Rogers, E.M, and Svenning, (Ed) (1969), *Modernization Among Peasants: The Impact of Communications*. Holt, Rinehart and Winston, New York.

Schultz, T.W. (ed.) (1964), *Transforming Traditional Agriculture*, Yale University Press. Newhaven. Conn.

Wilson, M. and Gladys, Gallup (1954), *Extension Teaching Methods* Extension Service Circular 495, Federal Extension Service, U.S. Department of Agriculture. Washington D.C.

4

Extension Teaching Methods and Communication

4.1 EXTENSION TEACHING METHODS

The basic as well as the ultimate aim of extension teaching is to change the practices of the people so that by adopting new scientific practices, they can benefit from them. In the earlier discussion on the concept of extension, it was made clear that Extension has to use its own combination of methods to convince people about the recommended new practices so as to enable them to take action in adopting these practices.

1. Extension Teaching Methods

In Extension work, the most common teaching methods used and listed in almost all text books on Extension are the following:

1. Farm and home visits
2. Office calls
3. Telephone calls
4. Personal letters
5. Result demonstrations
6. Method demonstrations
7. Leader training meetings
8. Lecture meetings
9. Conferences and discussion meetings
10. Tours and field visits
11. Schools
12. Miscellaneous meetings

13. Bulletins
14. Leaflets
15. News stories
16. Circular letters
17. Films
18. Radio
19. T.V.
20. Exhibits
21. Posters

Classification of Extension Teaching Methods

The Extension Teaching methods can be classified into two ways viz., (1) According to **Form,** and (2) According to **Use.**

According to Form: Under their classification, the extension teaching method, are divided into 3 categories:

1. **Methods involving symbols – either spoken or written**

Spoken: Farm and home visits
Office calls
Telephone calls
Leader training meetings
Lecture meetings
Conferences and discussion meetings
Schools
Miscellaneous meetings
Radio

Written: Bulletins
Leaflets
News stories
Circular letters
Personal letters

2. **Methods involving seeing**

Method demonstrations
Result demonstrations
Tours and field visits
Films

T.V.
Exhibits
Posters
Meetings at result demonstrations

3. **Methods involving seeing and doing**

Method demonstrations
Result demonstrations

According to Use: There are 3 categories under this classification as detailed below:

1. **Methods involving individual contacts**

Farm and home visits
Office calls
Telephone calls
Personal letters
Result demonstrations

2. **Methods involving group contacts**

Method demonstrations
Leader training meetings
Lecture meetings
Conferences and discussion meetings
Meetings at result demonstrations
Tours and field visits
Schools
Miscellaneous meetings

3. **Methods involving mass contacts**

1. Radio
2. T.V.
3. Bulletins
4. Leaflets
5. New stories
6. Circular letters
7. Exhibits
8. Posters

Some Fundamentals Underlying the Use of Extension Teaching Methods

1. Extension Must Use a Combination of Methods: Extension methods must always be used in combination for getting successful results. As Mosher puts it; "people learn more easily from what they see, next most easily from what they hear, less easily from what they read especially easily from what they actually do with their hands and minds. They learn best of all when several of these are brought to bear on the same subject matter". In other words repetition in a variety of ways is quite essential for successful extension teaching (an accepted educational principle). Research in many countries has shown that as the number of extension methods used increases from one to nine, the number of farm families changing behaviour increases from 35 to 98 per cent (Kelsey & Hearne, 1963).

A very important point to be noted in connection with the use of combination of methods is that not all or any combination is equally effective. The most effective combination is that which uses a combination of methods involving doing, seeing and oral exposure. This will be dealt again in para 2 following. This point needs to be stressed in all extension organizations.

2. Demonstrations are Basic Methods in Extension Teaching, Which Must be Used in Combination with Other Methods: Of all the methods extension workers use, the demonstrations have a fundamental place. The importance of demonstration methods in extension work is explained as under:

People who are to be educated in extension hesitate to believe and act on theory or even facts until they see with their own eyes the proof of them in material form. It is the responsibility of extension workers to bring this kind of work to the people's personal attention. This is the most challenging as well as satisfying test in extension education. Talking of the basic philosophy of demonstration work, Dr. Seaman A. Knapp, the father of demonstration idea in extension emphasized: "It has been said that farmers are a hard class to reach through press. That is not my experience. They are most trustable people if you have anything substantial to offer – but what they want is proof." David Houston, an extension administrator of the USA also highlighted this demonstration idea when he said, "It has been ascertained that the actual demonstration of a thing is the most effective. A farmer is rather prejudiced; he is conservative and rather harsh headed; he is a man of sense and wants to be shown and he is skeptical until he is shown."

* "Seeing is believing"
* "What a man hears, he often doubts
  What a man sees, he may possibly doubt
  What a man does, he will never doubt".

John Hutchinson Ex-Director, Virginia State Extension Service of the U.S.A. narrates the following experience to support the use of demonstration methods in extension.

"The Agronomists of our Experiment Stations found out more than 20 years ago that the highway to increase efficiency in the production of buffalo and dairy products in south western Virginia was to dress pastures with commercial fertilizers. Although they announced this through the press, through the bulletins and through public meetings, the net result over a period of 15 years was that less than 5 per cent of the cattle growers in that part of the State had top pastures in 1933.

South Western Virginia is in the Tennessee river watershed and about 7 years ago, representatives of the Tennessee Valley Authority came to the college wanted recommendations as to the best methods of soil and water conservation in that area. We recommended the fertilization of pastures and set the T.V.A to give at least 50 farmers in each country sufficient quantities of high phosphates were needed in local demonstrations. As a result of these demonstrations, more than 60 per cent of the farmers are now using phosphates and other fertilizers to top dress pastures. In our efforts to redefine extension job, I think many of us would do well to rediscover and apply to our work the principle of the demonstration.

These demonstration methods have to be used as basal methods in extension work around which all other methods are to be combined. Hence demonstrations are not just one of the several methods of extension. They had special consideration in extension work. That is why it is said that a well-rounded programme of successful demonstrations conducted and shown in an area may serve as valid evidence that a worthwhile extension programme is in progress in that area.

How demonstration methods could be combined with other methods is illustrated by the following guideline issued by the University of Missouri, College of Agriculture, Agricultural Extension Service, Columbia, USA in 1945 which reads as follows.

The Extension worker should draw up a teaching plan providing for time and methods of using the demonstration. This plan should be a part of the county programme and calendar of work. The agent and the demonstrator need to understand the teaching use to be made of the demonstration.

The teaching plan should at least show:

- What meetings are to be held in connection with the demonstration, and when they are to be held?
- What newspaper publicity is to be framed in connection with the demonstration and when it is to be released?
- What circular letters are to be written using the demonstration results, and when they are to be released?
- At what other meetings, the results of this demonstration or a compilation of other demonstrations are to be used, and when such meetings are to be held?
- What use is to be made of the demonstration results for charts, posters and other teaching methods?

To sum up, it could be said that the strategy in using Extension methods must be to use other methods to involve people to take up demonstration work or at least show them demonstrations. After the demonstration work is started or demonstrations seen, again use other methods to publicize the results of these demonstrations so that they also in turn can try them.

3. The Timing of Use of Extension Methods Should be Convenient to People and not to Extension Workers: It is commonly observed that this principle is not generally considered while using extension methods. A farmers' meeting is called in the morning or afternoon when most farmers are at their work in their fields and naturally very few farmers participate. A home visit is made at the farmers home when the farmer works at his farm. We then return with our observation that farmers' participation in extension method is low. The principle I is very important especially when we deal with small farmers particularly in the seasons. Small farmers will be free to attend extension meetings only in the evening after the days work is over off season time will be more convenient to involve farmers in extension methods like meetings, discussion, exhibitions. It is rather unfortunate that most research on the use of extension methods have come out with observation on farmers participation without examining whether extension methods used were timely to suit the convenience to farmers.

4. Use of Extension Methods Must Result in Indirect Spread of the Practice: The passing on of information and knowledge about a new practices from neighbour is one of the most powerful forces of work in extension and is popularly known as indirect spread of influence of extension teaching.

Research data available indicate that the indirect spread of influence accounts for more than 1/5th of all practices credited to extension.

An important point is to be noted in this context is that the enthusiasm of one farmer telling about the new practice to another farmer or his neighbour is closely associated with the economic advantage or other satisfaction growing out of the new practice. It is, therefore, necessary that extension methods like demonstrations should promote new practices, which are really economically sound and be of such nature that those adopting the practices are stimulated to tell others about it.

As a corollary, it is also suggested that when the trial of the recommended practice does not result in the indirect spread of it from neighbour to neighbour, it is necessary to check the teaching plan for coverage and re-examine the merits of the practice itself. Only a slight advantage of the newly recommended practice over the existing one may even lead to doubt upon its value and may not provide sufficient motivation to communicate about its advantages to others. In most of research studies in farm practice adoption, it has been pointed out that neighbours and friends are more reliable sources of communication. This is another indication that demonstration methods are important in extension so that a new farm practice is first tested and adopted or seen by few farmers in every community, who then will act as important sources of communication to spread indirect effect.

4.2 VARIOUS CONCEPTS IMPORTANT IN DEALING WITH EXTENSION METHODS

1. Definition—tools used to create learning situations.
2. Concept of methods, technique and device methods-way of organizing people—The problem of facilitating-learning devices—various mechanical instruments to augment the process employed.
3. Learning experience—-interaction between learner and external conditions.
4. How learning experiences should be set-up continuity, sequence, integration

   (a) Experience that gives opportunities to practice the kind of behaviour,
   (b) Obtain satisfaction,
   (c) Sequential,
   (d) Set standards attainable,
   (e) Motivation force.

5. Factors to be considered in selecting methods

   (a) Nature and complexities of subject matter,
   (b) Changes expected,
   (c) Relative importance of the changes,
   (d) Extent to which people already know,
   (e) Amount of time,
   (f) Number of people to be reached,
   (g) Economic, social and educational status of the people to be reached,
   (h) Kind and extent of local assistance,
   (i) Relative effectiveness,
   (j) Manner in which methods complement each other,
   (k) Character and stage of development programme,
   (l) Personality and skill of extension worker,
   (m) Local conditions,
   (n) Financial and other resources.

6. Relative merits of composite versus single factor demonstrations and their influence in changing behaviour.

7. Study of extension methods in respect of time, cost and their utilisation.
8. Suitable combination and sequence of extension methods for adoption of improved technology.

Important Research Results

U.S.A.

1. Individual methods: 17.5 per cent effective.
2. Group methods: 26.00 per cent effective.
3. Mass methods: 37.4 per cent effective.
4. Indirect influence 19.1 per cent.
5. People who had personal contacts with extension workers have adopted four times as many as improved practices as people who have no contact.
6. Methods must be suited to local conditions.
7. Subject matter to be taught becomes an important consideration.
8. Mass media only as the 1st source in awareness stage.

India

1. Different practices are influenced differently by different methods.
2. Mass media methods were used more by large farmers
3. Effectiveness of various methods differ with different stages of adoption.
4. Mass media as the first source of information has a very limited use except radio (Indian Institute of Mass Communication). In villages having radio forum, 20 per cent of the people were informed through radio.
5. Radio forums are not only an important source of information, but also an important method for accelerating adoption.
6. Mass media variables have lot of potentials.
7. Personal contact is more effective if followed by group discussion and demonstration.
8. Demonstration is the most important one of the most neglected methods.

9. Large-scale demonstrations are more effective.
10. Use of TV increased the knowledge in all types of farmers irrespective of their age, caste, and economic status. Economic status, more education leads to more knowledge. Viewers gained more knowledge than radio listeners.

New Areas of Research

1. Suitability of different extension methods and their combination to different stages of the adoption process.
2. In-depth studies in order to find out more effective use of individual methods.

Extension Methods

1. Definition

Extension teaching methods are devices used to create situations in which communication can take place between the instructor and learner. Coolie Varner makes a distinction between extension methods, techniques and devices, way of organising people for education i.e. individual group and mass, identifying the role of institution or organisation.

2. Techniques

The problem of facilitating learning identified the concept of techniques with the method determined, the second kind of relationship that must be established comes within the confines of the specific programme and its form is determined by the specific learning objectives at that programme. Techniques are identified with respect to their utility in facilitating learning objectives in terms of the outcomes. It is an operational decision to be decided by the Educator.

3. Devices

Various mechanical instruments to augment the process employed.

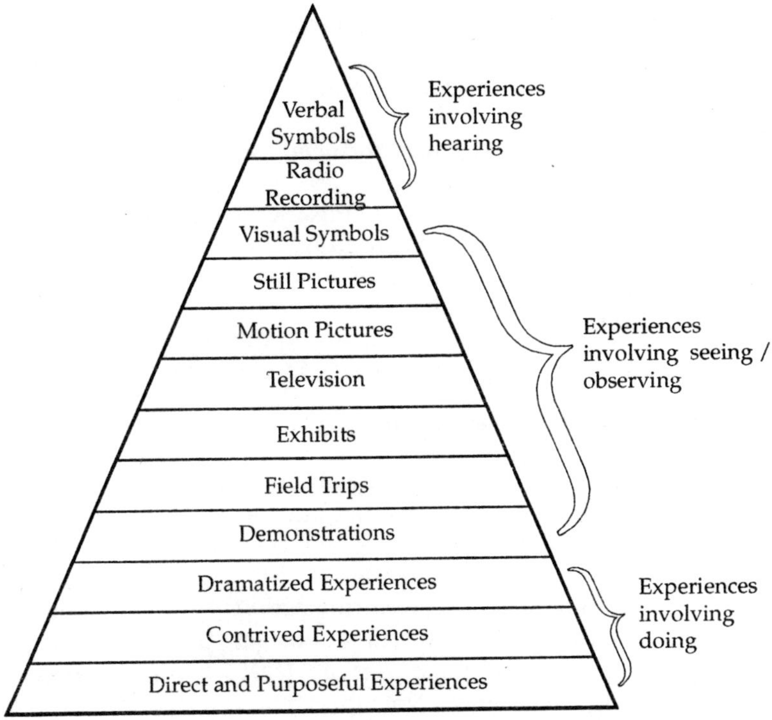

Cone of Experience (Edger Dale)

Principles in Setting up of Learning Experiences

1. Experiences that give a learner an opportunity to practice the kind of behaviour implied.
2. Obtaining satisfaction from carrying out the behaviour.
3. Motivation force is important.
4. Should have some guidance.
5. Ample and appropriate materials on which to work.
6. Time to carry on the behaviour to practice it until it becomes part of his reports.
7. Opportunity for a sequential practice.
8. Set standards beyond his present performance but attainable.
9. To study of his own, he should have means of judging the performance to be able to tell how well he is doing.

Learning Experiences to be Organized

Continuity, Sequence and Integration

Important Changes are not Produced Overnight

Continuity: Effective vertical organisation similar to repetition

Sequence: Goes beyond continuity

- Building upon the previous one with each successive experience going
- More broadly and deeply into the matter
- Emphasizing higher level of treatments

Purposes for Which Methods are Used

(a) Methods used in getting attention
(b) Methods used in creating interest
(c) Methods used in developing confidence
(d) Methods used in creating desire
(e) Methods used for ensuring action
(f) Methods used for maintaining satisfaction

Purpose of techniques: To create learning experience

Learning experience: Note the same as the content, which a course deals, nor the activities performed by the teacher-It refers to the interaction between the learner and external conditions in the environment to which he can react.

The student must be an active participant.

Elements of an Efficient Learning Situation

(1) Instructor, (2) Learner, (3) Content, (4) Equipment, and (5) Environment.

Factors to be Considered for Selection of Extension Teaching Method

1. Nature and complexity of subject matter
2. Changes expected
3. Relative importance of the changes
4. Extent to which people already know about and recommended practices
5. Amount of time that can be devoted

6. Number of people to be reached
7. Economic, social and educational status of the people to be reached
8. Kind of extent of local assistance
9. Relative effectiveness
10. Manner in which methods compliment each other.

Other Factors

1. The length of time the programme is underway
2. The character and stage of development of programme, personality and skill of extension worker
3. Age, sex, education motives and other complex human characteristics
4. Local conditions
5. Financial and other resources

Different Effectiveness of Methods

1. Subject Matter

The effectiveness of different methods is not the same in agriculture and have economic.

(a) Different practices are influenced differently by different methods
(b) Differences in effectiveness of extension methods in various subject matters
(c) Effectiveness index
(d) Utilization of sources of information by the farmers differ with the practices about which the information is sought
(e) Different sources differ in their use for the different practices.

Cost: Result demonstrations are the most costly of all methods, but can we avoid them?

2. Audience

(a) Age and effectiveness of methods
(b) Education: Mass media most used

(c) Farm size and income: Mass media used more by large farmers
(d) Farm participation
(e) Socio-economic status

Extension Methods and Stages of Adoption

Effectiveness of various methods differ with different stages of adoption

Time: Mass media takes less time while demonstrations takes more time

Demonstrations fail due to lack of full knowledge of purpose, process and technique of conducting Result Demonstrations.

4.3 DEMONSTRATION: THE BASIC METHOD IN EXTENSION

Demonstration is the Basic Method in Extension

Dr. Seaman A. Knapp, the father of American Extension Service said,

> "What a man hears he will doubt,
> What a man sees, he may possibly doubt,
> But what a man does, he cannot doubt."

The above saying also applies to our Indian farmers. When extension workers tell farmers to adopt improved practices, they are not convinced. Even when farmers are taken to Research farms, they start questioning the advantage of the practice and raise all sorts of doubts. But when farmers conduct demonstrations or undertake trials in their own fields at their own cost, they will be convinced.

This idea is expressed in very strong terms by Dr. Spencer Hatch an American Extension Expert who carried out extension work in Martandam in Kerala State for more than 25 years when he advised:

> "Farmers are not improved in India, or anywhere else by what they see on government show farms operated with public money not intimately connected with the farmer and not on a

self sustaining basis, but they are impressed by what they do themselves."

Good Demonstration Work Requires the Use of Combination of Methods

Although demonstration is the basic method in extension, we just cannot conduct demonstrations without using other extension methods. This is because,

1. It is not possible to conduct demonstrations with each farmer
2. Demonstrations cannot start by themselves. We need to use combination of other methods to establish demonstrations.
3. Demonstrations cannot be seen by large number of farmers unless we use other extension methods to bring farmers to demonstration plots. Similarly results of demonstrations cannot be made known to farmers without the use of other methods.

So good demonstration work requires the use of a good combination of extension methods.

Types of Demonstrations to be Conducted in the Villages

Trial Demonstrations or District Trials at Government Cost

These may be necessary in the first 2 to 3 years before a practice is recommended by research workers. Ten to twenty trial demonstrations per zone may be necessary in one year. The main purpose of these trial demonstrations at Government cost is to develop confidence in the new practice by the research workers.

Demonstrations or Trials at Farmers' Cost

When research workers have developed confidence about a new practice after setting up trial demonstrations at government cost, there should not be further demonstrations at government cost. Because farmers will not think in terms of the economics of the practice as long as these types of demonstrations are continued. It is only when farmers conduct demonstrations in their own fields at their own cost, they would start realizing the economic advantage of the new practice. Hence, other extension workers must start educating farmers and see that some farmers in each village start conducting demonstrations at their own cost. This type of demonstration work will also help in setting up large number of demonstrations in each block, which are necessary to create positive evidence about the advantage of a new practice.

How to Conduct Good Demonstrations and Use Them

If we want to convince farmers through the method of demonstration, we must establish good demonstrations. This is because one bad demonstration will destroy the advantage of ten good demonstrations. A practice which is really good may be discarded by farmers as useless if the demonstration fails to show the advantage of the same. If our demonstration must be good, we need to give attention to the following:

1. Sow or plant the demonstration plot in time.
2. Arrange a good check plot in the demonstration.

If a demonstration without check is established, it will be difficult to convince the farmer about the advantage of the demonstrated practice. The striking difference between the check plot and the demonstration plot cannot be shown. In many of these cases, the demonstrator farmer tries to compare his demonstration plot with good plots of other farmers grown without the improved practice and thus starts doubting the advantage of the recommended practice. That is why it is said **"Demonstration without a check is no demonstration".** When that is the case with the demonstrator farmer himself, imagine how difficult it is to convince other farmers in the village.

How to arrange a good check plot: A good check plot in a demonstration will help farmers to get convinced about the advantages of a new practice. A bad check plot will prejudice their mind and raises all sorts of doubts about the new practice. A good check plot should satisfy the following four requirements.

1. Check plot should be in the same field as the demonstration plot
2. Check plot should get the same cultivation as the demonstration plot except the practice involved in the demonstration.
3. Check plot and the demonstration plot should be perpendicular to the road or nearest field border.
4. Check plot should not be influenced by the border effect.

Farmers Should be Taken to the Demonstration Plots Which are Their Class Rooms

"Seeing is believing" goes a famous saying, Unless the farmers see the demonstration plot, they will not be convinced about the new practice. So help the farmers to observe demonstration plots and get convinced. Simple educational field days, that is collecting a group of farmers at the demonstration plots and explaining to them, are quite essential.

Harvest Demonstration Plots

Without harvesting demonstration plots and collecting the results, there will be nothing to show or explain the advantage of a new practice, over the local practice. So demonstration plots must be harvested and results obtained. Harvest demonstration plots should be in the presence of farmers.

If demonstrations are not harvested in the presence of farmers, they start doubting about the results. So at least involve few farmers who can support the results in meetings.

Get Visual Evidences to Serve as Proofs Later on

Extension workers have to work with farmers for more than six months when there will be no crop in the field. It is easy to convince farmers if some evidences from the demonstration plots can be shown to them. Photographs and specimen samples from the plots will be of great help in convincing farmers. So take photographs and collect samples of crops, or ear heads from the demonstration plots.

Use Demonstration Results in Meetings

Demonstration results being the local proofs have more value in convincing farmers. So in all village meetings the results of demonstrations should be used. Write on the black board and explain the results. Prepare simple charts or flannel graphs and use them in the meetings. Exhibit photographs and explain them.

4.4 CONDUCTING AND USING RESULT DEMONSTRATIONS

What is a Result Demonstration? A result demonstration is an extension method used to establish local proof that the recommended practice is applicable locally. It is based on the principle that which is seen and done is retained by farmers more readily.

Why is result demonstration important? Results obtained at the Experimental Stations alone often fail to attract the attention of farmers so as to build confidence in them. Farmers have more confidence in what extension workers teach if they are convinced that their recommendations are practical and are based on local demonstrations. This is specially so in underdeveloped countries to persuade the less informed and most skeptical families. The results obtained from the local demonstrations provide the basic information required to be used by extension workers. If film-shows and others are based upon such basic information, they stimulate much more interest than when used without them. The individual farmer who conducts the result demonstration in his field is the first person to learn about the new practice, by keeping a record of results. He then becomes his own teacher and teacher to many other neighbouring farmers. Extension workers can teach with more confidence about a recommended practice when that is locally proved to be a success in that area through local demonstrations.

How to conduct and use result demonstration? Result demonstration should be understood as an educational experience having a continuity. It must have a past as well as a future. It is not a routine item like supplies and sharp beginnings and ends. There are well defined steps in conducting and using

Result Demonstration which every extension worker must know and practice.

Step – 1: Decide the Practices Needed to be Demonstrated

This requires the analysis of the situation which should include the different projects listed in the extension programme of the area and the consideration of the most important practices to be taught in each project.

Step – 2: Specify the Purpose of the Result Demonstration

Result demonstration may be necessary to give confidence to the extension workers themselves so as to provide them the necessary teaching materials or to convince farmers in the practicability of new practices.

Step – 3: Workout the Plan of the Demonstration

The Extension workers should help the farmers in this job. If necessary, their superiors and or the research staff may also be consulted. The plan details should include the following:

(a) Number, nature and location of demonstration.
(b) Material to be used and records to be kept for each demonstrations.
(c) Methods to be used for estimating, summarizing and publicizing results.
(d) Procedures for laying out and supervising demonstrations.

Step – 4 : Select the Demonstrator

(a) Call a meeting of farmers who are engaged in the specified enterprise related to demonstration. For example Ragi growers in case of varietal demonstration on Ragi.
    (i) Impress on the minds of farmers that the demonstration is intended to establish local proof of the improved practice. Use suitable chart or other visual aid. Stress that the demonstration is not only

for the benefit of the individual farmer selected but also for the advantage of all farmers growing that crop.

(ii) Guide the farmers to select a suitable demonstrator, responsibility of a demonstrator and the requirement to be met by him should be clearly explained. Some of the factors involved which should be clearly explained are: convenient location where people generally pass by in their daily routine. For example Roadside, near a common well or temple. demonstrator should be respected by people as a good farmer. demonstrator must be willing to follow instructions in detail and demonstrator should be willing to have demonstration meetings in the field and allow others to visit and it.

(b) Where the extension worker finds difficulty in organizing a meeting, he should contact the farmers informally and try to explain the above mentioned factors before selecting a demonstrator. The purpose of the demonstration must be known to many farmers.

Step – 5: Starting the Demonstration

(i) Contact the demonstrator farmer. Discuss why, how and when the work is to be done.

(ii) Teach skills – if the demonstration involves the use of any skill which the demonstrator needs to be taught, a method demonstration meeting may be arranged to teach such a skill.

(iii) Plan with the demonstrator. This includes the measurement of the plot, layout of the plot leaving a check, deciding on the time of sowing or planting and calculating the requirements of seed, fertilizer, and other inputs.

(iv) Help the demonstrator to obtain services and materials. Assist the demonstrator to get the required seed, fertilizer, chemicals, signboard, implements, etc. well in advance.

(v) Assist the demonstrator in sowing or planting. Collect a bunch of farmers near the plot to see the starting. This will create more interest about the demonstration.

Step – 6: Put up a Signboard

Every demonstration plot should have a big signboard, to attract the farmers passing nearby the demonstration field.

The following details to be shown on the sign board in the local language are: Sketch of the plan showing the different treatments. Financial implications of the treatments, and some challenging questions to farmers.

Step – 7: Supervise the Demonstration

This is necessary to maintain the interest of the demonstrator and other farmers. It is common to observe that demonstrations become discouraged or loose interest and fail to complete the demonstrations unless they are closely supervised. Lack of supervision might also bring new difficulties, when insect or diseases attack appears on the demonstrated plot and if specific suggestions are not given to the demonstrator, the demonstration may fail.

Hence, the extension worker must visit the demonstration plot once in a week or two, and discuss with the demonstrator about the progress of the demonstration and the difficulties experienced by him. On such occasions, he should also take other farmers to the plot and discuss with them about the crop-growth in the demonstration plot and ascertain their reactions on the same.

Step – 8: Complete the Demonstration

This is the most important step to be followed and consists of the following:

(i) Hold result demonstration meetings. At least 2 to 3 meetings may be organised during the crop season. Those meetings will draw attention of the local farmers to the difference in growth of the check plot and the treatment plots. This will also give opportunity to the farmers to get their doubts clarified.

(ii) Take photographs: At least one photograph should be taken at each result demonstration meeting. This is needed to produce some evidence in the village meetings later on.

(iii) Organize the final demonstration meeting at the time of harvest. This is a must for every demonstration.

- Call local panchayat, taluk panchayat members and other leaders along with the village farmers;
- Show them the differences in the check plot and the treatment plots.
- Request them to estimate the difference in yields.
- Harvest to estimate the difference in yields.
  (A sample area might be selected uniform to the entire demonstration plots).
- Weigh or measure the produce carefully and record the same.
- Let the farmers estimate the yields and workout the economics.
- Get photographs of the harvested material for the use as visuals.

Step – 9: Summarize, Analyze and Interpret Results

More increased yields obtained in demonstrations will not be enough to convince farmers about the practicability of recommended practices. The yield data need to be summarized in a form that could be understood by farmers and details worked out, regarding the additional cost incurred in connection with the improved practice, additional returns obtained, net money saved, other advantages or disadvantages due to the improved practice and any other points. Incase the demonstration results are good, it is best to report the results with a statement that additional demonstration will be taken up. If the demonstration has suffered due to known conditions of unfavourable factors, the same may also be stated.

Step – 10: Follow-up Demonstrations

The practical value of result demonstrations depends upon the extent people see, hear or read about the results.

- Prepare photographs and slides showing the result of the demonstration.
- Prepare charts based on the results.

- Arrange meetings with local farmers and discuss the results obtained at the demonstrations with the help of such charts and slides.
- Request demonstrators to explain their experience to farmers.
- Report results of demonstrations in village planning meetings.
- Discuss the results of demonstrations in village planning meetings.
- Publish leaflets incorporating the results.
- Display photographs and specimens showing the demonstrations in extension offices and other organisations.

What Needs to be Remembered

It is not the number of demonstrations set up in an area that count but the way in which they are conducted and made use of. One result demonstrations conducted properly is more valuable than ten demonstrations set up without completing them. Result demonstrations are the most costly of all extension methods. They require more time of the extension worker. It is, thus, necessary to see that the result demonstrations which are started must be completed properly so that the time and money spent is not wasted. So, extension workers must be properly trained in planning, conducting and using result demonstrations.

4.5 FIELD DAYS

Man has been striving to get his basic needs from various sources since time immemorial. He obtained his requirements of food and clothing by harvesting products available in nature during hunting and fishing stage. Production has been increasing in different parts of the world to the extent to which science has been transformed into usable technology and actually adopted on farms. Process of agricultural development is a lengthy and complex one. It has deep roots in the laboratories where basic work is carried out in various fields of sciences like biology, chemistry, physics etc. Attempts to unravel mysteries of nature are in progress in many laboratories all over the world. New discoveries flow out continuously from these laboratories. Attempts are also going to make use of these discoveries to increase agricultural production.

Science has to be converted into usable technology. Technology thus developed for different areas has to be taught to users along with the scientific principles underlying these recommendations. The input required to practice technology have to be made available. It is not an easy task. Breeder may make available a handful of seeds of good variety when it is declared as released. The users are to be convinced about the superiority of new varieties over the old ones. Agronomic practices that are to be adopted are top be taught. Required quantity of seed has to be multiplied in stages and made available in pure form. Development and transfer of technology is possible only when it is done in a systematic manner through a communication system established for the purpose.

Field day is one of the links in this chain of agricultural development starting from scientific discovery and culminating from the usage of technology by large number of farmers. Field day is just a beginning of a long process of technology transfer from research station to farmers. Field days are organized to bring the agents of transfer of technology and potential users of technology to the place where science and technology are in the process of development. This provides an opportunity to get a preview of what is in the initial and later stages of development as well as what is ready for use and what is being used already by some progressive users. More than anything else, it gives an opportunity for the researchers to come in direct contact with the beneficiaries. The agents of transfer of technology have a chance to hear both sides. i.e. those who are responsible for creating new knowledge and convert the same into technology and those who are going to be ultimate users. The Field days provide a platform where researchers, extension and development agencies and farmers meet. It is always hoped that the discussions that would take place on this platform will be fruitful and satisfying to all those who participate in this.

On such occasions, every participant has a role to play. All the three parties, viz. researchers, technologists and users have got to play a role of transmitting as well as receiving. In this process of give and take, the utmost beneficiaries will be those whose receiving power is the highest. All those including researchers will be amply benefited if they observe keenly, hear patiently and absorb silently. Keen observation on the part of extension and development workers and farmers is necessary to learn what is placed before them by a research station. The researchers have to observe keenly from a distance the reaction shown by those who are observing what is exhibited by them. Patient hearing is inevitable on both sides. The result of keen observation and patient hearing will naturally result in good absorption. In doing so there are certain codes if followed will benefit all concerned immensely.

It is the duty of researchers to explain in clear terms the problems that they are required to tackle, viz. programmes taken up to solve the problems, results so far obtained and finally, their future plan of work. They should explain elaborately the barriers that exist in increasing the production in different sub-regions and which of them are more critical. Similarly, the scientific reasons for adopting a certain approach for solving these problems should be very clearly placed before the participants. The results obtained until them should be explained in a lucid manner. One should be modest in claiming successes. It is, however, necessary to indicate the potential benefit that the particular item of research is likely to offer. In doing so, neither high hopes should be created nor chord of despair should be struck. What is needed is to explain the approach adopted to solve certain problems and to give an idea of the stage reached so far, in getting solutions to these problems. It is necessary also to provide opportunity to participants, to know what the researchers future plans are. At this juncture, again it is necessary to be moderate and indicate only plans which are almost ready for implementation rather than paint a very bright future picture. In short, what is needed is to give a real picture of the past, present and future of the organization.

After presenting such a picture, the researcher should quietly observe the reaction of the agents of transfer as well as the users and make mental as well as written note of the same. They should hear patiently the expressions made openly and observe quietly unexpressed reactions. They should neither be elated by the praises nor depressed by drastic criticisms. The skill lies in knowing the real reaction. This reaction may be available with those who observe carefully and may not express. Such reaction has to be extracted by using various strategies. Some provocation and private discussion may bring out the reactions. All attempts should be made by researchers to get such opinions by using all ingenuity available with them. It is in this regard that one researcher is found to be more resourceful than the other and may also end up as a more successful one than the other.

It is not sufficient, if just mental or written note is made of the reaction. The comment should be analyzed carefully and required modifications should be made if necessary in the light of these comments that becomes available on occasions like Field Days. Specific mention should be made of the changes effected in the light of the comments on future occasions. This will help considerable in encouraging others to make useful suggestions.

The responsibilities of change-agents and farmers are more onerous than researchers in a meet of this kind. Plan of work presented should be carefully analyzed. More details should be obtained if necessary from researchers to enable such an analysis. The suggestions for improvement given at this stage go a long way in preventing fruitless and wasteful expenditure. No one should be little his role and think he has nothing to contribute in this regard since the programmes are supposed to have been drawn up by experts in the field. It is necessary that farmers should have a look at it from users' point of view and the change agents, look at it from sellers' point of view. These view points are of utmost importance to researchers who have a different point of view altogether. It is necessary that users' and sellers' points of views are brought to bear on the research programmes. Only then the results of such programmes are likely to be adopted much faster.

The programmes that are in progress should be viewed from different angle altogether. The users and change agents would be knowing what finished product is likely to come out. They should start thinking as to the areas where these results are likely to be useful and they should also think as to what steps are required to be taken to popularize the same quickly. Even at this stage, comments on the need for making any change in the studies can be given by the users as well as change-agents and accepted by the researchers with considerable advantage. At this stage thinking should be more on the steps required to be taken for adoption. It is at this stage that the input requirements have to be worked out. If any new input is required and steps should be initiated for their supplies in future.

The users should pick up ideas that they think would be workable under their conditions and try to get more details about the same so that it will be easy for them to adopt the same as soon as results become available in the form of recommendations. Considerable thought should be bestowed by change-agents also on the results that are likely to flow out soon. Doubts, if any, should be got clarified. It is an opportunity to have a preview of the finished product that is likely to be made available in the near future.

Lastly, the users and change-agents should put forward the problems that they are facing in adopting the recommended practices and what future improvements are necessary in making them more acceptable to users. They should also very bluntly say which recommendations should be modified and which should be withdrawn completely. This is where, plain speaking and courage of conviction are required. It is easy to say that certain recommendations should be withdrawn but difficult to justify such a statement. It is still more easy to say recommendations should be modified and, but, more difficult to list out the recommendations that should be dropped. Even today, there are many recommended varieties on the active list which should have been withdrawn long back. Similarly, there are many experiments or studies going on in the research stations which should have been discontinued long time ago. The process of discarding has to be gone through carefully but ruthlessly. Care should be taken not to throw the baby along with the wash water. But, at the same time filth is difficult to separate out of the useful from useless. Discarding has to be done with courage and discrimination. The courage in this regard has to be exercised by all very judiciously.

Finally, it must be said that the results of research which become available from research stations have to be modified by carrying on adoptive research in different parts of the region. The responsibility of carrying out adaptive research is cast on the State Departments. They, in collaboration with research agency, should draw adaptive research programme to test the findings and to know in which of the areas these findings are useful. The process of thinking should start during these Field Days on this aspect too.

A word of advice to the farmers is expedient at this stage. However perfect the recommendations are, it is necessary for the farmers to understand the principles underlying each recommendations so that it will be possible to them to make necessary changes to suit their own conditions. Our farmers have done this magnificently. They have shown their ability to understand most intricate scientific principles and modify the recommendations to suit their own conditions. Many modifications made in the hybrid seed production are a testimony to this ability. Researcher and change agents should know the farmers, though illiterate have the innate intelligence to understand most intricate scientific principles involved in various recommendations developed for their benefit. Only care that is to be taken is to see that he is convinced about the recommendations. Once he is convinced that the recommendation is advantageous to him, he will try to know scientific principles to the extent needed to understand the recommendation and modify them to suit his conditions. It is for the change-agents to actives his intelligence to such an extent that will enable him to make the required change in the recommendation to suit his condition.

This is the crux of the problem in carrying on extension work. It is no use conveying the recommendations in a routine manner to the doors of the farmers. They should be conveyed along with the principles. To enable the extension agency to do so, the adaptive research must be carried out by them only. Knowing of principles by extension workers is possible only when the researchers do some extension work in close collaboration with them.

Realization that agricultural development is a long drawn process in which many agencies are involved and that it cannot be done by only one agency, has is necessary so that the development takes place at a much faster rate than hitherto. Realization also has to come about that no one can coordinate the activities of these agencies from outside. Understanding should come from within and attitudes changed accordingly. Coordination has to be brought about by some one within these agencies themselves. Earlier the realization comes, better it is for one and all.

4.6 EFFECTIVE COMMUNICATION—TOOLS AND TECHNIQUES

In order to understand the tools and techniques required for effective communication by field workers, it is necessary that some of the fundamentals relating to communication for village work are also to be understood. Hence, while dealing with this topic, discussion under the following is needed:

1. What is Communication?
2. Is communication for village work same as ordinary communication?
3. Communication and stages in innovation-decision process.
4. Some fundamentals for effective communication.
5. Communication methods for village work.
6. Sources of effective communication.
7. Teaching aids needed for effective oral communication.
8. Some research results.

1. What is Communication?

Communication is not mere telling something to others. Communication must result in understanding of common meaning between two or more persons. Of course, words are the main media in this process. There are four elements involved in any communication, viz. source, message, channel and receiver. There are certain factors concerning each element, which influence the effectiveness of communication.

2. Is Communication for Village Work Same as Ordinary Communication?

Ordinary communication is primarily interested to change the behaviour of persons involving change in attitude, change in the knowledge and/or change in skills. Communication for village work also known as diffusion is a special type of communication where communication is in respect of a new idea and is aimed at in persuading people for taking action. In short, communication for village work is part of the process of educating rural people for changing their actions. Communication for educating people for changing actions besides requiring changes in attitude, knowledge and skills on the part of people, also needs building confidence in the new ideas or practices and methods to overcome the risk associated with them.

3. Communication and Stages in Innovation-Diffusion Process

The flow of technological information from its source to farmer is also not a one shot affair. This is achieved through well defined stages which form a part of the innovation-decision process. There are four stages in this process which are: (1) Knowledge (2) Persuasion, (3) Decision, and (4) Confirmation. The communication functions carried out during these four stages are indicated below:

Knowledge: The individual is exposed to the innovations existence and gains some understanding of how it functions.

Persuasion: The individual forms a favourable or unfavorable attitude towards the innovation.

Decision: The individual engages in activities which lead to a choice to adopt or reject the innovation.

Confirmation: The individual seeks reinforcement for the innovation decision he has made.

4. Some Fundamentals for Effective Communication

(a) Learning is the result of sensory experience.

(b) Although we receive new ideas through one or more of our senses, sight and hearing are the most active.

(c) It is estimated that 85 per cent of our learning is derived through the use of eyes and 10 per cent through the use of ears.

(d) Operation of the senses alone will not give the required perception unless the appropriate meaning is also simultaneously brought out.

(e) Communication will be more effective when maximum number of senses are involved.

(f) For confidence building situations, communication methods involving seeing and doing are best suited when compared to those involving only symbols.

5. Communication Methods for Village Work

There are different communication methods which can be used in fieldwork. Some important methods can be listed as:

1. Talking individually by personal visits
2. Meetings
3. Using newspapers
4. Using printed literature
5. Using radio
6. Demonstrations
7. Field trips
8. Exhibitions
9. Using televisions
10. Putting posters
11. Showing films

We should recognize that all communication methods do not produce the same results. Each serves a specific purpose. We should, therefore, know the various purposes involved in communication and the communication method ideally suited to meet each purpose. These methods could be classified under three heads, viz. (i) Involving symbols, (ii) Involving seeing, and (iii) Involving seeing and doing. Based on this classification, the methods could be arranged in a cone form. At the top of this cone will be the least effective methods while the most effective methods will be at the bottom. While using these methods, we should develop strategies of using more abstract methods with the underpinning of concrete experiences. It is always better to use a combination of methods in fieldwork. We must also understand what methods are most appropriate for the different stages of the innovation decision process.

Communication Methods for Knowledge Stage

Posters
Meetings
Talking individually
Printed literature
Newspapers
Radio

Communication Methods for Persuasion Stage

Exhibitions

Meetings with discussion
Literature with facts
Field trips
Films
Demonstrations
Television

Communication Methods for Decision

Meeting with discussion
Field trips
Demonstrations
Televisions
Films
Literature with local facts

Communication Methods for Reinforcement

Field trips
Literature with local facts
Television
Demonstrations

6. Sources of Effective Communication

More effective communication occurs when source and receiver are homophilous. Homophily is the degree to which pairs of individuals who interact are similar in certain attributes. One distinct feature in communication of innovations is that the source is usually quite heterophilous to the receiver. This highlights the role played by neighbours, friends and local leaders in the effective communication of innovations under village conditions. The two steps flow phenomenon in communication are also based on this principle.

Influence of sources of information on adoption of fertilizers: (i) At knowledge stage, the most frequently mentioned source was the personal type of formal sources followed by informal community sources and important formal sources (ii) The rate of adoption of fertilizers for farmer's reporting more than 3 different types of sources contacted at the persuasion and decision stages was found to be significantly higher than in case of farmers reporting less than 3 different types of sources contacted.

4.7 SOME FACTORS THAT INFLUENCE EXTENSION WORKERS IN CHOICE OF TEACHING DEVICES

Please check the principal methods that you would use if there is need in a village or group of villages for the following:

Checklist for Use of Principal Extension Methods for Different Purposes

Purposes	*Meetings*												
	Lecture method	*Discussion method*	*Method Demons. or lab method*	*Result demons.*	*Tour*	*Result Demons.*	*Home visits*	*Bulletins*	*Circulars*	*News papers*	*Radio/TV*	*Exhibition*	*Office call*
1. To teach skills													
2. To reach large number of people													
3. To give families timely information													
4. To motivate and stimulate action in some project													
5. To furnish cost data and other basic information of use in revising programme													
6. To furnish people in community local proof of the desirability of a good practice.													

(Contd.)

(*Contd.*)

Purposes	Meetings													
	Lecture method	*Discussion method*	*Method Demons. or lab method*	*Result demons.*	*Tour*	*Result Demons.*	*Home visits*	*Bulletins*	*Circulars*	*News papers*	*Radio/TV*	*Exhibition*	*Office call*
7. To promote individual and group thinking on problems of common interest.													
8. To stimulate acceptance of the improved practices through friendly competition.													
9. To develop tolerance with in the group and to help people to overcome prejudices.													
10. To help in selection of better leaders.													
11. To influence change at relatively low cost													
12. To have a good source of information for meetings, news items, pictures, radio talks													
13. To help rural people to feel satisfaction from success													
14. To provide change in environment, and worthwhile social contacts.													

(*Contd.*)

(Contd.)

Purposes	Meetings												
	Lecture method	*Discussion method*	*Method Demons. or lab method*	*Result demons.*	*Tour*	*Result Demons.*	*Home visits*	*Bulletins*	*Circulars*	*News papers*	*Radio/TV*	*Exhibition*	*Office call*
15. To furnish rural people definite, accurate, and detailed information.													
16. To influence people who do not and cannot go to meetings.													
17. To acquaint farmers and homemakers with improved practices.													
18. To stimulate interest and increase effectiveness of other means and agencies.													
19. To reach the largest number of people at the lease cost.													
20. To help rural people to establish confidence in the extension worker.													
21. To secure better and more efficient team work in meeting joint responsibilities.													

(Contd.)

(Contd.)

Purposes	Meetings												
	Lecture method	Discussion method	Method Demons. or lab method	Result demons.	Tour	Result Demons.	Home visits	Bulletins	Circulars	News papers	Radio/TV	Exhibition	Office call
22. To get the work before the public. To promote understanding of and goodwill toward extension work on the part of village and city people.													
23. To contribute to better understanding of good standards for farm and home products.													
24. To promote personal acquaintance between demonstrator and people.													
25. To help families to have broader, general information.													
26. To put information in hands of rural people.													
27. To acquaint the public with farmers' problems, promoting a better understanding.													

(Contd.)

(*Contd.*)

Purposes	*Meetings*												
	Lecture method	*Discussion method*	*Method Demons. or lab method*	*Result demons.*	*Tour*	*Result Demons.*	*Home visits*	*Bulletins*	*Circulars*	*News papers*	*Radio/TV*	*Exhibition*	*Office call*
28. To give the extension worker first-hand information regarding farmers' problems and activities.													
29. To assist rural families on a project when the worker has a relatively small amount of time to put on it.													
30. To help rural people to analyze their problems and prepare for intelligent action.													

4.8 FLOW OF TECHNOLOGICAL INFORMATION AND FACTORS AFFECTING ELEMENTS OF COMMUNICATION

New technological information must flow from its source and reach the ultimate users, viz. farmers. This process is popularly known as Diffusion of innovations. Diffusion of innovations is, however, a special type of communication. What distinguishes this from ordinary communication is that (i) in diffusion, the message is always a new idea which naturally carries with it some risk factors; and (ii) The communication process here is not only interested to transmit the message but it is concerned to see that the message results in some action, change of practice from the old to new.

Communication Stages

The flow of technological information from its source to farmers is also not a one shot affair. This is achieved through various stages and the entire process is known as Innovation-Decision process.

There are four stages in this process which are (1) Knowledge, (2) Persuasion, (3) Decision, and (4) Confirmation. The communication functions carried out during these stages are given below.

Knowledge: The individual is exposed to the innovation's existence and gains some understanding of how it functions.

Persuasion: The individual forms a favourable or unfavorable attitude towards the innovation.

Decision: The individual engages in activities which lead to a choice to adopt or reject the innovation.

Confirmation: the individual seeks reinforcement for the innovation decision he has made.

Different communication sources play their role during these different stages. Radio communication may provide new knowledge to a farmer but may not succeed in persuading him about its superiority. Personal discussion with a farmer may help in persuading him about the advantages of this practice but he may still remain indecisive about its use. A visit to another farmer's field where this new practice is being followed and a consequent favourable opinion from neighbours may ultimately help him in confirming about its superiority so that he continues to adopt it later.

Adopter Categories

The other side of this flow of technological information is that the reach of this technological, flow resulting in adoption varies from individuals to individuals. Research in this field has shown that individuals can be located differently on the time continuum of farm practice adoptions. These individuals can also be classified on the basis of their time of adoption. Five such categories of adopters are identified and their approximate percentage in a social system are given below:

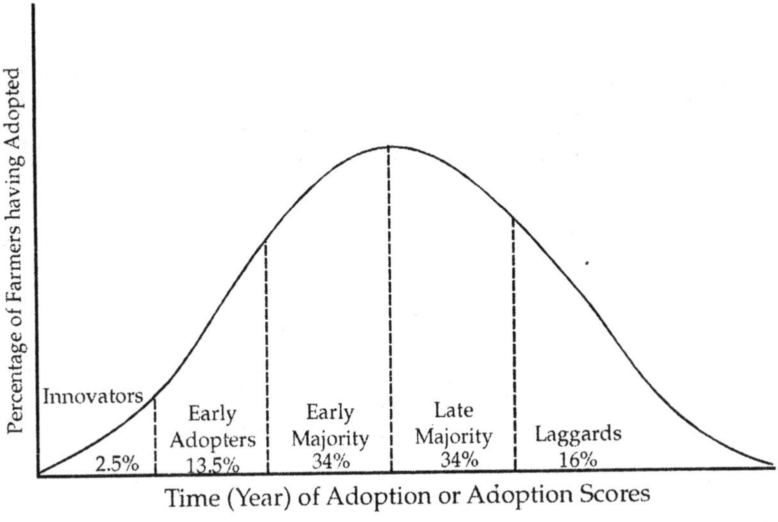

Adopter Categories

This aspect of the flow of technological information has lot of implications for developmental work. When a new programme is taken up it is desirable to work in as large an area as possible in order to encourage innovators in the entire area come under the fold of the programme rather than selecting a small area and attempting to bring majority of the farmers in that area to come under the programme.

Flow of Communication in Steps

The two-step flow of hypothesis which was formulated soon after the 1940 Presidential election in the U.S.A. challenged the growing belief in Mass Society and introduced a new concept of opinion leadership as a link between people and mass media in the transfer of influence of messages. In the field of flow of technological information relating to farming, the two-step flow has been found operating. In this model the receivers are a variable number of times removed from the message origin. The exact number of steps in the process depends on the intent of the source, the availability of mass media and the extent of audience exposure, the nature of the messages suitable to the receiving audience.

Mass Media Exposure and Modernization

There are certain antecedents which encourage mass media exposure. The mass media exposure has also its consequences which accelerates modernization. This can be shown in the below mentioned model.

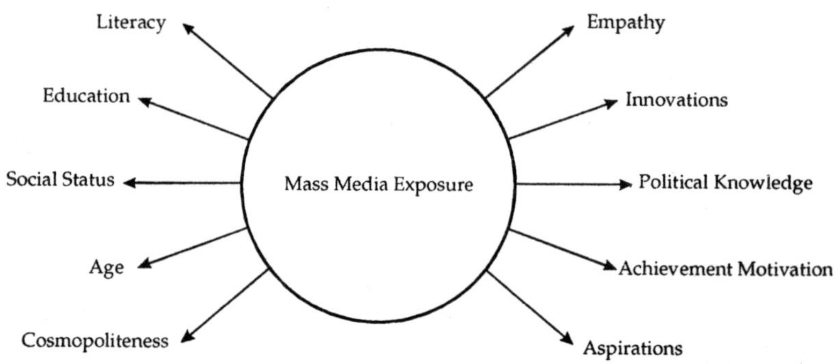

Communication Model and Important Factors Influencing the Effectiveness of Communication

There are 4 major elements in the Communication models, viz., (1) Source, (2) Message, (3) Channel, and (4) Receiver. There are certain factors concerning each element which influences the effectiveness of communication. These factors are listed element-wise.

4.9 MASS MEDIA AND ECONOMIC DEVELOPMENT

The Economic Development is the need for expansion of mass

media like newspapers, radio, television and movies in addition to the class media of books and travels. Why is it necessary to have such an expansion in mass media sources? The important reasons for this can be stated as follows:

1. Economic development requires that people should know new ideas and practices without any loss of time. Since majority of the people in India are still either illiterate or semi-illiterates, the cheapest and fastest method of reaching these people to fetch new ideas and practices is by transmitting the messages through mass media because these media have a unique ability to inform vast number of people quickly.
2. Mass media can also help to teach people by multiplying resources of knowledge. India, like other developing countries, is short of schools, short of teachers, short of literates, short of many kinds of informed and skilled people in places where information and skill would make differences. Although not all of the shortages can be met by the mass media, it follows more or less a two step in communication. Mass media are quite useful in changing attitudes to which audience members are not particularly committed – a fact which explains much of the media effectiveness in advertising.

   Mass media are not equally effective in all diffusion stages. When an idea or practice has to change; a person has to pass through 5 stages – awareness, interest, trial, evaluation and adoption. Research has shown that mass media are only important in the awareness stage. While other interpersonal communication sources like friends, neighbours, extension workers influence more at other stages like interest, trial, evaluation and adoption. Communications research has consistently revealed that people tend to read, watch and listen to communications which present points of view with which they are themselves in sympathy and tend to avoid communications of a different line. Thus, people are exposed to mass communication selectively. They select material, which is in accord with their existing views and interests.

3. Mass media assist to a certain extent in the decision function by presenting alternate viewpoints, feeding discussions and presenting discussions once made.
4. Mass media teach new desires and new satisfactions. They depict situations in which the good things of life which most people never dreamt before they are taken for granted. They portray roles in which these rider lives are lived and provide clues as to how these roles can be enacted by others.
5. Mass media can have profound characterological effects. This is possible because media provide the capacity to convince of situations and ways of life quite different from those directly experienced.
6. Certain types of media content especially in children's literature can actually rise achievement motivation which is in turn a major necessary condition for development.
7. Exposure to mass media operate directly upon attention, information, tastes and images of individuals.
8. Uses of mass media bring about changes in the structure of influence in the society. This process occurs when the audience number is predisposed to change.

The social effects of mass communication will, therefore, depend primarily on the society as a whole and in particular such institutions as the family, schools and churches – fashions the audience numbers whom mass communication serves.

Media are quite effective in changing attitudes to which audience members are not particularly committed.

Mass media are of tremendous importance to persuasive communicator today because it has reached audiences that are otherwise unavailable to them. But the mass media are by no means a panacea for all their problems. Persuasive communication through the mass media still depends for a high ratio of success of the interpersonal efforts of opinion leaders.

In spite of the earlier stated advantages of the mass media, there are also certain limitations, which we need to recognize.

Limitations

1. Mass media alone do not effectively change people. It

takes a combination of media and direct personal contact to move people to action and practices. To stimulate action mass media exhilaration need to be coupled with the organization of face to face leadership. This point has been most dramatically demonstrated in a series of UNESCO sponsored studies of radio listening and TV viewing groups. For example, in radio studies, the radio programmes listened by people under normal fashion had visually no effect while, radio listening groups were organized and discussions for the programmes encouraged in the villages, the ideas communicated through the radio were followed by the people. The same results have been reported even with television communication.

2. Mass media follows more or less a two-step flow of communication; i.e. mass media information is mostly used by few leaders in the society for changing ideas and practices. When such leaders provide further persuasion or set personal example, the common man starts changing his idea or practice. This is true even in the case of advanced society. Hence, interpersonal channel of communication play an important role.
3. Mass media participation in every country exhibits a centripetal tendency i.e. as different mass media channels like radio and press diffuse through different social strata and geographical areas they tend to converge on the same people in the same places. This may explain why hopes for achieving quick millennia of modernization through the media alone usually have been disappointed.

To sum up, it could be said that mass media alone unlike the word of mouth communication fail in producing action, but do create information and desires. Without an effective political organization at the grassroots to provide word of mouth support for the messages in the mass media, the latter do not produce the desired action results.

The theory of communication that underlies the media investment pattern in most non-communist development countries is one which says: that the media do not seem to produce major changes in action, other changes in the short run as changes in beliefs and values unaccompanied by appropriate changes in practices tend to be destructive. Despite the impracticability and dangers of trying to produce changes in the minds of men, it is recognized that such changes are needed for modernization.

There is a two-step flow of communication. That is to say the mass media do not lead to adoption directly. They create an awareness of the existence of the new practices and they provide guidance to innovating leaders.

However, actual adoption of a new practice, requires either personal persuasion or personal example by a respected opinion leader.

Thus, the spread of an innovation can be traced from an initiating centre by direct personal contact out to the periphery. It can also be traced from younger, well educated some what alienated and relatively cosmopolitan individuals in a community to older, highly entrenched, above average educated individuals with whom the farmers are in touch and then finally to other people in the community who follow the leaders. The adoption of their innovation advocated in the mass media has been shown to depend on interpersonal discussion of it.

The last point has been most dramatically demonstrated in a series of UNESCO sponsored studies of radio listening and TV viewing groups.

A study of Village Radio Broadcasts in India has shown that in the controlled situations where these broadcasts were listened by individuals in usual fashion, the radio programmes had virtually no effect. Where, however, listening groups were organized and discussion of the programmes took place immediately after, the suggestions were often followed. The same thing was followed with the TV viewing groups in France and the other countries too. Similar results on the role of the word-of-mouth communication in clinching media advice have been detained in marketing studies.

To stimulate action, mass media exhortations need to be coupled with the organization of face-to-face leadership.

Very few studies have looked at the role of the mass media in producing transformations in values and personality. Although it is said that changes in men's actions are the really important objectives and that changes in attitude are but a means towards the desired actions, it may be the other way round. It is, for example, relatively easy to get peasants to plant a particular kind of seed one foot apart instead of six inches apart, this action can be induced by many payments, by terror, by authority, by persuasion, by proving it to be the will of the Gods and by many other means. But improvement of one such practice does not mean that the peasant has been in any way modernized. A far more significant change would be the development of a scientific attitude towards the adoption of new practice. It is only that kind of internal change in the latent structure of his attitudes that would produce self-sustaining movement towards modernization.

In this area the most notable contributions have been by Daniel Herner and David Mclelland. They have both put forward the daring thesis that the mass media can have profound character logical effects. Learner argues that as the traditional rules crumble, some of the basic relationships among human beings undergo transformation. The ancient power of the village elders declines to respectful difference while real influence goes elsewhere. The traditional rule that age brings wisdom probably work well in immobile isolated villages where change was slow and experience was the only teacher. The longer one lived, the more experience he gained and the greater his title to wisdom. Now the young men no longer wait their patrimony. They go off to the cities, take jobs under the modern discipline, learn from newspapers and movies. On many matters they are better informed – perhaps more than the old timers. As these are the matters of current interest, others turn to the young men for opinion and advice. The structure of influence thus changes in the community and in the family.

The media teach new desires and new satisfactions. They depict situations in which the good things of life, which most people never dreamt, before are taken for granted. They portray roles in which these richer lives are lived and provide clues as to how these roles can be enacted by others.

The modernity acquires what it considers news mainly through the media systems, recalling equally radio and newspaper items. The traditionals receive their news mainly through the oral system. The transitional participate in both systems.

As radio and press diffuse through different social strata and geographical areas, they tend to converge on the same people in the same places. This may explain why hopes for achieving quick millennia of modernization through the media alone usually have been disappointed.

1. Central to modernization is in modes of communicating ideas, attitudes – for spreading among a large public vivid images of its new ways is what modernization distinctly does. Not the class media of tabloids, radio and movies are now the dominant modes. Nevertheless, encouraging reports have come where the use of mass media have shared the best teaching, supplemented the resources of local schools, multiplied the content possible for field workers.
2. Speeded up learning and encouraged people to expose themselves and their children to other learning opportunities. In many cases, it has also been possible to do all the teaching by using these mass media. For example, in Japan there are radio television high schools which combine the use of radio, television and correspondence for teaching. Similarly in Australia mass media are used for home teaching and distant students. It is also reported from Africa that mass media have been used for giving in-service training to teachers.
3. Mass media can also help to a certain extent in the decision function by presenting the material, which is not in accord with those views and interests.

Mass communication seldom works directly upon its audience. So mass communication usually serves as an agent of reinforcement. This does not mean that mass communication can never produce changes in the ideas or the tastes or the values or the behaviour of its audience. The factors of reinforcement sometimes maximize the likelihood of mass communication serving in the interests of change. Mass communication is widely believed to be quite effective in creating opinion leaders who are particularly likely to be exposed to the mass media appropriate to the sphere in which they lead. Fashion leaders read more fashion magazines, leaders of opinion regarding motion pictures read more movie magazines etc.

Social Effects of Mass Communication

The audience for mass communication consists of people and that these people like among other people and amid social institutes. Each of these people has become subject and continue to be subject to numerous influences besides mass communication. It is obvious that a simple movie or radio or TV programme is not very likely to change existing attitudes of audience members, particularly if these attitudes are relatively deep seated. The practitioner must know which specific medium or media use. He must know too the rules of the game. He must have a planned programme for use on coordinated basis, using one to reinforce and supplemented the others.

Newspapers

Newspapers reach more people more often than any other medium. A person buys his newspaper as something he wants, not as something thrust on him. Newspapers are read at the readers' leisure and convenience. This is in sharp contrast with the broadcast media where a programme missed is gone forever. An average reader reads only a portion of his daily newspaper. Thus, it is a mistake to assume publicity in the press is publicity received by all readers.

In conclusion, it could be said that the development of mass media is of course one of the requisites for and signs of a modernizing society but the traditional media on social communication – the bazaar, the coffee house, the puppet show, local meeting and others continue to be influential long after the newspaper and broadcasts are available. Interpersonal channels of communication play an important part in mediating and effects of mass media even in the most advanced societies. A variety of the strategies and tactics through which both mass and interpersonal communication are put in the services of economic and social change.

4.10 TRAINING AIDS—MATERIALS AND EQUIPMENT

Commodity marketing involves a special type of communication, which we call salesmanship. It differs from ordinary communication in that, here the communication should immediately result in some specific action on the part of the audience-purchase and use commodities.

Requirements of communication for salesmanship in marketing should meet the following requirements:

1. Development of a favourable attitude towards commodities.
2. Clear understanding of the knowledge regarding commodity use.
3. Retention of commodity knowledge for a longer period.
4. Development of the needed skills involved in commodity use.
5. Development of confidence so as to result in action to use commodities.

It is, thus, evident that mere verbal communication as is generally practiced in ordinary communication will not be adequate to meet these requirements. The type of communication needed for salesmanship should result in good training that is education for action. Training aids also help in this important task.

Some Fundamentals Behind the Use of Training Aids

1. Learning is the result of sensory experience.
2. Although we receive new ideas through one or more of our senses, seeing and hearing are the most active.
3. It is estimated that 85 per cent of our learning is derived through the use of eyes and 10 per cent through the use of ears.
4. Operation of the senses alone will not give the required perception unless the appropriate meaning is also simultaneously brought out. Learning will be more effective when maximum number of senses are involved.
5. For confidence building situation, learning experiences involve seeing, and doings are the best suited when compared to those involving only symbols.

What Training Aids Will Do?

1. Overcome language barriers.
2. Add interest and involvement.
3. Reduce verbalism.
4. Develop continuity of thought by assisting in understanding proper relationships of component parts.
5. Make learning easier by assisting in forming correct images. Make learning real.
6. Make learning permanent by adding retention of information and visual images.
7. Provide a wide variety of teaching tools.

What Training Aids Will Not Do?

Training aids cannot do the job of communication by themselves. They must be thought of as "aids" only.

Different Types of Training Aids

1. Charts and Graphs

These are very handy training aids and are useful in presenting abstract information in a graphic, easy to understand way. They can make relationships clear and explain the steps in a process. Charts and graphs can also tell story in detail. There are various kinds of charts, each embodying a specific visual pattern.

2. Photographs

The value of a photograph as a training aid is immense. The saying that "a picture is worth one thousand words" is more than true because a photograph can be used to communicate directly with learners in spite of language differences. Other advantages of photographs as training aids are:

(i) Speak a universal language
(ii) Compel attention
(iii) Help building attitudes
(iv) Simple to prepare or obtain

(v) Anything can be photographed
(vi) May be used in different communication situations.

3. Models

These are replicas of real objects. Models as a training aid have a reality that can never be duplicated by a verbal description. Many times, models may be better than real things particularly when there are difficulties of getting the real things for communication. The advantages of using models as training aids can be listed as follows:

(i) Can be handled, examined and operated
(ii) Show how things look and work
(iii) Show relationships
(iv) Simplify complex mechanisms
(v) Enlarge small objects for group study
(vi) Reduce large objects for easy manipulation

4. Samples

These are the real objects that have been mounted or treated in some special way to preserve them. They offer the opportunity to use the object when it might be personally or otherwise unavailable. Samples are mounted and preserved either in glass jars, on cards, in boxes or on boards. It is to be remembered, however, that demonstration with specimens does not substitute for actual demonstrations in the field.

5. Slides and Film Strips

These are projected teaching aids and therefore magnification often helps to get across an idea. Slides are also flexible training aids. The communicator can use all of the set or select the few that will do the best job for him. Because slides and film strips are compact, a large amount of teaching material can be carried from place to place and stored for repeated use. Other advantages of the slides are:

(i) Project pictures for a large audience
(ii) Can be held on the screen as long as needed

(iii) Concentrated attention can be expected
(iv) Can be arranged in any order to suit the specific need
(v) Can generally be produced locally

6. Films

These training aids have the potential to create powerful emotions and urges. People who will not attend any kind of meetings will go to see films. Because of these, films are one of the most effective means of arousing interest, we can still use films primarily to get people to attend meetings. Other good points about the use of this training aid are:

(i) It brings the distant past and the present into learning situation.
(ii) Excellent for showing the steps necessary in doing a task or for showing continuous action.
(iii) It can provide an easily reproduced record of an event or an operation.
(iv) It builds a common denominator of experience.
(v) It can influence change of attitude.
(vi) Can reach literate as well as illiterate people equally effectively.

7. Books

Very few of us generally think of books as training aids. Books are however very useful in training. If small and cheap books can be produced, they can also be used for training groups of people. Not only the pictures in a book are visual aids, but the whole book itself is a good device to aid learning through the eyes. Other advantages of using books as training aids are:

(i) The average teacher cannot organize his own material in as good a form as the book.
(ii) Books place in the hands of a learner something which can guide and stimulate his thinking.
(iii) Neither taking of notes nor mimeographed material can be substitutes for books.
(iv) Helps the average teacher.
(v) Guarantees the uniformity of content to be communicated.

Other Useful Training Aids

1. Flannel Graph

It is a simple training aid with an appeal in its action and suspense. Most useful in communication for a group. In this method, information is written on pieces of paper or cardboard which have flannel or sand paper pasted at the back. These can be pressed against a flannel board for presentation. Flannel graph is like a dream. It has a story or plot. It has a background or set. It has parts that can be moved about the actors.

2. Flash Cards

These are brief visual messages on poster board cards, displayed to emphasize important points in a presentation. Drawings, cartoons and photographs can also be used with brief messages on flash cards. The story is told as each card is held before the group.

3. Flip Charts

It combines some of the advantages of chalkboard, flannel graph and flash cards. It consists of a series of papers stapled together on which information or message is written or drawings are made. The chart can be hung on an easel and the sheets used one by one by turning them back or flipping while presenting the ideas.

4. Chalkboard or Black Board

The most common and simple training aid which can be used every-where. Very useful in meetings and group discussions. Its use needs to be encouraged. A roll up blackboard can be taken wherever we go and used.

5. Demonstrations

Demonstrations are such a common method of training that their values are sometimes overlooked. Demonstrations made the communicators less dependent on words. There are two types of demonstrations; "the Method' and 'the Result'. The first one can be taken to a group and in the second one, the group can be taken to a demonstration.

Demonstrations can combine many other training aids. They often make use of real objects and specimens, models, charts and pictures.

6. Field Trips

It includes a series of demonstrations by taking the learners on a tour. This method may appeal to man's desire to go places and see things. It offers people an opportunity to see for themselves concrete evidence of the value of ideas which are being communicated.

Equipment for Using Training Aids

There are two kinds of equipment-projection equipment and non-projection equipment.

1. Projection Equipment

Like slides and movie projector are needed when we use training aids like slides, film strips and films. The opaque projector or Epidiascope is another common equipment used since a long time. Any photograph or sheet of printed or boldly written information can be projected with this. Complete darkness is, however, necessary to use the above mentioned projection equipment.

Another projection equipment which has come into popular usage in recent years is the overhead projector. The advantages of this, over the opaque projector are that it can be used without darkness and it can be used by the communicator himself as he is giving information. However we have to use only transparencies with it.

2. Non-projection Equipment

The non-projection equipment needed in using several training aids are: (i) chart stand, (ii) flannel boards, and (iii) bulletin board.

4.11 THE ROLE OF AUDIO-VISUAL AIDS

Master teachers are a few and may be encountered only now and then in a lifetime, but if the elements of their abilities could be separated and analyzed, a major portion of their success would most likely be found not in what they say but in how they say it and the method used in communicating their ideas.

Audio-visual aids are no panacea for all our ills, but if effectively utilized, they become very handy in communicating ideas. In the last analysis, teaching and learning is nothing more than the transmission or communication of ideas by the teacher and the understanding and assimilation of these ideas by the learners. If these ideas have been clearly understood, we can assume that the learner will translate them into desirable and accepted patterns. We must, therefore, utilize every process, device and method by which we can be assumed that our ideas have been communicated. A critical analysis of our own instructional methods and procedures will illuminate areas where learning has been non-existent or ineffective. It is these points that audio and visual media can and will assist in the clarification of concepts and the improvement of instructions.

'Don't tell them, show them'.

"We are using slide films, motion pictures, charts, graphs and photographs to carry our sales messages" say sales promotion and advertising manager.

If the system works in explaining sales, there should be no reason why it should not apply equally well in demonstrating effective agricultural methods.

It has always been difficult to set a large number of persons to see demonstrations when they were at their best. So in order to present the results of extension work to many who otherwise might never see or hear of them and get many of whom might need such information most, the results are recorded using several visual, audio and audio visual aids.

Average attendance at meetings when it is known that these pictures are to be shown has been much better than in many other types of meetings. All classes of persons in the community are attracted, including old and young, rich and poor. Thus, refuting to some extent the common comment that extension work often reaches only a select group.

Suggested use for miniature slides is to replace charts, tables, maps, graphs, plans, mounted photographs and diagrams when used in connection with lectures. These could be photographed and prepared into slides.

The value of a slide or film strip and other visual aids depends largely on local application. To have the greatest local application these should be made from pictures of local people, events, homes, fields, gardens, orchards, fairs, streets, schools, roads and neighbourhood scenes.

Charts and Graphic Presentation of Facts

A table helps to fit in mind a mass of numerical facts. A graphic form may further crystallize those facts in one's memory. The justification of tables and graphs of any kind in extension work is that they instruct and influence.

The proven contributions of audio-visual materials:

1. They supply a concrete basis for conceptual thinking and hence reduce meaningless word responses of learners.
2. They have a high degree of interest for students.
3. They make learning more permanent.
4. They offer a reality of experience which stimulate self-activity on the part of learners.
5. They develop a continuity of thoughts; this is especially true of motion pictures.
6. They contribute to growth of meaning hence to vocabulary development.
7. They provide experiences not easily obtained through other materials and contribute to the efficiency, depth and variety of learning.

REFERENCES

Anonymous (1970), *Symposium on Field Days*. Mimeo prepared by the University of Agricultural Sciences, Bangalore.

Anonymous (1970), *Whole Farm Demonstrations*. Mimeo prepared by the University of Agricultural Sciences, Bangalore.

Anonymous (1955), *Result Demonstrations, Some examples*, Federal Extension Service, USDA.

Anonymous (1950), Surveys and Reports Section, Div. of Field Co-ordination, Extension Service, USDA.

Anonymous (1957), Result Demonstration Manual, USDA Dept. of Agriculture, Handbook 123, USDA Federal Extension Service, Washington D.C.

Anonymous (1945), Guidelines issued regarding Demonstration Methods. Agricultural Extension Service, College of Agriculture, University of Missouri, Columbia, USA.

Coolie Verner (1964), "Definitions of terms" in the book Gale Jensen *et al.*, *Adult Education*, Chicago, USA.

Dale Edgar (1954), *Audio-visual Methods in Teaching*, Revised Edition The Dryden Press, New York. pp. 534.

Hutcheson John R. (1952), "Redefining the extension job and field of action in R.K. Bliss *et al.* (eds.). *The Spirit and Philosophy of Extension* Work. Graduate School, USDA, Washington D.C.

Jalihal, K.A. (1964) Effective Result Demonstrations necessary for progress in Extension Work. Paper presented at Extension Education Seminar conducted by the University of Tenesse, Indian Agril. Programme at Bangalore.

Jalihal, K.A. (1964) Block Demonstrations. Paper presented at the International Seminar in implementing public programmes in Agriculture at East West Food Institute, Hawai, USA.

Jalihal, K.A. (1963), Procedure followed in effecting a breakthrough from Demonstration stage to Adoption stage in fertilizing Dryland Ragi in Mysore State, Agricultural College, Magazine, Dharwad.

Knapp, S.A. (1952), His Philosophy, objectives and methods in R.K. Bliss (eds.) 1952, *The Spirit and Philosophy of Extension Work* Graduate School, USDA and EPSILON SIGMA PH1, National Honorary Extension Fraternity, Washington D.C.

Leagans Paul (1961), Characteristics of Teaching and Learning in the book "Extension Education in Community Development" Directorate of Extension, Ministry of Food and Agriculture, Government of India, New Delhi.

Rao, Y.V.L. (1966), *Communication and Development*. Univ. of Minnesota Press, Mineapolis, USA.

Smith and Wilson, (1930), *The Agricultural Extension System of the United States. op. cit.*

Wilson, M.C. and Lionberger, H.F. (1960), *Adoption of New Ideas and Practices*, The India State Univ. Press, India.

Wilson, M. and Gallup, G. (1955), *Extension Teaching Methods*. Extension Service Circular 495, USDA, Washington D.C.

5

Broad Functions and Responsibilities of Extension Subject Matter Specialists

5.1 WHO IS AN EXTENSION SUBJECT MATTER SPECIALIST?

"The term specialist as defined in the dictionary refers to a person who engages himself in some special field of activity, interest, business, knowledge, art or science."

But the term Extension Subject Matter Specialist as has been developed has a still specific and more exclusive definition.

According to Egger (1948), a specialist is one who has been trained for a special technical or professional calling and who possesses technical and professional qualification which do not ordinarily form a part of the normal equipment of every public servant. To be an extension subject matter specialist, his duties should require the use and exercise of these qualifications.

Extension Education is directed towards disseminating research tested knowledge which should be useful and practical to the people and also is concerned with encouraging its application. This requires that the results of experimental work have to be studied, selected and simplified for the use of farm people. This job cannot be done by the research workers themselves or by the extension workers as this is a job special by itself. This special job needs training in technical fields as well as training in extension. The extension personnel who carry out this job are popularly known as Extension Specialists or Extension Subject Matter Specialists.

Extension Subject Matter Specialists are generally not research workers conducting research work in the laboratories or experiment stations. They also do not carryout extensive field trials.

But they are the people who have to prepare popular bulletins and conduct inservice training programmes for the extension field personnel. Extension Subject Matter Specialists are also required to assist the Information section on the preparation of news releases and visual aids.

Hence, the Extension Subject Matter Specialists provide specialized help to field extension staff. This specialized assistance besides making the subject matter available is also concerned with: (i) the methods of teaching, (ii) of presenting the information, and (iii) of organization.

Extension Subject Matter Specialists generally devote their full time to a particular subject matter aspect of extension such as agronomy, nutrition or dairying. The subject matter with which they are concerned also enters into their title, the specialist dealing with extension methods is known as Extension Methods Specialist. Similarly, there are extension Agronomists, Extension Plant Pathologists, Extension Animal Husbandry specialist and others. Sometimes an Extension Specialist also deals with a few closely related areas in place of a single field. This is possible because some specialists' work is closely associated or related to the work of other specialists or because most of them have training in other fields than the one they give major attention to.

The Extension Subject Matter Specialist is also a member of extension service with certain special prerogatives and duties unlike an ordinary advisory member. He should not only specialize in his subject matter but also fit his speciality into practical life situation. If he cannot specialize and view his speciality in relation to its use to rural people, he belongs to research and not to extension. The specialists' supreme challenge is, therefore, to be narrow and broad at one and the same time.

5.2 IMPORTANCE OF EXTENSION SUBJECT MATTER SPECIALISTS

We can list five important duties of extension specialists to show their importance.

1. They bring up the technology from the State Agricultural College, the Departments of Agriculture, Animal Husbandry and others.

2. They are the men and women the University extension director relies on to help him in developing a wide extension programme in their respective subjects.
3. They are the people the field extension workers depend upon to keep them up-to-date on the latest findings in science as they apply to agriculture and help them to develop sound local extension programmes.
4. They take the complicated results of agricultural research and simplify them so that the farmer may understand and apply them to his everyday affairs.
5. They tone up the whole extension system keeping the field extension workers and their training accurate.

They are as essential as are the specialists in medicine and surgery to those professions.

5.3 QUALIFICATION AND TRAINING OF EXTENSION SUBJECT MATTER SPECIALISTS

The specialists needs much more formal training than other extension staff and that is not all. As with the other extension workers, he has also to qualify himself for the special requirements of extension work. Some of these are:

1. Basic grounding in the physical and social sciences of importance to rural life.
2. Knowing the reliable sources of important information.
3. Understanding the background, philosophy, objectives, policies and organization of the extension system.
4. Possessing the skill in applying psychological and educational principles to extension teaching, supervision and administration.
5. Ability in organizing rural people and stimulating leadership.
6. Understanding the process by which rural people and Extension workers co-operate to analyze local problems, arrive at possible situation and develop a local extension programme.
7. Knowing the problems and procedures of adult and out of school youth education.

8. Skill in organizing, interpreting and presenting basic economic, social, technical and scientific data and knowing their implications in rural life.
9. Knowledge of the techniques and processes of Extension evaluation.

It is on account of the above mentioned requirements that the Extension Subject Matter Specialists besides their technical subject matter need training in such subjects as education, economics, sociology, journalism, public speaking, office organization and management, extension organization and methods of teaching.

The qualifications of Extension Subject Matter Specialists are generally stated under five heads (1) Background, (2) Training, (3) Experience, (4) Characteristics, and (5) Philosophy.

Background: Rural background with farm experience is desirable. Extension Subject Matter Specialists themselves have indicated that their practical experience in farming and home making have aided in their work.

Training: Extension Subject Matter Specialists benefit by college training beyond a bachelor's degree in their subject matter area. Other special preparation is also desirable to meet the problems peculiar to the specific field of extension teaching.

Experience: As explained under the heading background, farm experience is desirable. Field experience of extension work is also desirable. In cases where it may not be practicable for some specialists, experience in working with the public in a related area may take its place.

Characteristics: Extension specialists need to possess the following eight characteristics for efficient work,

1. Effective teaching ability:
   (a) Able to assist field extension workers in organizing and developing programmes.
   (b) Able to use effectively applicable teaching techniques.
   (c) Able to evaluate his own and field extension programmes.
2. Ability to plan and co-operate with others. Must be able to analyse his field in relation to the whole field of agriculture, to prepare his plan of work and be able to successfully correlate his work with that of other extension worker.

3. Vision and leadership.
4. Sympathetic attitude towards associates.
5. Clear and systematic thinking.
6 Effective speaking and writing. Should be able to interpret and present ideas through bulletins, reports and otherwise in a language understandable by and applying to the public.
7. Tact.
8. Enthusiasm.

Philosophy: Extension Subject Matter Specialists' work should not aim at the promotion of his work alone. He should be a contributor to a general plan for the betterment of rural life and aim at the welfare of the living community.

To conclude, the Extension Subject Matter Specialist is the extension worker who leads his or her line of work, not by authority but by reason of the fact that he knows; he has a fountain of knowledge, his foundations are sure; he gives of his stories abundantly; he anticipates the needs of the fieldworker; he offers help before the request is made; he gives his all to others that they may succeed and of course doing, so grows most himself.

5.4 BROAD FUNCTIONS AND RESPONSIBILITIES OF EXTENSION SUBJECT MATTER SPECIALISTS

The job of Extension Subject Matter Specialists is as follows:

1. Serving as a bridge between research divisions and field extension workers; interpreting research results in order to help solve farm and home problems.
2. Keeping the extension workers up-to-date with regard to the findings of Research.
3. Outlining a state-wide programme in his or her subject-matter area.
4. Helping field extension workers and their project groups to develop sound extension programmes with regard to a particular enterprise.
5. Assisting field extension workers in the proper use of appropriate teaching methods, suitable to his or her subject matter field.

6. Supporting the local extension programmes with state-wide publicity.
7. Conducting studies to identify successful and unsuccessful methods of extension teaching in the particular subject matter field.
8. Outlining measuring devices and procedures pertaining to the subject matter problems being attacked and helping extension workers in their use.
9. Handling direct extension teaching to train the extension worker and to strengthen his position.

The above kinds of jobs can be classified under few broad groups.

The following six broad groups of functions should be performed by subject matter specialists:

(a) Planning functions
(b) Training functions
(c) Direct teaching
(d) Field studies
(e) Preparation of teaching materials
(f) Relationships

5.5 ROLE OF EXTENSION SUBJECT MATTER SPECIALISTS WITH REFERENCE TO DIFFERENT FUNCTIONS

(a) **Subject matter authority:** The Extension Subject Matter Specialist must be the most outstanding authority in his subject matter field considering the people with whom he must work, the natural climatic and soil conditions and the economic circumstances under which his work is to be conducted.
(b) **Training:** A specialist's job is to discover, assemble and make available most of the facts and skills that all extension workers should possess.
(c) **Direct teaching:** The function of the specialist calls for direct teaching in highly specialized fields in addition to preparation of materials for bulletins, for radio and press and training local personnel.
(d) **Programme planning:** The Specialists' service should be fully utilized in the preparation of programme planning and in the preparation of the local extension programmes.

(e) **Evaluation:** This function of the specialists assists in improving the extension work. Authorities on evaluation work have stated that evaluation is a process of vital importance to the specialists. This is because the specialist deals with teaching programme. It is the specialist to whom we look for subject matter. A sound evaluation plan is included as one of the essential steps of every programme or project.

(f) **Relationship:** Good working relationships are essential as knowledge of subject matter to the success of all extension workers. This is particularly so for extension specialists in view of their specialized work and hence forms a part of their responsibilities. Relationships are the sum total of our experience with people, individually and collectively. The efficient and effectiveness of specialist teaching is based to a great extent on relationships with all individuals or groups with whom we come in contact. The creation and development of the best possible relations is one of our basic responsibilities. It is recognized that most failures of specialists can be traced to their inability to work with others.

To sum up, it may be said that the specialists should be considered as a trainer of teachers and should minimize his activities of direct teaching with the farm people.

As the situations vary from time-to-time and from place to place, it would be desirable for the administration to inform the extension specialists which of their functions need more emphasis and which less and which the least and also make available the required facilities to carryout these functions satisfactorily.

ANALYSIS OF FUNCTIONS AND RESPONSIBILITIES OF EXTENSION SUBJECT MATTER SPECIALISTS

I. Programme Planning

Extension Subject Matter Specialists have great opportunity and responsibility in the programme planning process. They can make important contributions to both programme and plan of work.

A clear understanding of the nature of this job is quite essential for the specialist. As a pre-requisite, specialists must necessarily possess a clear and workable concept of the basic principles and philosophy of extension programme planning process and also should know the importance of such a process to the total effectiveness of extension work. To be more specific, Extension Subject Matter Specialists need to understand the following:

(i) Definition of an Extension programme
(ii) Difference among State, district, taluk or village .programme
(iii) Definition of a plan of work
(iv) Programme development cycle or extension teaching process
(v) Role of programme building in guiding and directing all kinds of work
(vi) Continuous nature of programme planning process
(vii) Importance of all rural classes, sections, and enterprises – men, women
(viii) youth, participating in programme building
(ix) Other principles. involved in programme planning process

The job of the Extension Specialist in programme planning work is mainly to provide educational leadership in a subject matter area. Unlike the supervisor, he is not to deal with the entire extension programme. In doing so, he is required to work with the extension workers.

The Extension Subject Matter Specialist is required to assist the local extension workers in the following items of work in relation to programme planning in his subject matter area.

(a) Recognizing the local problems and setting up major objectives.
(b) Reviewing the recommended plans and programmes.
(c) Publicizing the programme.
(d) Considering the most effective methods and techniques to be used in executing the programme including the selection and training of leaders.
(e) Evaluating programmes and achievements.

(f) Determining the adjustments and changes required in programmes to take care of special problems as they develop.

Although Extension Subject Matter Specialists are experts in their own subject matter areas, their approach in programme planning activity needs to be a generalistic one – that is co-ordinated and integrated efforts by all different specialists.

Specific Duties of the Specialists in Extension Programme Development

The specific duties of the Specialist may be discussed as below:

1. Duties in relation to the development of local extension programme
2. Duties as a member of the University Programme Committee
3. Duties in developing a plan for himself

1. Duties in Relation to the Development of Local Extension Programmes

The specialist helps in programme development in three main ways:

(a) He assists the field extension workers in getting the subject matter information and thus keeps them up-to-date on the latest development.

(b) He is able to interpret the situation in his subject matter area to the local extension workers. This is possible because of his statewide activities and contacts. In addition, he transmits good ideas about programmes from area to area.

(c) He supplies the background information that is used by the extension workers in developing the programme.

The above functions can further be spelled out as follows:

(a) Review of annual reports and plans in order to determine assistance that is needed for local extension workers to see and understand situational problems and solutions.

(b) Collecting information on situation, bringing it in usable form and make the same available to field staff.
  (i) From research sources.
  (ii) From local conditions, based upon previous experiences.

(c) Helping extension staff prior to planning meetings.
  (1) To ascertain local information.
    (i) Preparing instruments such as questionnaires, check sheets or meetings to register the interest, ideas and thinking of the people.
    (ii) Assisting leaders in analyzing situation to identify problems.
    (iii) Analyzing problems with agents and local leaders.
    (iv) Obtaining the help of leaders and other groups that might supply the required information.
    (v) Helping people to form community committees to study problems.

(d) To interpret local and background data collected in light of the latest state findings and to draw the proper conclusions pertaining to his subject matter area.

(e) Assisting local extension staff at programme planning meetings.
  (1) By serving as advisors.
  (2) By correlating local developments with state-wise developments.

(f) Working with extension workers after planning meetings.
  (1) By scrutinizing of local programmes for purpose of future suggestions.
  (2) By assisting to evaluate the progress of local programmes towards objectives.
  (3) By supporting the local extension programmes with the necessary publicity.

2. *Duties as a Member of the University Programme Committee*

The main role of the Extension Subject Matter Specialists is to act as an advisor to the University Extension Director. He has an important part to play in the second stage of the programming operation when plan is to be developed and schedules designed for the collection of the basic data and information upon which local and State programmes must be built. The function of the specialist in this respect can be broadly stated as follows:

1. To serve as a member of the Committee.
2. To collect, interpret, analyze and make available all factual information pertaining to his subject matter area.
3. To advise on the progress of work in respect of his field.
4. To review the proposals from the stand-point of technical feasibility and thus assist the Director.
5. To assist in finding out effective methods and techniques of programme execution.
6. To aid in publicizing the programme.
7. To aid in programme evaluation.
8. To get acquainted with the total programme so as to understand his relation to the whole.

II. Teaching

A. Subject Matter Authority

1. Extension Specialists must be an outstanding authority in his particular subject matter field.
2. He also needs to be a generalist so as to fit his speciality into the overall programme.
3. A broad knowledge of the entire extension programme is also necessary for the specialist.
4. Subject matter information of a specialist can be developed through four ways.
5. The subject matter can be collected through different channels.

B. Preparation of Teaching Materials

1. Subject matter information of the specialist needs to be translated into simple teaching aids or materials in order to be used.

2. Research results indicate that specialists should devote more time for preparing teaching materials.
3. More and more visuals should be developed as a part of this work.
4. Specialists require to work with the information department in this connection.
5. Some teaching materials have to be supplied to the local workers.

C. *Training Extension Workers*

1. The specialists success depends mainly on how well he trains the agent.
2. A thorough understanding of the nature of extension teaching is a must for each specialist.
3. Training the Extension Worker should be problem oriented.
4. Variety of techniques are needed in this task of training extension workers.
5. Different methods could be used by the specialist in training Extension.
6. In view of the large number of specialists, it is necessary to have co-ordinated programmes in training the Extension Specialists.
7. Obstacles to teaching extension workers can be recognized into several types and each requiring to be analyzed.

D. *Direct Teaching of the Farmers.*

The Extension Specialist should take to direct teaching of farm people only for special purposes.

III. Evaluation and the Specialists Role

1. The process of evaluation of an extension programme is a major responsibility of the Extension Specialist as compared to other extension staff.
2. Six essentials required by the specialist in evaluation work are:

(i) Must know teaching objectives.
(i) Be familiar with what has been done.
(iii) Know who can provide evidence.
(iv) Study methods of collecting evidence.
(v) Interpret collected information.
(vi) Have the evaluation scheme built in the programme and plan of work.

3. Continuous evaluation schedule is desirable.
4. Specialists can conduct evaluation by the methods – informal and formal.
5. Time spent on evaluation is time well spent.

IV. Relationships

1. Good relationships are as important as other qualifications of the specialists.
2. Maintaining good relationships with diverse groups is not an easy job.
3. Knowledge, understanding and application of psychological principles are helpful in maintaining good relations.
4. Good relations with Administrators are more likely when there is co-ordination, understanding and integration between the specialists and the administrators.
5. Specialists can develop good relationships with the supervisors by keeping them posted with the project information from time-to-time.
6. Appreciation of other Specialists' work will develop healthy relationships with them.
7. Conduct all work in the operational area with and through the local extension workers.
8. Maintaining a close contact with the related subject matter departments in college and Experimental stations.
9. Constant contacts with the state level specialists are also helpful.
10. Co-operate with all agencies that have plans or objectives relating to extension work.
11. Special services with industry, co-operation and commercial interests should be avoided.

12. Contact farm people always through the local extension staff. Avoid developing as a mere agency for continuous supply and service.
13. Handle all formal contacts with farm people politely, effectively and efficiently.
14. Evince keen interest in the people's problems, respect their opinions and interests.

REFERENCES

Boone, Edgar J. (1959), "The Role of Extension Specialist" Report on Cernell Extension Specialists' Workshop, Cornell University Extension Service, Ithaca, USA.

Brunner, Edmund des and Yang, E.H.P. (1949) – *Rural America and the Extension Service,* Teachers College, Columbia University, New York. Davidson, J.B. *et al.* (1933), *A Study of the Extension Service,* Iowa State College, Ames, Iowa, USA.

Egger Rowland (1948) Public Administration and Extension Work, Extension Service Circular, 451 U.S.D.A. Washington, D.C.

Kelsey, L.D. and Hearne, C.C. (1966), *Co-operative Extension Work* (3rd Edn.) Comstock Publishing Associates, Ithaca, New York.

Mathews, J.L. (1952), "How to Develop Programmes" Talk at the Tennessee and Virginia Annual Extension Conference August 27 and 28, 1952. Washington D.C. U.S.D.A. Extension Service.

Stutz, F.H. (1959), "The Art of Teaching and the Specialists" Report on Cornell Extension Specialists' Workshop, Cornell University, Extension Service, Ithaca, New York.

Smith, C.B. and Wilson, M.C. (1930), The Agricultural Extension System of the United States, John Wiley & Sons, New York.

Warren, H.M. (1957), Functions and Responsibilities of Extension Subject Matter Specialists in the Extension Service New York State Extension Service, Ithaca, USA.

6

Programme Planning in Agricultural Extension

6.1 PROJECT MANAGEMENT CYCLE

For understanding the project management cycle, we need to know the definition of few terms and some concepts.

Development Programme

This is an understanding arrived at co-operatively by the local people and development staff which includes information on:

(a) the situation in which people are located,
(b) the problems and needs that are part of the situation,
(c) the objectives in relation to the people, and
(d) recommendations to reach the objectives both on a long term basis as well as a short term basis.

Development Project

A project can be defined as one of the many developmental programme activities taken up for the benefit of an area, e.g. dairy project, pulse production project etc.

The Project – Management Cycle

It is an application of the overall programme planning cycle with special reference to the management of factors identified as important in the implementation of the project. In other words, the steps suggested in the programme planning cycle must be examined in relation to the factors determining success of the agricultural project.

Factors Determining Success of Agricultural Projects

Six major factors have been identified which play a crucial role in the success of an agricultural project. These are:

1. Simplicity and clarity of the objectives.
2. Availability of an economically attractive technology to promote the product.
3. Integration of the basic production services especially those of extension, input supply, credit and marketing.
4. Access to the necessary specialists and provision for the training of needed personnel.
5. The ability to recognize potential constraints and to design contingency plans to overcome them.
6. Compatibility of the project with existing administrative structures.

Programme Planning Cycle

This consists of two parts, viz. (1) Determining the programme, and (2) Carrying out the programme. The cycle is generally thought of as consisting of 8 steps (See Appendix A).

6.2 ROLES AND TECHNIQUES OF EXTENSION WORKERS IN PROGRAMME PLANNING

The Supervisor

Role

1. Support all roles of the director.
2. Development own philosophy and understanding same as the director.
3. Function as a member of a team.
4. Inform people one supervises.
5. Assist taluk panchayat staff in establishing priorities.
6. Report to the director and others on progress, problems, etc.

7. Be the voice of the taluk staff to the director.
8. Act as coach to taluk staff in teaching and training by arranging learning situations.
9. Advise on use of resource people in helping coordinate taluk activities.
10. Work with taluk staff in evaluating the programme and its progress.
11. In general, assume the role of the director in informing those one supervises and securing acceptance and activation of policy.

Techniques

1. Become informed about the programme.
2. Supervisory teams agree among themselves on procedures and job assignments to do job.
3. Make a plan with co-workers.
4. Supervisory team maintains continual communication with steering committee and other supervisory teams.
5. Conduct district training conferences for taluk panchayat chairmen and taluk staffs with director assisting.
6. Meet with taluk panchayat chairmen and staffs individually and collectively.
7. Evaluate the persent taluk programme and show need for programme projection.
8. Evaluate taluk personnel available to do the job and assist in developing procedure to be followed.
9. Examine the existing planning structure in terms of the job to be done.
10. Assist taluk in developing a taluk plan of work that is integrated with the taluk programme.
11. Design routine tools and methods in such ways that will accomplish these objectives.
12. Secure commitments from taluk panchayat chairmen as to when each phase will be accomplished in each taluk.
13. Secure from taluk panchayat chairman his dicisions on follow-through timing.
14. Develop a calendar of work that will assure adequate supervision.

The Specialist

Role

1. Serve, when needed, as a resource person in methodology and techniques.
2. Providing subject matter information for use by planning groups.
3. Provide vision concerning trends, needs and possibilities in one's specialized field.
4. Suggest possible solutions or methods for developing solutions to problems raised by planning groups.
5. Provide on-the-spot assistance when the programme gets down to specifics.
6. Understand the importance and philosophy of the programme, one's role, how one can contribute.
7. Attend taluk meetings to learn the process and determine one's role as project leader.
8. Serve when asked, as a member of State steering committee or special committee.
9. Keep informed of the progress of the planning effort in each taluk.
10. Exercise initiative in providing guidance for individual taluks.

Techniques

1. Plan with taluk staff before programme projection starts.
2. Send personalized letters to extension workers concerned in specific taluks covering such items as:
   (a) Taluk situation as viewed by the specialist.
   (b) Trends in the subject-matter field concerned that are pertinent to the taluk.
   (c) Problems in the taluk which the specialist believe should have atttention.
   (d) Programme ideas which the specialist believes would be appropriate for consideration in the particular taluk.
3. Adapt one's work habits to new situations which programme projection creates.

4. Study committee minutes and send suggestions to taluk staff for future committee consideration.
5. Suggest other resource people that committee might call upon for assistance with particular problems it faces.
6. Reserve time in one's schedule for servicing committees.
7. Work with extension workers in developing plans of action for carrying out the program planned with committees.

How Administration Can Aid the Specialist to Understand and Perform His Role

1. Orient the specialist on the importance and philosophy of the programme.
2. Give the specialist opportunity to attend meetings in taluks to observe the planning process and get first-hand experience with it.
3. Provide opportunity for specialists to work together to correlate and integrate their programmes.
4. Provide for an exchange of programme projection outlines developed by various specialists for their projects.
5. disseminate information from the steering committee to other state staff members.

The Village Extension Worker

Role

1. Be a part of the team.
2. Accept the taluk panchayat staff chairman as the leader.
3. Act as a professional person (resource person, counsellor).
4. Recommend people for advisory group and contact them.
5. Recommend resource sources.
6. Assist organizations to find their place.
7. Create understanding in local groups.
8. Act as liaison between local people and the rest of the taluk extensions staff.
9. Prepare himself for his professional role.

Techniques

1. Know, understand and accept one's role.
2. Participate as a member of staff team in arriving at decisions.

3. Accumulate and contribute appropriate kinds and amounts of information material needed to support programme projection.
4. Serve as secretary or leader of category groups (if he serves as secretary, the staff member may have to train lay leaders in objectives and methods. In the role of secretary he may also act as resource person).
5. Actively participate with the rest of the staff in arriving at an overall taluk plan.
6. Suggest names of leaders who meet qualifications and criteria and who will serve in commodity or category groups.
7. Develop an annual plan of work for one's own activities which integrates into the taluk plan.
8. Spread information in necessary form to appropriate groups (lay people, mass media representatives, specialists, taluk panchayat chairman).
9. Use portions of preliminary information required to attract local people for interest and participation. This results in local person seeing importance of contributing to programme projection.
10. Establish and maintain communication with appropriate specialists and other resource people.
11. Evaluate process and results.

APPENDIX A

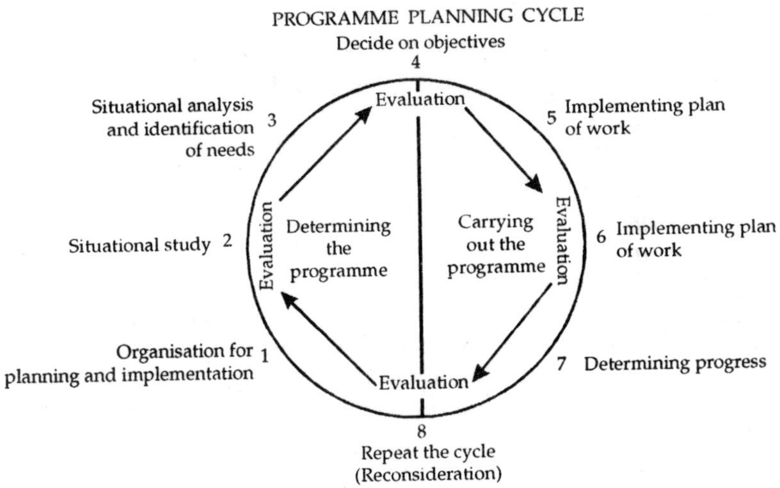

Some Ideas Relating to the Steps of the Programme Planning Cycle

1. Organization for Planning and Implementation

Project development and implementation cannot be the responsibility of only development workers. For successful project implementation, a local committee with representatives of local leaders and the various organizations – extension, input supply, finance, marketing, processing etc., is a must which has to function right from the planning stage.

2. Situational Study

In relation to project implementation, the study of the local situation is required to understand the following:

(i) Local practices followed by people with reference to the project.
(ii) Study of local organizations and their working-Input supply and credit supply organizations.

(iii) Study of the existing technical competency of development workers who will be required to implement the project.

(iv) Study of local leadership with reference to the project work.

Both development workers and local leaders must be involved in this work by constituting a special project development committee.

3. Situational Analysis

A mere collection of situational facts will not help in project implementation. Local situation has to be carefully analyzed comparing what is with what should be. Help of specialists is needed in this stage. The idea of situational analysis is to assist in identifying immediate problems or needs, for undertaking solution through project implementation. Needs identified may be of different kinds viz., (i) Generated need, (ii) Ascertained felt need, (iii) Solicited felt need, and (iv) Demonstrated felt need.

For a successful project implementation, there is a necessity of transforming generated need into demonstrated felt need. This might require work for a period of years.

4. Deciding Objectives

Objectives are the statements expressing the ends towards which efforts are to be directed. For a successful project implementation, clear-cut formulation of objectives is necessary which describe the changes in people's attitude, skill and knowledge that are expected to be achieved through the project. Two kinds of objectives have to be kept in view in relation to a project viz., (i) Project objectives, and (ii) Working objectives. For each project objectives, we must develop the related working objectives.

5. Develop Plan of Work

Unless a careful plan of work is developed and carried out, no project can be implemented. The plan of work tries to answer the questions what, where, when and how the project will be implemented. The action planned must include:

(a) People to be reached.
(b) Goals, dates and places.
(c) Teaching procedures to be followed.
(d) Duties, training and recognition of local leaders.
(e) Part to be played by development workers.
(f) Part to be played by other agencies.
(g) Plans for measuring results.

6. *Implement Plan of Work*

While implementing plan of work, flexibility, co-ordination, co-operation, peak loads of work, seasonal interests of the people and a host of other considerations have to be kept in mind. PERT method should be used with advantage.

7. *Determine Progress*

It is no use implementing the project without determining progress at each stage and at different periods of time. This step is necessary for determining how far the project has progressed and how much further it should be carried to accomplish objectives.

8. *Repeat the Cycle*

The project work is rarely completed in one year. Hence, the work has to be repeated with new look at the situation. Even when a project appears to have been successfully completed, the situation might change through economic and social trends, through action of people locally or of governments, and otherwise. Problems change, emphasis changes and phases may be completed. Solutions change; new and improved practices and materials are found. Objectives change; people may see more clearly what they need. Hence, repeat of the project cycle is necessary.

REFERENCES

Creech, L.G. (1959), A Report of the Proceedings of the Seminar on Extension Supervision for the Western Region. The National Agricultural Extension Centre for Advanced Study, University of Wisconsin, Madison, Wisconsin.

Green, B.C. (1976), A systems perspective of the agricultural programme management process. Unpublished paper, East-West Food Institute, Honalulu, Hawaii.

Kelsey, L.D. and Hearne, C.C. (1966), *Corporative Extension Work*, Comstock Publishing Associates, Ithaca, New York.

Radhakrishna Setty, (1973), "Knowledge of Gramasevaks about Extension Programme Planning and the nature of agricultural extension programme development at the Gramasevak Circle level" Unpublished M.Sc., Thesis in Agril. Extension, University of Agricultural Sciences, Bangalore.

Sanders, H.C. (1966), *Co-oporative Extension Service.* Prentice Hall, New York.

Schaefer, K.W. (1977), Approaches to the design of agricultural projects. International Development Institute, Indiana University, Bloomington, Indiana, USA.

Woods, John L. (1976) Working paper on Programme Planning and Work Plan. Development Support Communication Service, UNDP/DSCS, Bangkok, Thailand.

PART – II

MANAGEMENT IN EXTENSION

7

Broad Areas Relating to the Concept, Principles, Theories, Roles and Functions of Management in Agricultural Extension

7.1 CONCEPT, PRINCIPLES AND THEORIES OF MANAGEMENT OF DEVELOPMENT PROGRAMMES

Concept of Management

Management is a complex process involving many varied responsibilities and activities required for the successful accomplishments of objectives of an organization through the efforts of others. At the total organization level, the concept of management is synonymous with the concept of administration. In its totality the functions of management or administration are best described by the popular term POSDCORB, each letter of which indicates one management function. These are: (1) Planning, (2) Organizing, (3) Staffing, (4) Directing, (5) Co-ordinating, (6) Reporting, and (7) Budgeting. In recent years two more functions have been added, viz. (1) Innovating, and (2) Representing or Linkage.

At the middle level, the term "Management is more appropriately be called as Supervision". Supervisor is a person who is responsible for the work done by others. In this way supervision is defined as the art of directing the efforts of human beings. Although the practice of supervision is in itself an art, the methods and procedures of good supervision are defined from the science of human relations. Under this topic of supervision the functions of Direction and Co-ordination are included. Motivation is also part of Direction and Supervision. Communication, Training employees and Maintaining a good morale in the organization are also part of Supervision function.

Principles and Theory of Management of Development Programmes

There are two main schools of thought on organization; the **classical theory** and **modern theory.** Both these theories provide certain principles for the guidance of effective management of development programmes.

Classical theory gives us some principles which are long standing while modern theories have provided new principles primarily related to human relations.

Principles from Classical Theory

The most commonly cited principles from classical theory are those whose initial letters spell the name "OSCAR" – Objectives, Specialization, Co-ordination, Authority and Responsibility. The nine principles are generally stated which have origin from the classical theory. They are:

1. The organization should have a clearly defined objective and each position should have an objective logically related to it.
2. The work of each person should be confined to a single function and related functions should be grouped under one specialization.
3. Means of coordinating all efforts towards the common goal must be provided.
4. The organization must have a supreme, authority and a clear line of authority should run from that person to every individual in the organization, a principle known as "Scalar Principle".
5. Authority should be equal to responsibility – that is, when any one is given responsibility for a task, he should be given enough authority to accomplish it successfully.

6. Authority and responsibility should be delegated as far down in the organization as possible.
7. Each person should be accountable only to a single supervisor.
8. No superior should have more than six immediate subordinators.
9. There should be as few levels of management as possible between the supreme authority and the rank and file.

Principles from Modern Theories

Modern theories are less concerned with laying down exact rules. They are conscious that in an organization made up of human beings, there are a great number of variables and the attempt to alter any one of them is likely to start a sort of chain reaction. The modern theories also point out that orders and policies no matter how plainly stated will be subject to reinterpretation in the light of the psychological set of those who transmit them or carry them out, the environment in which they find themselves, and the conflicting pressures to which they are subject to. Nine important principles from modern theories can be stated as under:

1. Employees can be basically self-directed and creative at work if properly motivated.
2. Motivation occurs at the social, esteem and self-actualization levels, as well as physiological and security levels.
3. It is not desirable to have a close supervision over the work environment for employees.
4. Supervision is creative not prescriptive. It determines procedures in the light of the needs of each situation.
5. Supervision should provide opportunity for originality and self-expression by employees.
6. Supervision seeks improved methods of teaching and creates a physical, social and psychological climate favourable to learning.
7. Supervision substitutes leadership for authority. However, there is no one best style of leadership, which can be used in management.

8. There are at least three areas of skills necessary for carrying out the process of management – technical, human and conceptual.
9. The capacity to exert influence upward is essential if a supervisor is to perform his supervisory functions successfully.

7.2 ROLE AND RELEVANCE OF MANAGEMENT IN AGRICULTURAL ADMINISTRATION

All agricultural administrators have been entrusted with the stupendous task of bringing about agricultural development in their respective areas. They are technically competent persons and their staff. This technical competency can further be improved if needed. Inspite of their high technical competency, no progress can be achieved unless all the staff equally function effectively. Similarly the progress further depends on how well other related agencies and organizations also function. In short, the real progress depends on group effort i.e. efforts to be made by each member of the group. To improve this group effectiveness, the application of management principles and concepts are necessary. When a group of district staff get together to achieve a given objective, somebody that is the group leader has to direct, co-ordinate and control the activities of others. In other words, there is a management component in his work.

Traditionally we all think that agriculture has not progressed in a particular area because of lack of resources – men and materials. However, mere provision of the same will not automatically lead to rapid economic development. The most important missing link is this vital management input. This input, has however, been neglected in our country and as a result the progress has been slowed down.

According to John Servan Schreiber who has written a book "American Challenge", the United States developed technologically economically and militarily primarily because of its managerial competence resulting from investment in human resources. In industry as well as in agriculture, the U.S.A. has shown how physical capital and manpower resources have to be optimally and judiciously employed through management input to increase productivity.

Three factors are involved in relation to management input which influence group effectiveness. These are: (1) Individuals,

(2) Organization, and (3) Systems. Of course, in this discussion we will emphasize on the first factor – not that others are not important but because we do not have a direct control over them.

A good organization should be developed incorporating a number of management principles such as unity of command, span of control, necessary authority for the responsibility given, delegation of authority at the appropriate levels, co-ordination, rewards commensurate with performance, opportunities, recognition of merit etc.,

There are several managerial skills to be developed by managers which have to be developed along with the specialization or technical skills. The mix between specialization skills and the managerial skills at various levels will be different. More managerial skills are required at the top levels as compared to lower levels.

Some of the managerial skills needed may be listed as: (1) Conceptual skills and attitudes, (2) Skill to supervise and co-ordinate, (3) Human relations skill, (4) Understanding of social costs and social benefits, (5) Empirical knowledge and experience and (6) Decision making skill.

The management has several facts. It is a combination of all these skills. The relevance of each aspect and their proportion will be different for different undertakings and at different levels.

The management and administration skills are important resources which have to be developed in our organization. These skills together with appropriate organization and systems could contribute a great deal to hasten the process of agricultural development in our country.

7.3 TASKS AND FUNCTIONS OF MANAGEMENT IN AGRICULTURAL EXTENSION

Institutions promoting Agricultural development are organs of society. They primarily exist to fulfil a specific social purpose to see that agricultural technology is transformed and made applicable in rural areas as a result of which agricultural development takes place. It is therefore necessary that when we discuss management functions, it should be recognized that they are not ends in themselves, but means. The right question to ask about these functions is not what they are? But what are they supposed to be doing and what are their tasks?

Major Tasks and Dimensions

There are three major tasks or dimensions which extension management has to perform. These are:

1. Fulfilling the primary purpose of bringing about agricultural development in the area it is serving.
2. Making work in the organization productive and the worker achieving.
3. See that farmers it serves are educated and benefited from the application of agricultural technology.

The functions of management in agricultural extension which we discuss today require to be ultimately analyzed with reference to the three major tasks listed above.

Functions of management in Agricultural Organizations

Agricultural Administration or Management

All administrators or managers should understand what is administration or management and how agricultural administration or management differs from the regular administration or management.

P — Planning		Co — Coordinating	
O — Organizing		R — Reporting	
D — Directing		B — Budgeting	
S — Supervising			

Many times these functions are also classified under the four broad functions of planning, organizing, supervising and controlling.

In recent years two more functions have been added, viz. innovation and establishing linkages or representing.

Special Responsibilities of Management Functions in Agricultural Extension

Extension administrator's work is not limited to the four walls of the office or an industry as in case of other administrators.

They have a task of not only seeing that their employees work properly but also have a responsibility of reaching hundreds and thousands of farmers in far off villages and educating them to develop agriculture. This special work requires networks of small field offices and special logistical operations. Programme needs and outcome are often difficult to forecast, no only because of weather, yield and price changes but also because of the uncertainty of how farmers and agri-business people will respond.

Classification and Meaning of Management Functions

The management functions are some times listed under two main classes or headings, viz. (1) The mechanics of management, and (2) The dynamics of management. Functions under the dynamics of management involve more than human relations as compared with those under the mechanics of management.

Meaning of Different Management Functions

Planning: It involves selecting objectives and the strategies, policies, programmes and procedures for achieving them either for the entire enterprise of for any organized part thereof. Planning also involves decision making.

Organizing: Involves the establishment of an internal structure of roles through determination and enumeration of the activities required to achieve the goals of an enterprise and each part of it, the grouping of these activities, the assignment of such groups of activities to a manager, the delegation of authority to carry them out and provision for co-ordination of authority and informal relationships horizontally and vertically in the organization structure.

Supervision: It is often defined as the art of directing the efforts of human beings in an organization. It includes the functions of direction and co-ordination.

Controlling: It is the measuring and correcting of activities of subordinates to assure that events conform to plans.

Innovating: It is the introduction of new methods in working of the organization in order to bring about improvement and increasing the efficiency.

Representing: It is the establishment of linkages with the other institutions so that the work of the organization is co-ordinated with them effectively.

Management Functions More Relevant in Implementing Agricultural Programmes

1. Defining the technical practices to be followed in the operating units and sub-units.
2. Formulating, operating policies for an action organization, budgeting and accounting.
3. Establishing operating objectives and targets, with some effort of setting standards.
4. Determining and appraising the systems of operating divisions, sections and units.
5. Organizing the facilities and equipment needed to do the job.
6. Co-ordinating internally the various sub-systems and externally with and to other systems.
7. Directing the work of sub-ordinates; reporting to superiors.
8. Monitoring and appraising performance.
9. Modifying and adjusting internal systems.

Administration or Management as a Process

The term administration or management refers to the work carried out in any organizations. An organization is assemblage of two or more interacting human beings collectively seeking to attain some common goal. Administration or management on a broad level refers to asocial process which involves guidance, leadership and control of the efforts of a group of individuals towards some common goal. In this broad way both these terms are used synonymously. The term administration was popular in the past while in the present times, the term management has been very commonly used.

The process of administration or management should encourage the organization to reach its purposes in an effective way. All definitions seem to agree that management is (1) a process, (2) is related to resources such as people, money and equipment, and (3) is aimed at helping the organization accomplish its goals.

As a Function

When administration or management is viewed from functional angle, the term, gives different meanings.

The work carried out by the head of an organization is called administration while management has several meanings depending on the level at which it is used. Middle management or supervision refers to the function carried out by people who are neither at the top of the organization not at the bottom as workers.

Management is Both an Art and a Science

The process of managing like all other arts makes use of underlying organized knowledge – science – and applies it in the light of realities to gain a desired practical result.

Why Management?

The work of an organization will not depend only on the technical competency of its employees but requires sound management practices.

Functions of Management

Administration or management of an organization or part of it includes carrying out of various functions. The famous word "POSDCORB" denotes the various functions of administration or management.

Management Functions in Agriculture Requires Blending

The management of agricultural programmes is clearly composed of many functions and related tasks embodied in various persons including farmers. The system must also include the underlying formal and informal processes of communication and co-operation linking these persons. Thus the management functions in agriculture include an institutionalized blending of several functions. A systems perspective of the agricultural programme management process should be recognized.

7.4 MANAGEMENT SKILLS NEEDED BY SUPERVISORS IN EXTENSION ORGANIZATIONS

All extension supervisors should understand that there are at least three areas of skills necessary for carrying out the progress of Management: (1) Technical, (2) Human relations, and (3) Conceptual.

Technical Skill

It involves understanding of and proficiency in a specific kind of activity. It includes specialized knowledge, analytical ability within that knowledge and use of specific techniques.

Human Relations

It is the person's ability to work effectively as a group member and to build a co-operative effort within the Team he leads and outside. It includes such functions, which involve communication, motivation, understanding, leadership and counselling.

Conceptual

Ability to see the organization as a whole. It includes recognizing how the various functions of the organization depend on one another and how changes in anyone part affect all others. Co-ordination, establishing linkages and integration are parts of this skill.

Levels of Management and Skills Needed

The appropriate mix of the three kinds of skills required in management varies at different levels of management as indicated in the following diagram.

For good management, people at higher levels should concentrate more on conceptual skills as compared to technical skills and *vice versa*. The common denominator that is crucial at all levels is human relations skill.

Some Examples of Specific Functions Under Each Area of Skill

Joint Director of Agriculture

Technical

1. Inspection of crop demonstrations and trials.
2. Conducting training programmes at district level.
3. Organizing training programmes at taluk level.
4. Publishing popular literature and success stories.

Human Relations

1. Participating in seminars, meetings etc., organized by private sector organizations.
2. Accompanying Officers of other departments of both the State and Central Government on their tour in the district.
3. Reviewing the work of Assistant Directors and other technical staff, counselling and instructing them to do a better job.
4. Conducting monthly meeting of the subordinate technical staff and guiding them in their programme.

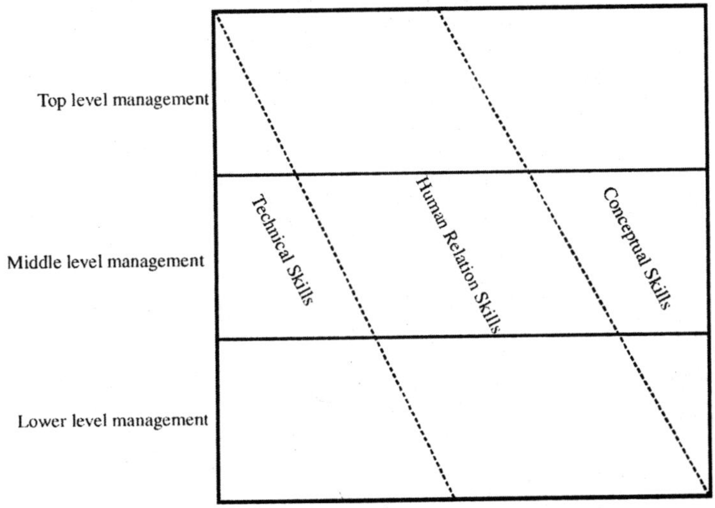

Skills required at different Levels of Management

Conceptual

1. Participating in co-ordination committee meetings at the district level.
2. Participating in sub-committee meetings involving other departments.
3. Meeting the Officers at the Department of Co-operation and ensuring timely and adequate supply of inputs to farmers.
4. Meeting the credit providing agencies and ensuring timely loan advancement to farmers.

Administrator's Ability to Listen

Of all the sources of information a manager has by which he can come to know and accurately size up the personalities of the people in his department, listening to the individual employee is the most important.

Items Related to Bad Listening

1. Calling the subject uninteresting
2. Criticizing the delivery
3. Getting over stimulated
4. Not listening to facts or ideas
5. Outlining everything
6. Faking attention
7. Tolerating distraction
8. Evading the difficulty
9. Submitting to emotional words
10. Wasting thought–power

Some Sources of Communication Difficulties

There are 6 major sources of communication difficulties in organizations. These are:

1. Misunderstood expectations.
2. Mismatched frame of reference.
3. Mis-use of internal communication channels.

4. Strict controls over communication.
5. Role conflict.
6. Norm conflict.

REFERENCES

Brath, S.J. (1986), *Basic Managerial Skills for All,* II Ed.

Chatterjee, S.S. (1983), *Principles and practice of Management.*

Dale, E. (1973), *Management – Theory and Practice* III Ed, McGraw-Hill, Kogakusha Ltd., Tokyo.

Green, Donald, (1976) *A Systems Perspective of the Agricultural Programmes Management Process* – A mimeo, unpublished paper, East-West Food Institute, Honolulu, Hawaii, USA.

Hersey and Balanchard, K.H. (1972), *Management of Organizational Behaviour – Utilizing Human Resources,* Prentice - Hall of India Pvt. Ltd., New Delhi pp. 1-8.

Hodgetts, R.M. (1979) *Management Theory – Process and Practice.* W.B. Sanders Co., London.

Katz, Robert L. (1955) Skills of an Effective Administrator. *Harward Business Review,* pp. 33-42.

Koontz, H. and O'Donnel, C. (1972), *Management.* McGraw-Hill, Kogakusha Ltd. Tokyo.

Mcgrath, E.H. (1986), *Basic Management Skills for All.* Prentice-Hall of India (Pvt.) Ltd., New Delhi.

Newman, W.H. *et al.* (1973), *The Process of Management.* Prentice-Hall of India (Pvt.) Ltd., New Delhi.

8

Administrative Functions Required in Extension Management

8.1 PLANNING AS A FUNCTION OF MANAGEMENT

Planning is a very important management function, since it determines the nature of the Manager's other functions. Planning involves choosing an objective, plotting a course of action, and moving along the course to the desired goal. Frequently, planning takes valuable time, but planning ensures a much greater chance of success. In most cases, managers who fail to plan, plan to fail. Regardless of how competent and well-trained employees may be, changes and improvements cannot be successful unless careful planning takes place. Often managers will complain that they do not have enough time to plan a job thoroughly, but they always find time to do the job when everything goes wrong. After all, it does not matter how fast you are going if you are on the wrong-road.

There are two basic elements in planning: (1) assessing the future or deciding what is likely to happen or what should happen, and (2) providing the means to see that the plan is carried out. Whether you are planning for tomorrow's agenda or for the next 10 years, your plans will include these two parts. "Planning is essentially choosing."

Planning is the process by which a manager looks to the future and discovers alternative courses of action. Planning pervades management. Planning at all levels of the organization is desirable. Planning at the top level may be overall or broad, whereas at the lower level, it may be detailed day-to-day type, important to the individual manager at that level.

Planning involves predetermining a course of action to be taken. The process of planning may begin with a vague hunch or an element of intuition on the part of a manager and his group, yet good managers visualize quickly a clear pattern for handling current thought about future actions. Plans become promises for decisions to be made in the future. Planning provides frame of reference for decisions of individuals in an organization. The increased importance of planning in an organization is the direct result of the changing environment in which the enterprise operates. The modern manager must continuously anticipate changes which will require discarding old ways and adopting new ones. Thus, the need for planning results from various changes in the environment. The aspects of this changing environment are:

1. Changes in technology
2. Changes in Government policy
3. Changes in overall economic activity, including prices, inputs, etc.
4. Changes in the nature of competition
5. Changes in social norms and attitudes

Useful Generalizations of Planning

1. A plan should be directed towards well defined objectives, otherwise, performance in the future cannot result in purposive effort.
2. Plans made by different units should be coordinated through adequate communication.
3. Planning is a pre-requisite to other functions of management since each other function depends upon thinking in advance of execution.
4. Adaptation of plans to current action demands continuous redrafting of plans.
5. Planning pervades the hierarchy of an organization. Planning at lower level tend to be detailed and for short periods in the future; planning at higher levels tends to be general and for long periods of time.
6. A manager should relate the degree of commitment of his resources to the need for definite plans.
7. Plans should retain flexibility. Planning tends to present a rigid course of action unless change is incorporated in plans. Alternative courses of action will help provide flexibility, though often only at extra cost.

Planning allows us to design for an uncertain tomorrow with some assurance of meeting our goals. This assurance is the "bridging the gap" between what is desirable and what can be accomplished. Management of most organizations can be divided into three groups according to their ability to bridge the gap. Mcconkey has classified organisations as the "Pussy cats", "Fat cats" and "Tigers".

Pussy cats assume that today and tomorrow are the reflections of the past.

Fat cats realize future is not the same as the past, utilizes resources better.

Tigers: Future is what you make it. Monitor for new ideas and adopt them.

Phases of Planning

The planning function can be divided into four phases:

1. Establishing the goals and objectives of the organization.
2. Formulating policies to reach the goals and objectives.
3. Developing intermediate and short-range plans to implement the policies.
4. Statement of detailed procedure for implementing each plan.

Types of Plans

1. Strategic or long range planning to be done at the upper levels.
2. Operational planning to be done at lower levels. "Plan the Work; Then Work the Plan".

8.2 ORGANIZING AND PRINCIPLES OF ORGANIZATION

Organizing function relates to the assignment of duties and the co-ordination of efforts among all the organizational personnel to ensure maximum efficiency in the attainment of predetermined objectives. Organizing is also grouping of work and people, defining working relationships, building spirit or morale and balancing work structure so as to achieve desired results.

Organizing involves: (a) determination and enumeration of the activities required to achieve the objectives of the organization, (b) the grouping of these activities, and (c) assigning of the activities and authority to carry them out.

The following paragraph from American Management Association will highlight the importance of organizing function in Management.

"Each member of an organization must know what he is supposed to do and to whom he is accountable. Most personnel conflicts are due to faculty organizational relationships and poor communication. Frequently, even those in executive positions do not understand their responsibilities, their authorities and their relationship to others in the organization. The result is overlapping responsibilities or authorities with resulting conflict, or just as bad, a no man's land where no one takes responsibility or assumes authority."

The managerial task of organizing obviously deals with people as well as equipment and other facilities. Satisfactory performance of the organizing function exists when:

(a) there is a plan for arranging and relating resources
(b) resources have been determined
(c) provision has been made for assembling resources
(d) factors to be appraised have been defined
(e) means of measurement have been established

Four Foundations of Organization

1. Division of work
2. Scalar and functional process
3. Structure
4. Span of control

Functions of Organization

The organization has the following functions to perform in management.

1. It divides work among its members and provides each employee particular task, limits and concentrates his attention on that task.

2. It establishes standard practices and works out detailed procedures to relieve the employee of the need to determine such procedures each time he uses them.
3. It transmits authoritative decisions downward, upward and cross ways providing employees with information/ messages they need in the course of their work.
4. It provides a communication system to make known all kinds of information to its employees.
5. It trains and indoctrinates its members and provides for the internalization of influence relating to knowledge, skills and loyalties. Training enables employees to make decisions as the organization would like them to be made.

Principles of Organization

1. There must be clear lines of authority running from top to the bottom of the organization.
2. No one in the organization should report to more than one line supervisor. Everyone in the organization should know to whom he reports, and who reports to him.
3. The responsibility and authority of each manager should be clearly defined in writing.
4. The responsibility should always be coupled with corresponding authority.
5. The responsibility of higher authority for the acts of its subordinates is absolute (not limited, unconditional).
6. Authority should be delegated as far down the line as possible.
7. The number of levels of authority should be kept minimum.
8. The work of every person in the organization should be confined as far as possible to the performance of a single leading function.
9. Whenever possible, line functions should be separated from staff functions, and adequate emphasis should be placed on important staff activities.
10. There is a limit to the number of positions that can be co-ordinatsd by a single manager/executive.
11. The organization should be flexible, so that it can be adjusted to changing conditions.
12. The organization should be kept as simple as possible.

Bureaucracy

It is a familiar term. It originally signified an approach to organized government, in which a "bureau" was appointed to handle each aspect of a given job. In the olden days, bureaucracy was considered a praiseworthy arrangement. To German Sociologist, Max Weber, it symbolized a "consistent system of rules and procedures designed to achieve organizational goals". In recent years, however, bureaucracy has become synonymous with the tendency of large organizations to over organize, so that the process becomes more important than the product.

The main characteristics of the Bureaucracy are the following:

1. High specialization
2. Rigid hierarchy of authority
3. Elaborate rules and controls
4. Impersonality

Bureaucracy has the advantage of stability and unified focus on the objectives.

8.3 SOME ASPECTS OF ADMINISTRATIVE COMMUNICATION

Communication is an exchange of ideas, facts, opinion or emotions by two or more persons resulting in the transfer of meaning.

Paradigm of Administrative Communication

Administrative Communication

Administrative Process		**Functions of Communication**
• Planning		• Informative
• Organizing		• Evaluative
• Directing	Line of Communication	• Instructive
• Controlling		• Persuasive
• Co-ordinating		• Integrative

Role of Communication in Administration

1. To keep employees informed up-to-date.
2. To provide guidance to employees regarding their task roles.
3. To enable employees to become interested in their respective jobs and in the work of the organization.
4. To motivate employees to commit themselves to the organizational objectives.
5. To solicit information and ideas from employees.
6. To install in members a sense of pride in belonging to the organization.

Some Fundamentals of Administrative Communication as related to Source and Receiver

During his daily activities, the administrator acts as both a source and a receiver. How the source and receiver operate depends on the attitudes, knowledge, communication skill and socio-cultural context of both.

Communication and Decision Making

Information and knowledge that has a bearing on decisions arise at various points in the organization. Effective communication is concerned with how to channelize knowledge and information to the appropriate decision points.

Feedback in Communication

By feedback, it is meant to the evaluation by the source of messages received from others. Indirect feedback is obtained when direct observation of the receiver is impossible. To acquire indirect feedback is one of the most difficult and yet one of the most important administration tasks.

Difficulties in Getting Correct Feedback

1. Psychology of source.

2. Psychology of receiver.
3. Rationalization.
4. Socio-cultural context.
5. Delay and distortion.
6. Difficulty to use one feedback to interpret what is needed.

Communication in Organization

Communication is important in all phases of management and particularly important in the function of directing.

Communication and Decision Making

In the decision making process and in implementing decisions, communication has a vital role to play. A supervisor cannot make proper decision unless information available at various levels reaches him in time. Similarly decisions reached in the higher ranks of the organization hierarchy will have no effect upon the activities of operative employees unless they are communicated downward.

Levels of Information Flow in Organizational Communication

There are three levels of flow of information viz., (1) Upward flow, (2) Downward flow, and (3) Lateral flow.

Areas of Work Where Communication Operates

Communication in organization is needed in various activities of an organization and the purpose. However, different communication is needed in :

(i) Recruiting, (ii) Orientation, (iii) Operation information, (iv) Individual appraisal, (v) Personal safety, and (vi) Enforcing discipline.

Major Problems in Communication

There are six major issues involved in relation to the problems in communication. These are :

1. Getting ready to communicate

2. Barriers in communication
3. Principles of communication
4. Choice of techniques in communication
5. Cross-wise communication
6. Written versus oral communication

Getting Ready to Communicate

Very few supervisors pay adequate attention in getting ready to communicate. The evidence is everywhere that people start talking and writing without thinking. Many things are involved in getting ready to communicate. The objective must be clear, the premises known, the alternatives weighed, and the messages selected. Thereafter the choice of communication techniques and who is to execute the message become critical.

Barriers in Communication

There are number of factors which create barriers in organizational communication. Some of the important factors are:

1. Faulty translating
2. Loss by transmission and poor retention
3. Inattention
4. Unclarified assumptions
5. Insufficient adjustment period
6. Distrust of communicator
7. Premature evaluation
8. Fear
9. Failure to communicate

Principles of Communication

1. Principle of clarity
2. Principle of integrity
3. Principle of strategic use of informal organization

Choices of Techniques in Communication

Supervisors must often choose between presenting information in narrative, statistical or graphic forms. Trend datas are easiest to understand in a graphic presentation; some items are more easily grasped in statistical form; and the unusual or complicated may be clearer in a narrative form.

Cross-wise Communication

Supervisors should not only permit but insist on voluntary cross-wise or horizontal channels of communications at all levels, to speed information and improve understanding.

Written versus Oral Communication

Both written and oral communications have advantages and disadvantages. A supervisor cannot depend on either the written or the oral method of communication. He has to use a judicious combination of both methods while communicating with employees.

8.4 ADMINISTRATIVE COMMUNICATION IN EXTENSION MANAGEMENT

Extension service, as a goal seeking system, operates in conformity with certain organizational principles, processes and procedures. A social system comes to existence with an interacting group of individuals. Such a system survives through time by maintaining an acceptable pattern of interaction. Human communication is involved in most of this interaction.

An administrative organization is a special type of social system. All formal administrative communication is directed towards this element. Organizations vary in their effectiveness. To a certain measure this effectiveness is related to the communication system obtaining in the particular organization. Much depends upon the pattern and quality of communication involved. Since organizations are hierarchical in structure and since they are oriented to the attainment of some goals, there is a constant need for making and transmitting decisions, circulating information and regulating performance. All this means efficient communication.

Extension organizations have at least three special problems.

1. They have to process and transmit highly scientific and technical information with least possible distortion and delay.

2. Since they are spread over a large geographical area, they have to depend upon a limited means of communication, particularly in developing countries.
3. By the nature and their spread and the clientele they serve, the problems they have to handle are greatly diversified and intricate.

Therefore, if communication needs attention in a small compact organization, it deserves greater attention in large diffuse organizations like extension service. Still this matter has not received enough attention, so far. Most frequently it is taken for granted, if not neglected. The principal trouble in this matter of communicating is that so many people think it is really no problem at all. Administrative communication has become more important in modern life, as the organizational role in society is changing. Communication is seen to be a pervasive process in organizational performance. Organizational effectiveness, therefore, to a certain degree, depends upon the efficiency of the concerned communication system.

Communication is basic to successful extension management. Good communication allows us to get our ideas across, find out what other people have to say, and solve problem quickly and effectively. For the Extension Manager, an understanding of the communication process and the different methods of communication will help to prevent misunderstanding which can make professional career miserable and unproductive.

Men and women in organizations spend 10 per cent of their communication time writing, 15 per cent reading, 35 per cent speaking, and 40 per cent listening. This pattern holds true for most people. Talking and listening are particularly important communication skills for a manager. They must be able to give clear directions and also learn to listen effectively in order to understand subordinate's ideas and complaints. In addition, they must maintain open communication channels between workers and management.

Communication is clearly a vital key to supervisory effectiveness. The supervisor receives and sends oral and written messages – informal and formal in a continuing communication interchange with others. Supervisors must be able to interpret the messages of top level management correctly and transmit these messages accurately to workers in a language they will understand.

Concept of Communication

Communication is the transfer of information and understanding from one person to another. It is a way of reaching others with ideas, facts, thoughts and values.

SOURCE : Communication skills, attitude, knowledge, social system, culture

MESSAGE : Content, element, treatment, structure, code

CHANNEL : Seeing, hearing, touching, smelling and tasting

RECEIVER : Communication skills, attitude.

Importance of Communication

Organizations cannot exist without communication. If there is no communication, employees cannot know what their associates are doing. Management cannot receive information inputs, and management cannot give instructions. Coordination of work is impossible and the organization will collapse for lack of it. Co-operation also becomes impossible, because people cannot communicate their needs and feelings to others. We can say with some confidence that every act of communication influences the organization in some way.

From management's point of view, all management acts must pass through the bottleneck of communication as shown in the following figure. Great management ideas are strictly armchair thoughts until a manager puts them into effect through communication. When communication is effective, it tends to encourage better performance and job satisfaction. People understand their job better and feel more involved in them.

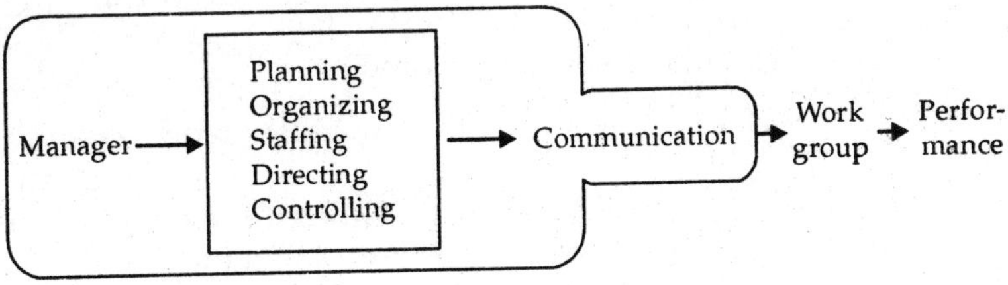

The Rule of Five

The entire set of five receiving steps in communication often is called the Rule of Five. The Manager (Sender) wants the receiver to receive, understand, accept and use the message and to provide feedback. If a communication accomplishes these five steps with a receiver, it has been fully successful.

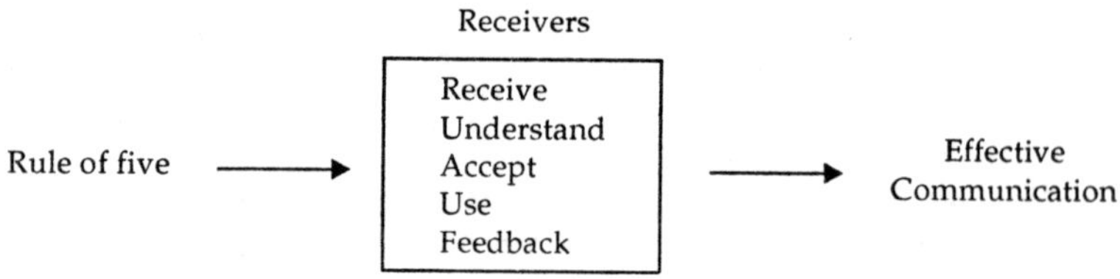

Transplanting Ideas

Most of the things, managers do involve the transplanting of their ideas into the minds of other people and allowing them to transplant their ideas into theirs. The Manager sends messages as well as receive them. He communicates his desires to others every day. His tone of voice, the words he speaks, his facial expression, his gestures and his manner of acting, all communicate what he wants to communicate to other people.

Ways People Communicate with Each Other

Thinking, Action, Observation, Speaking and Listening are the ways people communicate with each other.

Ten Commandments for Good Listening

1. Stop talking. You cannot listen if you are talking.
2. Put the talker at ease. Help him feel he is free to talk.
3. Show him that you want to listen. Look and act interested. Do not read your mail or perform other paperwork chores while he talks. Listen to understand, rather than to oppose.
4. Remove distractions. Don't doodle. Lap, or shuffle papers. It might be quieter if you shut the door.

5. Empathize with the talker. Try to put yourself in his place so that you can see his point of view.
6. Be patient. Allow plenty of time. Do not interrupt him. Don't start for the door or walk away.
7. Hold your temper. An angry man gets the wrong meaning from words.
8. Go easy on argument and criticism, which will put him on the defensive. He may clam up or get angry. Don't argue; even if you win or lose.
9. Ask questions. This encourages him and shows you are listening. It helps to develop points further.
10. Stop talking. This is first and last, because all other commandments depend on it. You just cannot do a good listening job while you are talking.

Communication Styles

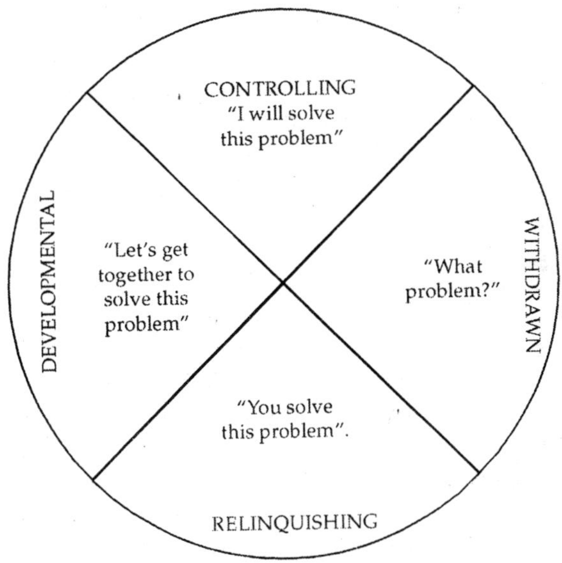

The Development Communicator: He does not assume that he is always right. He is willing to give advice and to listen to opinion of others, but he does not attempt to force his own ideas on others. Instead, he tries to develop joint understanding of the problem or issue and lead the discussion towards a joint conclusion. He understands the two-way process of communication. He explores, experiments, look for new approaches.

The Controlling Communicator: He uses high pressure approach to communication. He is convinced that his idea is the only right one, and, further, that no one else could add to it or find fault with it. He never experiments or considers alternatives, because for him, there are no alternatives. He sees two-way communication as a waste of time. Since he knows all answers, he needs only to tell people, what to do. Many managers are strong controlling communicators. They consider their memos the last and only word.

The Relinquishing Communicator: He insists that others should take lead in decision making and discussions. He is humble and unsure and believes that he can offer no worthwhile contributions. When some one else presents a new idea or solution, the relinquisher is happy to accept it. This type of communicators will not actively participate in discussions or problem-solving sessions. They are quite content to let someone else do the thinking, guide the discussion or vocalize a group decision.

The Withdrawn Communicator: Of all the styles of communication, this type usually involves the least amount of actual communication. They assume that nothing can improve situation. They do not ask for or give advice and avoid interaction of any type.

The Five Cs of Communication

The five Cs of Communication are: Clear, Complete, Concise, Concrete and Correct.

Is it Clear? The message should be straightforward and logical. There should not be too many messages.

Is it complete? Clarity will not help others understand the message if important information is omitted. An incomplete message will be dangerous. Message should be complete.

Is it concise? Most of us use too many words to convey our messages. If the messages ramble on, contain words whose meanings are unclear or stretch to great lengths, it is quite likely that they will be misunderstood.

Is it concrete? Concrete facts should be given and not abstract terms and broad generalizations.

Is it correct? If the message is not correct, it does not matter how well it is worded or how concise it is. Accurate information should be given.

Methods of Communication

In handling information in organizations, two major types of channels are used.

Downward Channels

1. Handbooks, manuals, pamphlets, statutes.
2. Periodicals.
3. Annual and special reports.
4. Chain of command—orders, memos, circulars, meetings, conferences.
5. Information racks, bulletin boards, notices.
6. Staff associations.
7. Grapevine.

Upward Channels

1. Chain of command
2. Welfare committees
3. Suggestion system
4. Staff associations
5. Personal discussions
6. Staff periodicals and representations
7. Grapevine

8.5 DECISION MAKING AND COMMUNICATION IN EXTENSION MANAGEMENT

Management at Supervisory level is considered as the art of getting things done. Generally not very much attention is paid to the determining of what is to be done. The task of deciding pervades the entire administrative organization with as much as does the task of doing. It is indeed tied up with the letter.

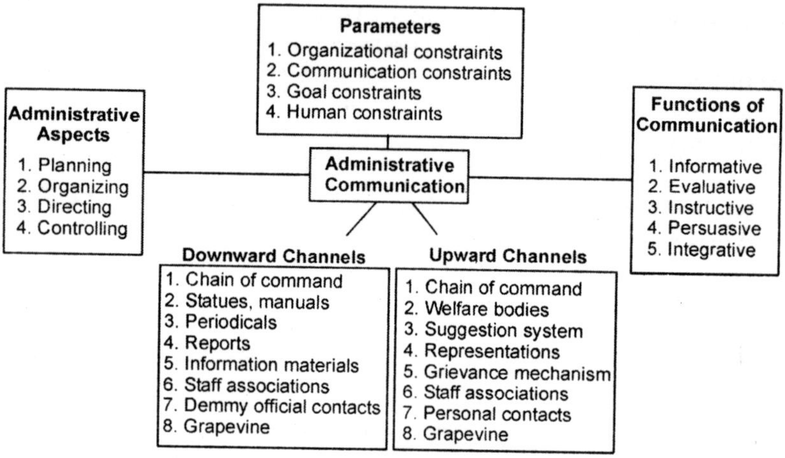

A Paradigm of Administrative Communications

Decision making within Extension Organization calls for several procedures, each of which is useful and appropriate in its place. The supervisor who fails to delegate finds himself so involved in a mass of minor decisions that the big issue may go unattended.

Well defined policies permit much delegation. The subordinate who is conversant with policy feels confident in making decisions within the field of his responsibility knowing that he has adequate policy guidance for his actions.

Some broad guidelines related to decision making as spelled out by Chester Barnard are : "From the point of view of the administrator, one of the main decisions he must learn to make is what to select for decision from the endless demands on his attention and his authority and what not to decide himself but delegate to others."

The Process of Decision Making

There are five rather distinct phases in the decision making process :

1. Getting the problem clearly defined
2. Making a thorough analysis of the problem
3. Developing alternate solutions
4. Selecting the most acceptable solution
5. Taking appropriate action to implement the decision

Decision Making in Extension Organization

There are two major areas in Extension Organizations which require decision making:

1. Decision making in the organization for the purpose of management of employees.
2. Decision making for the benefit of farmers for the purpose of deciding agricultural programme to be implemented.

Decision Making in the Organization

Who should take a decision? It is a difficult question to answer. It is said that the autocratic supervisor is likely to perform each step in the decision making process himself without involving his staff. In some cases this may be the only logical course to follow. However, in most cases decisions should be more frequently the result of staff discussion and occasionally it may be prudent to submit a question to the staff for a group decision..

Continuum of Administrative Decision Making and Communication

There are ways and means of taking administrative decisions and communicating them to employees. These methods could be classified on a continuum of administrator's behaviour in the process of decision making and communication, the two ends being authoritarian and democratic. These are shown in the diagram below:

Methods of Decision Making

Use of Authority by the Administrator

Tells	Sells	Presents and invites question	Presents tentative decisions	Presents problems and gets suggestions	Asks the group
(1)	(2)	(3)	(4)	(5)	(6)

Area of freedom for employees

It is rather difficult to say which method a good administrator should use in making and communicating administrative decision. It depends on the individual case. It should, however, be recognized that whenever it is possible to follow more democratic way, it may be done. Who decided that? The more nearly such a question can be answered "We did", the closer the organization will come to good morale and high productivity.

Decision about Agricultural Programmes at the Local Level

The most important question about implementing agricultural programme is who and how agricultural programmes are decided or determined. A common complaint about agricultural programme implementation is that there is poor people's involvement.

Agricultural programmes cannot be mere demonstrative programmes but have to be developed as adoption programmes. Without involving local people especially the local leaders, agricultural programme decisions cannot be implemented successfully. The concept of extension Programme Development and Execution Cycle requires to be understood by all extension supervisors so that all extension workers at the operating level could be trained and guided in following the correct procedure in determining agricultural extension programme at the village levels and also in implementing them.

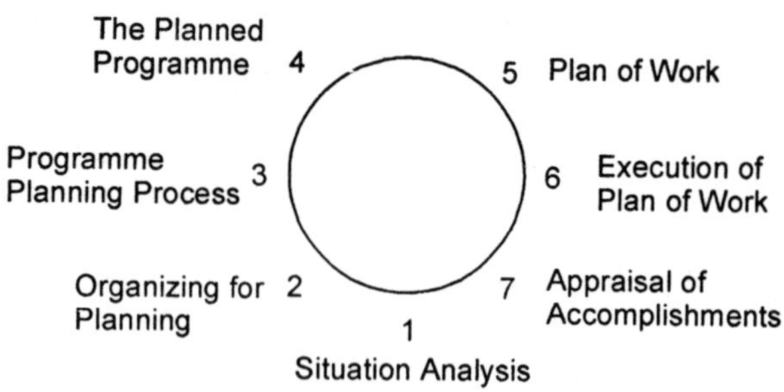

Local peoples' involvement in extension programme determination and implementation is a must.

1. **Situation analysis:** It uses facts gathered by staff at all levels, meetings with local leaders, local resource persons and suggestions, survey conducted by local leaders, consultation with various interest and commodity groups, and other devices.

2. **Organization for planning:** It is developing and agreeing on procedure or structure through committees and meetings of staff and local leaders to understand the sequence of events at different levels and stages.
3. **The programme planning process:** It begins by making certain that all concerned understand the various roles and functions of the persons and committees involved. The time the extension workers spend with local leaders in analyzing and identifying important problems, and agreeing on objectives is well spent.
4. **The planned programme:** Must be written, reproduced and distributed to everyone who has a present or potential interest. This includes extract for the public press.
5. **The plan of work:** Is primarily for extension staff and participating local leaders.
6. **Execution of the plan:** Is the first responsibility of extension staff, who must keep in mind the need for flexibility, co-ordination, co-operation, peak loads of work, seasonal interests of the public, and a host of other considerations.
7. Appraisal of accomplishment may bring both surprise and disappointment but is quite sure to show a new situation which starts the cycle again.

8.6 TIME MANAGEMENT

Management is a complex process involving many varied responsibilities and activities required for successful accomplishment of objectives of an organization through the efforts of others. Further, the quality of managers' performance is a major determinant of the effectiveness of the organization. This being the case, a most crucial issue to resolve is that of determining how managerial ability and performance can be developed and improved within an organization.

It is necessary to know what managers do, how they manage their time and how deeply they are involved in their job. As the organization becomes more complex and the scope of the organization's activity expands, it becomes increasingly important to know how managers are spending their time. Of all resources, it is the scarcest, the most perishable and the most elusive.

Managers who know how to use time will achieve results by planning. Some managers accomplish more than others, yet each manager has exactly as much time as everyone else. The problem lies not in the actual number of hours available, but in how well the managers use their time. Time is a unique and valuable resource. It can be managed wisely or misused, because every individual enjoys control over personal use of time.

Planning and using time wisely is a challenge to every manager. The time squeeze on each manager is a wide spread problem, since very few managers have learned how to manage their time effectively.

Time is an unusual commodity.
One cannot save it.
One cannot borrow it.
One cannot lend it.
One cannot leave it.
One cannot take it.
One can do only two things with it: use it or loose it.

A manager can learn to get more work done in the same time or as much done in less time. The choice is his. "Time is the scarcest resource. Unless it is managed, nothing else can be managed".

Assessing How Managers Use their Time?

To take stock of just how one's time is being used with respect to many different specific types of activities, it is necessary to know how much time is spent on the following:

1. Reading and replying to correspondence.
2. Conferring with office staff/personal staff and immediate subordinates.
3. Conferring with visitors who come uninvited.
4. Attending meetings called by one's superior officers.
5. Arranging and attending self-initiated meetings.
6. Attending ceremonial functions.

7. Reading reports and memoranda.
8. Signing routine approvals.
9. Writing reports.
10. Preparing and making speeches.
11. Lunch, tea and coffee breaks.
12. Personal reading and study.

Managers Need More Time

There never seem to be enough hours in the day to handle all the tasks, problems, administrative details, routine work and crises that occur. Most of the managers wish for a time extension each day.

A study has revealed that out of 1000 supervisors 10 of them admitted having enough time, 100 of them wanted 10 per cent more time, 400 of them wanted 25 per cent more time. Rest of them wanted 100 per cent more time.

Since no one has any more time than, anyone else, using it well is of utmost importance. Though we all have different personalities, talents and skills, there is one thing each of us has in exactly the same amount, that is time.

Major Time Wasters

The problem of time management is universal. There are many time wasters—ways in which other people waste the manager's time and how the supervisor wastes his own time.

Executive Time Wasters—External and Internal

List A	List B
1. Incomplete information presented for solutions to problems	1. Attempting too much at once
2. Employees with problems	2. Unrealistic time estimates
3. Lack of delegation	3. Procrastinating
4. Telephone	4. Lack of organization
5. Routine tasks	5. Failure to listen
6. Lunch	6. Doing it myself
7. Interruptions	7. Unable to say no

List A	List B
8. Meetings	8. Refusal to let others do the job
9. Lack of priorities	9. Delegating responsibility without authority
10. Management by crisis	10. Involving everyone
11. Personal attention to people	11. Bypassing the chain of command
12. Outside activities	12. Snap decisions
13. Poor communication	13. Blaming others
14. Mistakes	14. Personal and outside activities

Most people blame others for their poor use of time. A manager has to realize that managing himself is essential to manage his time.

Plugging Time Leaks

The following is the troubleshooting chart for time wasters

Time waster	*Possible causes*	*Solutions*
Lack of planning	Failure to see the benefit of planning	Recognize that planning takes time but saves time in the long run.
	Orientation towards action	Emphasize results, not activity.
	Success without planning	Recognize that success is often in spite of not because of, lack of planning.
Lack of priorities	Lack of goals and objectives	List goals and objectives. Discuss priorities with employees.
Over commitment	Too broad interests Misplaced priorities, Failure to set priorities	Learn to say no. Put first things first. Develop a personal philosophy of time. Relate priorities to a schedule of events.
Management by crisis	Lack of planning	Use the same solution as for lack of planning.
Haste	Impatience with routine	Take time to do it right. Don't waste time doing it over
	Dealing with the urgent	Learn the difference between urgent and important

(*Contd.*)

Time waster	*Possible causes*	*Solutions*
	Lack of planning ahead	Take time to plan. It will be well worth the effort.
	Trying to do too much in too little time	Attempt less, Delegate more
Paper work and reading	Information overload	Read selectively, Learn to speed read.
	Failure to screen	Delegate; reading to subordinates
Routine and unimportant (detail)	Lack of priorities	Set goals and stick with them. Delegate non-essential tasks.
	Over supervision of subordinates	Delegate; then give subordinates responsibility. Expect results, not particular methods.
	Inability to delegate; feeling of greater security dealing with trivial routine.	Recognize that without delegation, it is impossible to get anything done through others.
Visitors	Enjoyment of socializing	Do it somewhere else. Meet visitors outside your office. Go to lunch if necessary; Hold on-the-spot conferences.
	Inability to say no	Screen visitors, say no. Be unavailable.
Telephone	Lack of self-discipline	Screen and group calls. Don't talk long
	Desire to be informed	Stay uninvolved with all but essentials.
Meeting	Fear of responsibility for decisions	Make decisions without meetings
	Indecision	Make decisions even if some facts are missing.
	Over communication	Don't plan or attend unnecessary meetings.
	Poor leadership	Stick to the subject. Prepare minutes immediately afterwards.
Indecision	Lack of confidence in the facts	Improve information – gathering procedures
	Insistence on getting all the facts	Accept some risks. Decide without all facts
	Fear of the consequences of a mistake	Delegate the right to be wrong. Use mistakes as a learning process.

(*Contd.*)

Time waster	*Possible causes*	*Solutions*
	Lack of a workable decision making process	Get facts, set goals, investigate alternative actions and consequences, make the decisions; and put into operation.
Lack of delegation	Fear of subordinates' inadequacy	Train them well. Allow mistakes. Replace if necessary.
	Fear of subordinates' competence	Delegate fully. Give credit.
	Work overload on subordinates	Balance the work-load. Create new positions. Set priorities in proper order.

8.7 CO-ORDINATION OF EXTENSION ACTIVITIES OF THE STATE DEPARTMENTS AND AGRICULTURAL UNIVERSITIES

Agricultural Development work requires efforts of various nature like research, research testing, educational work based on demonstrations, supplies, services, regulations etc. This need of developmental work is met by organizing activities by various institutions and agencies like the Central and State Government Departments, the Agricultural Universities, and many private agencies. A co-ordinated effort of all these institutions and agencies is necessary to teach the common objective of agricultural development.

Two kinds of institutions are primarily kept in view in this regard: (1) The State Government Departments, and (2) The Agricultural Universities. Basic principles involved in co-ordinating the extension activities of these two kinds of institutions could as well be extended for co-ordinating with other agencies with slight modifications. This is discussed below under the following headings:

1. The concept of inter-institutional co-ordination
2. Guidelines for promoting inter-institutional co-ordination
3. Factors which impede inter-institutional co-ordination
4. Some problems relating to co-ordination in extension work
5. A Suggested Plan for Promoting Inter-institutional Co-ordination

1. The Concept of Inter-Institutional Co-ordination

The concept of co-ordination has several dimensions. Co-ordination may be vertical or horizontal, inter-departmental or inter-institutional type. Fesler (1968) has stated that co-ordination is a fundamental element in institutional co-operation.

Why is it so important?: Every book on administration or management has given reasons why co-ordination is important. However, statements made by Simon (1957) and Dale (1965) are more pertinent. According to Simon, "Co-operation will usually be ineffective – will not reach its goal whatever the intentions of the participants – in the absence of co-ordination". Dale is more categoric when he states "Without constant effort towards co-ordination, there is likely to be duplication of work and work at cross purposes". He further states that co-ordination is needed to relieve difference of opinion.

Definition and Meaning: It might be necessary at this stage to understand what is co-ordination. According to Fesler (1968), there is no such thing as co-ordination in general. It must always refer to something like a definable subject matter of problem. Again co-ordination is not so much a function as it is a set of working relationship. Newman (1951) states that co-ordination involves the synchronizing or dovetailing of inter dependent activities and demand harmonized programmes and policies. Considering these view points, inter-institutional co-ordination can be broadly defined as the process of developing working relationship between or among institutions in order to synchronize their programmes and activities so as to reach common objectives.

Elements involved: Based on Simon (1957), we might state that inter-institutional co-ordination involves the following elements:

1. The relations of the institution's objectives and intermediate goals to those of other institutions.
2. The institution's assessment of the alternative available to it and to the other institutions.
3. The institution's expectations as to the courses of action that will be followed by other institutions.

More specific list of activities related to co-ordination given by Fesler (1968) are as follows:

1. Inform each representative of the other's activity and plans.
2. Help to achieve agreement on removal of superficial frictions.
3. Promote action on matters whose solutions is of relative indifference to the agencies principally involved.

Undesirable Co-ordination: Attempts to implement a single programme by co-operative efforts of different institutions is commonly referred to as co-ordination. However, such activities only require a continuous attention to special co-ordinating devices for implementing a programme. According to Gulick and Urwick (1937), "whenever an organization continuously resort to special co-ordinating devices in the discharge of its regular work, it is a proof that the organization is bad".

2. Guidelines for Promoting Inter-Institutional Co-ordination

A number of useful guidelines have been suggested by different authorities for promoting inter-institutional co-ordination. The following list of guidelines drawn from these various sources might serve useful for this discussion group:

1. The success of inter-institutional co-ordination depends on the unifying forces of doctrine, spirit and morale.
2. Clearly written objectives and programme description will roster co-ordination.
3. Full and mutual understanding of the objectives and organizations of the administration and operating personnel at all levels, promotes co-ordination.
4. In several circumstances, the objectives of one institution need to be formulated with partial sacrifices for some time to promote better co-ordination.
5. Co-ordinated action directed towards a set of objectives requires plans that everyone recognizes as official.
6. Constant appraisal of the objectives and programmes of the organizations to see that they are following the pattern for which they were created is helpful in co-ordination.
7. Consistency and compatibility are necessary even in relatively more independent activities.

8. Actions of different institutions must synchronize whenever their work inter-locks.
9. Co-ordination requires the consideration of the systems of authority, status and specialization, the system of technically necessary inter-dependence in regard to the organization's goal.
10. Authority, if any, used in co-ordination must be disciplined by reason and reality.
11. In organizing, in dividing the work and delegating jurisdiction, authority must submit to the needs of speciality.
12. Co-ordination would be futile if it were to be confined to laying down the law. It must seek consensus. It must convey reasons. It must elucidate identification with its objectives. You can't legislate co-operation and team work. It must be earned through leadership and demonstrated sincerity.
13. The recognition of mutual inter-dependence is capable of providing as broad a basis for co-ordination as is technically needed.
14. Co-ordination based upon the mutual recognition of need, cannot, of course, be arbitrarily imposed by authority.
15. Memoranda of Understanding or agreements between or among different institutions help in co-ordination.
16. Mutual acquaintance of personnel belonging to different institution is necessary to promote understanding which is helpful for co-ordination.
17. Maintenance by each institution of a sincere attitude and willingness to develop plans for co-operative action with other organizations, without relinquishing its own responsibilities helps in co-ordination.
18. An agreed programme of reporting and interpretation should be developed giving all institutions their just credit for the progress and accomplishments of the co-ordinated endeavour.
19. Administrative meetings of personnel of concerned institutions should be called frequently enough for evaluation and for correcting personnel clashes which might come in the way of co-ordination.

3. Factors which Impede Inter-Institutional Co-ordination

Along with the understanding of the above mentioned guidelines it may also be necessary to get acquaintance with the factors which impede inter-institutional co-ordination. The following list attempts to indicate such factors which impede co-ordination:

1. Institutions which spend their time on speciality often come to regard their activities as ends in themselves rather than as means to another and bigger end.
2. Institutions which are independent are likely to make decisions without regard to what is done or needed in other institutions.
3. Conflict arises when rights or competencies are allocated or demanded in disregard to technical needs.
4. The rules and regulations may increase tension if they constitute and impose division of work emphasizing jurisdiction or rights rather than abilities.
5. The existence of authority to ignore the needs of specialization, this possibility of pure acts of political power, opens the way for inter-personnel and inter-group competition for authority and jurisdiction.
6. Co-ordination becomes a shame when it is attempted to operate by first.
7. Co-ordination will be difficult when feelings run deep, institutional prestige is at stake and views of public policy diverge.
8. There is danger that some institutions will attempt to improve their showing at the expense of other institutions.
9. Clashes arise from difference in dynamic personalities misunderstanding in programme function and operation, selfish publicity on programme and programme contribution and apparent disregard of clause of agreement and the likes.

4. Problems Relating to Co-ordination in Extension Work

1. The functions of the Departments of agriculture have not been redefined in most of the States where Agricultural Universities have been set up. The expert opinion as

evidenced through the recommendations of different national committees seems to be divided on this issue. The Agricultural University Committee (1962) and the Educational Commission (1966) have recommended that the University should take over the entire educational aspects of extension work from the State Departments. The Agricultural Study Team of the Administrative Reforms Commission (1967) has suggested that the responsibilities for the field extension educational work should not he entrusted to the Agricultural University. The Fourth Evaluation Team or the intensive Agricultural District Programme (1969) has cautioned the Agricultural Universities in respect of programmes to substitute the extension work presently being carried out by the State organization and experience in doing effective extension work.

2. In several States, Agricultural Universities are slowly establishing their own field extension units without clearly defining their extension roles *vis-a-vis* those of the State Departments through the accepted Memoranda of Understanding. Such actions appear to have already resulted in some duplication of resources as pointed out by the report of the Fourth Evaluation Team of the ICAR.
3. Agricultural universities are demanding through the resolutions passed in National Committees and Conferences that certain extension activities should be transferred from the State Government Departments to the Universities. Many State Government Departments are contesting such resolutions.
4. In some States, Co-ordinating Committees operating at the Department level and the Secretariat level appear to be not functioning effectively and as an alternative committees at the Minister's level are being set up.
5. Due to the introduction of new extension activities sponsored through the centre, new problems of co-ordination between the State Departments and the Universities have also cropped up.
6. Efforts made to identify the various stages involved in implementing agricultural programmes and to delegate the responsibilities of implementing different stages to

different institutions like the University and the State Departments depending upon their specialists and the resources available, seem rather inadequate.

5. A Suggested Plan for Promoting Inter-Institutional Co-ordination

1. The State Departments and the University should both recognize each other's statutory responsibilities regarding the extension function and accept their mutual inter-dependence.
2. The role and responsibilities of the Agricultural University and the State Departments in carrying out the agricultural programmes through various stages should be clearly defined and mutually agreed to.
3. Memoranda of understanding between the State Departments and the university must be drawn in respect of extension functions stating clearly the following :
   (a) Expectations of the institutions to fulfil their statutory responsibilities relating to the extension role.
   (b) Clearly stated list of objectives in respect of their extension functions.
   (c) Specifications of different extension programmes of the institutions to reach their objectives indicating how these fit in with the accepted specialties and the resources available at the institutions.
   (d) Category of extension personnel to be employed by the institutions and a clear statement of their job descriptions relating to the various extension programmes to be undertaken.
   (e) An agreed programme of reporting the progress of work in order to avoid any possible conflict with other institutions.
   (f) An inter-institutional committee should be set up to promote co-ordination for: Mutual acquaintance of personnel of the different institutions, informing each institution of the other's programmes and plans, constant appraisal of the objectives and programmes of the institutions from time to time, and discussing differences of opinion if any which might come in the way of co-ordination.

8.8 PROJECT EVALUATION AND REVIEW TECHNIQUE (PERT)

The PERT (Project Evaluation and Review Technique) is one of the specialized control techniques used in management. PERT employs what is called a time event net work in building the net work, events and activities are first identified. An event is a point in time when an activity is begun or finished and is generally represented in the net work by a circle. An activity is an operation required to accomplish a particular goal and is represented in the net work by an arrow. The method explained in a simple way involves steps in logistic analysis. The basic steps involved are :

1. Break the activity necessary to achieve the objective into steps or parts.
2. Note the relationships between each of these parts.
3. Determine the resources that will be needed for each step.
4. Find out when each resource will be available.
5. Estimate processing time for each step.
6. Assign definite dates to each step.

For control purpose, the critical path, i.e. the sequence of activities and events that is longer than any other is worked out. The next method of control is to find out the path which is shortest.

For getting the task performed, we were required to do the following things:

A. To find out the important steps involved in using PERT.
B. To indicate the types of agricultural extension projects where the PERT can be used effectively.
C. To prepare calendar of operations taking advantages of PERT to avoid the problems of (i) Late supply of inputs for demonstrations and trials and (ii) Late receipt of credit by the farmers.

A. Steps involved in PERT

1. Division of the task into series of activities.
2. Determination of the relationships and sequence of the activities.
3. Identification of the resources needed.

4. Determination of the time when the resources are required and when these would be available.
5. Processing time for each activity and allocation thereof.
6. Development of calendar of operations.

B. The Types of Agricultural Extension Projects Where PERT Can be Used Effectively

PERT can be used for all agricultural extension projects. However, here are some of the types of such agricultural extension projects :

1. Crop demonstration and trials.
2. Crop development projects, e.g. NODP, SAAP etc.
3. Horticultural and spices development programmes, i.e. coconut development programme, spices development programme.
4. Watershed development projects.
5. Special area development programmes.
6. Coordinated programmes ITDP, IRDP etc.
7. Command Area Development Project.
8. Programmes of the voluntary agencies.

C. Development of Calendar of Operation

1. For Supply of Inputs

The object of this task is to ensure timely supply of inputs for conducting demonstration and trials. Supply of inputs means :

(i) Supply of seeds
(ii) Supply of fertilizers
(iii) Supply of pesticides
(iv) Supply of irrigation etc.

For supply of any kind of inputs, the following activities need to be involved :

(a) Assessment of requirement
(b) Placement of indent with the supplying agency/agencies
(c) Receipt of supply
(d) Distribution to the farmers

Supposing a task was to supply paddy seeds for conducting demonstrations, the following calendar has to be developed using PERT system:

Supply of paddy seed——0————0————0————0————0
10/9[a] 15/9[b] 20/9[c] 30/9[d] 30/10

2. *In the Matter of Credit Supply the Following Activities are Found to be Involved*

(a) Checking credit worthiness with cooperative societies
(b) Preparing list of eligible farmers
(c) Assessment of their credit requirements
(d) Processing of document
(e) Release of funds from the apex body
(f) Distribution of loan through cooperative societies

With an object to get the activities done in time, the following calendar under PERT has been developed.

0————0————0————0————0————0————0
10/7[a] 20/7[b] 1/8[c] 15/8[d] 1/9[e] 20/9[f] 30/9

It is to be mentioned in this connection that in a task there may be certain activities which are inter-related. In PERT system that relationships can be shown. Here the supply of credit is inter-related with supply of inputs, so, the calendar has been prepared in such a manner that distribution of credit is completed before the commencement of distribution of inputs to the farmers at the target date for completion of the previous one commencement of the later has been timed as end of September.

REFERENCES

Koontz, H. and O'Donnel, C. (1972), *Management* (6th Edition), McGraw-Hill Kogakusha Ltd., Tokyo.

Dale, E. (1973), *Management – Theory and Practice* (III Edn.). McGraw-Hill, Kogakusha Ltd., Tokyo.

Davis, K. (1981), *Human Behaviour at Work.* Tata McGraw-Hill Publishing Co. Ltd., New Delhi.

Flippo, E.B. (1981), *Personnel Management* (6th Edn.) McGraw-Hill Publishing Co., New York.

Fulmer, R.M. (1976), *Supervision – Principles of Professional Management.* Glencoe Press, London.

Glueck, W.F. (1977), *Management.* The Dryden Press, Illinnois.

Hodgetts, R.M. (1979), *Management – Theory, Process and Practice.* W.B. Saunders Co., London.

McGrath, E.H. (1986), *Basic Managerial Skills for All.* Prentice-Hall of India (Pvt.) Ltd., New Delhi.

Newman, W.H. (1983), *Administrative Action – The Techniques of Organization and Management* (II Edn.) Prentice-Hall *INC.* New Jersey.

Nadler, L. (ed.) (1984), *The Handbook of Human Resource Development.* John & Wiley and Sons, New Delhi.

Newman, W.H., Summer, C.H. and Warren, E.K. (1973), *The Process of Management* (III Edn.) Prentice-Hall of India (Pvt.) Ltd., New Delhi.

Richards, M.D. and Nilander, W.A. (1971), *Readings in Management* (III Edn.) D.E. Taraporevala, Sons & Co. (Pvt.) Ltd., Bombay.

Scanlan, B.K. (1973), *Principles of Management and Organizational behaviour.* John Wiley and Sons, Inc., New York.

9

Socio-Psychological Aspects Involved in Extension Management

9.1 SOME ASPECTS OF PSYCHOLOGY OF LEADERSHIP

We presume that leaders must have more intelligence than followers or group members. However, leadership research has pointed out that intelligence is not the major determinant of leadership. Although leaders must have more intelligence than followers, the difference must not exceed the followers, by too large a margin for, great discrepancies between the intelligence of leaders and followers, militates against the emergence of the leadership relationship. Research has indicated that measures of leader intelligence showed the highest relationship with unit effectiveness. Some other studies have also shown that if leaders have high job knowledge, even those who had low intelligence scores could provide good leadership.

Important Qualities of Leadership

1. **Empathy**: Ability to step into the shoes of others, i.e. to see others problems assuming their position.
2. **Considerate**: Able to help in very practical ways; to be ready to explain actions; to give detailed instructions to improve the welfare of its followers relative to their work or activity in the group. Who can help with anyone of a hundred practical problems with efficiency and skill if not warmth and sympathy?
3. **Surgency**: Enthusiasm, expressiveness, talkativeness, alertness and originality particularly for elected leader is important.

4. **Emotional stability**: Well adjusted, integrated person with competence to move during good and bad times with poise and serenity.
5. **Personal adjustment**: This is directly related to effective member participation. Personal adjustments are necessary because individuals meet with blocks to full participation in groups:
   (a) Not knowing goals and objectives.
   (b) Disapprove the means used.
   (c) Feeling of insecurity.
   (d) Concern whether the group will accept him

A responsibility of all members in a group is to help others to analyze themselves objectively so that they can overcome their blocks and frustrations and participate more effectively in the group.

A person has many ways to help adjust these blocks mentioned above. Some are rational and at conscious levels while others are not.

Aggression: When one's ideas are not accepted he may strike back blindly. He may show his aggression by gestures, words or even physical violence. He may feel or say "Well, you, people, are not interested in good ideas."

Compensation: To divert energies into another field of substituting another goal. If a member has difficulty in communicating in group discussion, he may not talk but devote a tremendous amount of energy to the legwork in carrying out actions decided by the group.

Rationalization: If one finds it difficult to attain a goal, he may unconsciously explain the situation away by denying to himself that he ever wanted to attain it.

Identification: Imitate the behaviour and mannerisms of the person with whom they identify themselves.

Idealization: Adjusting to such feelings as one's own inadequacy by over-evaluating himself his ability, attainment, importance.

Displacement: Transfer the feelings he has for one person to another.

Projection: Transfer to another his own feelings of inadequacies or frustration.

Conversion: Transfer of energy after or during a wish frustration into some physical symptoms or complaints.

Regression: Retreating from an existent complex situation to a simple one revert to a less mature approach in anticipation of being dealt with on this level.

Negativism: Frustrated individual responds to all subsequent alternatives in a negative way.

Fantasy: Imagining of situations in which one's goals are achieved when frustration takes place – day dreaming.

Importance to groups: Minority in a group often feels frustrated. The group member or group leader who recognizes this and attempts to create social interaction patterns within his group, which will minimize frustrations, will find that group morale will remain higher and the group will move more rapidly towards achievement of its goals.

Interpersonal sensitivity: It is related to empathy. It is a kind of skill or empathetic ability to observe facts about people and draw proper inferences. Presumably, some people have more sensitivity than others. Give them an opportunity to see people and listen to them and they will come up with many more accurate perceptions than with others who are not as sensitive.

The degree of accuracy with which people perceive others would seen to depend upon personal factors that are not as yet to well planned down.

Eight Rules in Training Leaders

1. Atmosphere

Physical atmosphere conducive to problem orientation. Large enough to permit maximum experience background, small enough to permit maximum participation and minimum threat.

2. Threat Reduction

Pleasant interpersonal relationships, reduce threat and permit shift of orientation from interpersonal problems to group goals.

3. Distributive Leadership

Distribution of leadership maximizes problem involvement and permits maximum distribution of member growth.

4. Goal Formulation

Explicit goal formulation increases a group 'We' feeling and increased involvement in the decision making process.

5. Flexibility

Groups should formulate agenda, which should be followed until new goals are formulated on the basis of new need.

6. Consensus

The decision making process should continue until the group formulates a solution upon which it can form a consensus.

7. Process Awareness

Awareness of group process increases the likelihood of goal orientation and arouse more rapid modification of goals or sub-goals.

8. Confined Evaluation

Permits catharsis and intelligent modification of the problem solving process at any stage of decision making.

9.2 LEADERSHIP STYLE AND GROUP BEHAVIOUR

Leadership involves personal relationship in which one person directs, co-ordinates and supervises others in the performance of a common task.

Leadership style: The concept of leadership style refers to the pattern of leadership behaviour working with groups. Three broad styles of leadership have been identified viz. (1) Autocratic, (2) Democratic, and (3) Laissez-faire. The basic difference in these styles is the location of the decision making function.

Leadership Style Influences the Group Behaviour

Some fundamental studies on leadership style have indicated that group behaviour varies under the influence of different leadership styles. A study by White and Lippit (1960) indicated the following:

1. Laissez-faire was not the same as democracy.
2. Democracy can be efficient.
3. Autocracy can create discontent that does not appear on the surface.
4. There was more dependence and less individuality in an autocracy.
5. There was more group mindedness and more friendliness in democracy.

The above results should not, however, be interpreted in favour of democratic type of leadership style on all occasions. This is because research has also revealed to support different leadership styles under different conditions which we will discuss little later.

Leader Authority versus Group Freedom

In a completely autocratic style, the leader authority dominates while under a completely democratic style, the group freedom is maximum. When a leader, however, acts in a group, he cannot be completely autocratic or completely democratic all the time. The styles of his leadership varies from time to time which will also have effect on his authority as well as on the freedom of the group. This can be explained by illustrating five kinds of leadership styles (1) Telling, (2) Selling, (3) Testing, (4) Consulting, and (5) Joining, as shown in the following diagram:

Telling	*Selling*	*Testing*	*Consulting*	*Joining*
Administrative Authority			Freedom of Employee	

Leadership Styles

These various leadership styles may have to be used depending upon the particular situation.

Factors Determining Leadership Styles

According to Fiedler (1967), there are three important dimensions present in a group at a particular situation which will determine the leadership style to be used. These are: (1) Leader member relationships, (2) Task structure, and (3) Position power. Research by Fiedler indicated 8 different situations involving different combination of these three factors. The style of effective leadership varied under these 8 situations. The indication was that autocratic style might be tolerated when all these three factors are positive or negative. When these factors are at intermediate level, democratic way might be useful.

Some Implications for Extension Work

1. The leader must be aware of all dimensions of the situation in order to decide about the leadership style.
2. Leadership style must be adjusted to engineer the most desirable conditions that result in high quality decision that are based on relevant data and facts and rational reason.
3. Leadership role should be dynamic.
4. Leadership style must clarify task structures provide procedures for group operation, identify resources that will make task achievement possible and open goal paths early in the planning process.
5. Leadership style must objectively evaluate group progress, individual differences, disagreement, and divergent ideas through recognition, and application to new dimension of the problem and innovations valuable to group goal achievement.
6. Leadership style must objectively evaluate group progress, individual contributions and provide boundaries that lead to task on accomplishment.

To sum up, the effective leader is the one who can correctly identify the leadership function and utilize the appropriate leadership style.

9.3 MOTIVATING EXTENSION WORKERS

How to Motivate an Individual to Work?

Meaning of Motivation: A motive is an inner state that energizes, activates or moves (hence motivation) and that directs or channels behaviour towards goals. Motivation is a general term that applies to the entire class of drives, desires, needs, wishes and similar forces. Motivators are those things which induce an individual to perform.

Man and animal need alike—food, shelter, security, sleep and sex. But, in addition, man requires many other things such as knowledge, interesting work, recognition and opportunity for creative work. Animals do not need these things.

Approaches to Behaviour Motivation

The Classical Approach: The basic idea is to make it possible for workers to earn more by producing more. This approach usually establishes production quotas for particular jobs. If the workers produce their quota, they are rewarded accordingly. If they exceed the quota, rewards are proportionately increased. Thus, workers can greatly increase earnings by increasing production. Money is clearly considered as the best motivator in classical approach. In some situations, opportunities for increased earnings bring definite improvements in production. There is danger, however, in believing that only money motivates people.

The classical approach to motivation attempted to establish money as the simple solution to production problems. But it is not a simple solution. Money is certainly a motivator and usually good one, but the classical approach failed to take into account other factors that affect an individual's motivation.

The Human Needs Approach: There is more to life than earning money. The human needs approach takes into account other factors affecting motivation on the job.

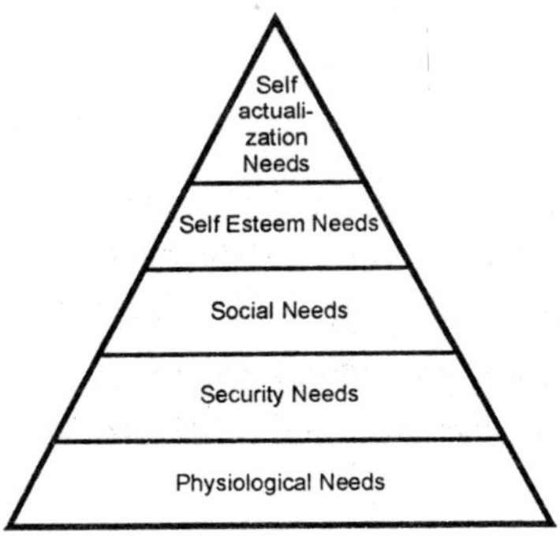

Maslow's Need Hierarchy

Once the basic needs for air, water, food, shelter and clothing are satisfied, man requires security as well as safety. Social needs for companionship and acceptance are the next to be fulfilled. Next, he seeks to gain the respect of the group to which he belongs (peer, neighbourhood etc.) The highest level of need—self actualization can never be completely fulfilled, because no one ever develops abilities to their fullest capacity. There are gradations of needs among human beings.

The Human Relations Approach: Top three levels of human needs approach exert the greatest influence on human motivation. Social, esteem and self actualization needs make up the human relations approach. Highly productive department is characterized by good human relations:

- Workers get along well with one another and with superior.
- They like their work and they are happy with the organizational establishment.
- People who are involved in pleasant, productive relationships with others are likely to be motivated toward goal fulfilment.

Therefore, the supervisor should encourage workers' participation in decision making and allow them to use their creative and leadership abilities to work toward organizational goals. Worker should be seen as a part of the team and not just a person to carry out simple, uncomplicated assignment. If an individual feels like a significant member of the group, it will provide the highest form of motivation.

The Two Factor Approach: Maintenance and Motivation

There are 10 maintenance characteristics which must be present before the worker can begin to be motivated.

- Organizational policy and administration
- Technical supervision
- Interpersonal relations with peers
- Interpersonal relations with superiors
- Interpersonal relations with subordinates
- Salary
- Job security

- Personal life
- Work conditions
- Status

The Second factor consists of motivational characteristics. Once the maintenance needs were satisfied, the following six factors become critical in developing worker motivation and dedication.

- Achievement
- Advancement
- The work itself
- The possibility of growth
- Recognition
- Responsibility

What really motivates a worker involves the job itself, not peripheral matters.

Maintenance Factors = Lower Level Needs
Motivational Factors = Upper Three Need Categories

What Motivates Workers to Work Effectively?

A challenging job that allows a feeling of achievement, responsibility, growth, advancement, enjoyment of work and recognition.

What Dissatisfies Workers?

Factors peripheral to the job such as poorly conceived work rules, poor lighting, regimental breaks, over emphasis on seniority rights, and inadequate raises or fringe benefits.

When do Workers Become Dissatisfied?

When opportunities for meaningful achievement are eliminated, they are sensitized to their environment and begin to find fault.

KITA – Does it Motivate Workers?

KITA literally means "Kicking the employees". It has several grave disadvantages. The possibility of the employee kicking back is ever present. This is a mental torture in the form of reprimand and demotion. It does not motivate. The employees resent humiliation and loose interest in work.

Job Enrichment: People work better only when the work is intrinsic, interesting or when there is scope for initiative, creativity and when the job is challenging. The job should provide opportunity for psychological growth of an individual knowledge, understanding, creativity and capacity to deal with ambiguous situations and maturity.

It is through work that a person develops himself psychologically. If he stops taking interest in work, his psychological development, stops and he degrades himself and destroys himself.

Intrinsic Motivation: Motivation within self.
Extrinsic Motivation: Motivation due to external factors.

On the Job Training to Motivate Employees

1. If the leader moves forward quickly, his followers have to do likewise.
2. The job should be challenging.
3. The staff should be continuously trained since today's work is increasingly knowledge work.
4. Management must encourage employees to assume responsibility. Employee participation must be encouraged.
5. An organization should be built on the strength of the people not on their weaknesses.
6. The emphasis should be on working smarter not merely harder.
7. Top management roust be strictly impartial in matters of promotions.
8. Manager should not blame or praise any one before other employees
9. Guide the employees and entrust them with important work.

9.4 FACTORS INFLUENCING THE PERFORMANCE OF INDIVIDUALS IN ORGANISATIONS

Extension Supervisors are expected to get good work from their subordinates. The performance of extension workers in organizations depends on two major sets of forces: (1) Factors related to individuals, and (2) Factors related to organization. The task of a good supervisor is to understand them carefully and promote their interplay.

1. Factors Related to Individuals

Basically three aspects determine the performance of individuals in extension organizations, viz. (i) knowledge and skill, (ii) Motivation, and (iii) Resources. This can be shown through a triangular model.

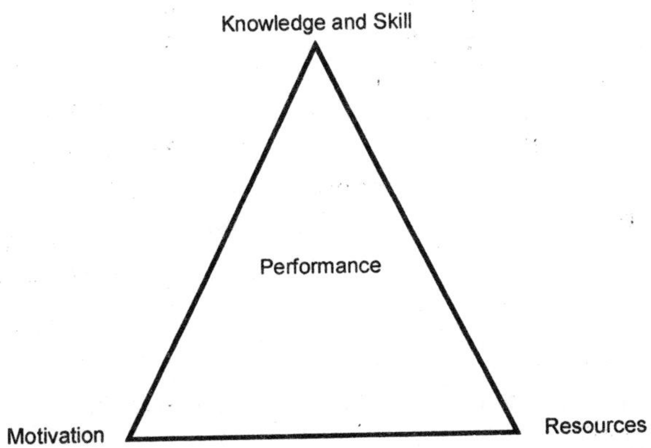

Three aspects determining performance of individuals in organizations

Knowledge and skill: Extension worker has to influence farmers through his authority of knowledge and skill which we generally call as subject matter authority. This subject matter authority has to be developed by the each field worker. A newly recruited worker in spite of his academic qualification is not fully equipped with the knowledge and skill required for his specific job. The supervisors have to assist them to develop their knowledge and skill. The knowledge and skill required by a field worker is in respect of the subject matter, extension methods and techniques and the skill needed in working with people.

Motivation: The motivation is defined as the interest and will to do the job. This primarily depends on the attitudes of individuals towards the work and their morale in the organization. Although individuals vary in their motivation levels, the general motivation levels of personnel could be maintained at high level by special supervisory techniques.

Resources: In spite of the required knowledge and skill and the motivation, individuals will not be able to perform their job effectively unless adequate resources are made available to them. These resources include physical facility as well as the required authority commensurate with their responsibility. The supervisors must ensure that the extension workers have access to these resources.

2. Factors Related to Organization

In administration what the supervisors try to do to improve the performance abilities of personnel has been called as personnel development or personnel management. This requires: (a) Commandments of good organization, (b) Methods to be used for personnel development, and (c) Model for personnel management.

Commandments of good organization: There are several commandments of good organizations which will help to improve the performance of individuals. They are the following:

1. Definite and clear-cut responsibilities should be assigned to each executive,
2. Responsibility should always be coupled with corresponding authority,
3. No change should be made in the scope of responsibility of a position, without a definite understanding to that effect on the parts of all concerned,
4. No individual occupying a single position in the organization should be subject to definite orders from more than one source,
5. Orders should never be given to subordinates over the head of a responsible executive,
6. Criticisms of subordinates should, whenever possible, be made privately and in no case a subordinate be criticized in the presence of executives of employees of equal or lower rank,

7. No disputes or difference between executives or employees as to authority and responsibility should be considered too trivial for prompt and careful adjudication,
8. Promotions, wage changes and disciplinary action should always be approved by the executive immediately superior to the one directly responsible,
9. No employee should be required or expected to be at the same time an assistant to and critic of another,
10. Any person whose work is subject to regular inspection should, whenever practicable, be given the assistance and facilities necessary to enable his to maintain an independent check on the quality of his work.

Methods to be used for personnel development: Three major methods to be used in personnel development are: (a) Counselling, (b) Training, (c) Performance appraisal.

REFERENCES

Fred, F.E. (1967), "Styles of Leadership" in Hollander and Hunt (Eds.), *Current Perspectives in Social Psychology* (2nd Edition), Oxford University Press, London.

Scanlan, B.K. (1973), *Principles of Management and Organizational Behaviour*. John Willey and Sons, Inc., New York.

White Ralph and Ronald Lipit (1960), "Leader behaviour and member reaction in three social climates" in Cartright and Zander (eds), *Group Dynamics* (2nd Edition), Harper and Row, London.

10

Human Resource Development and Training of Extension Personnel

10.1 HUMAN RESOURCE DEVELOPMENT IN EXTENSION ORGANIZATION

Increasing productivity is a worldwide concern of all nations. Human Resource Development (HRD) is a major factor in productivity. The basic relationship is that training can contribute directly to productivity. The human resources are assuming increasing significance in modern organizations. A majority of problems in organizational setting are human and social rather than physical, technical and economic. Since productivity is associated with human resources, it calls for a need to develop them. Organizations must invest wisely in both things and people. Of all resources of an organization, the human resources are probably the most critical and difficult to manage. Human resources are most critical because these are the only active resources at its disposal and the effective use of all other resources directly depends on efficient use of them.

Human resource development is the process of helping the personnel of the organization to acquire competencies. It is the process by which the employees of the organizations are helped in a continuous and planned way to: (a) acquire or sharpen capabilities required to perform various functions associated with their present or expected future roles, (b) develop their general capabilities as individuals and discover and exploit their inner potential for their own and/or organizational development purpose, and (c) develop an organizational culture in which superior-subordinate relationships, team work and collaboration among sub-units, are strong and contribute to the professional wellbeing, motivation and pride of employees.

Why HRD?

People need competencies (knowledge, attitude, values and skills) to perform tasks. Quality of performance of tasks requires high level or degree of skills. Competent and motivated employees are essential for organizational survival, growth and excellence.

Any organization that is interested in improving its services and its effectiveness in other ways (cost reduction, reduction in delays, improved quality and promptness of services, clientele satisfaction etc.) needs to develop its employee competencies to perform tasks to bring about improvements.

HRD in Extension Organizations

Extension organizations are non-formal educational organizations and their personnel have the responsibility of organizing learning situations in rural areas. The main purpose of HRD in Extension organizations should be the development of change agent system and improving competence of village extension workers from time-to-time. The HRD should aim at:

(a) Creating human resource base to absorb high-tech solutions in rual areas.
(b) Creating human resource for scientific management of rural extension.
(c) Develop a corps of effective and effcient rural trainers.
(d) Create competent research force in extension education.

Human Resources

Human Resources Development	**Human Resources Management**
Training	Recruitment
Education	Selection
Development	Placement
	Salary
	Appraisal
	Information Systems
	Benefits
Human Resources Environment	**Human Resources Others**
Organisation	Human Resources Planning
Development	Superior-Subordinate
Employee Assistance	Relations
Programmes	Research
Quality of work life	Carrier Development

10.2 TRAINING OF EXTENSION PERSONNEL

Extension Training is very important in Agricultural Extension work. This is because Agricultural Extension aims at bringing about changes in farmers' behaviour focusing attention on their immediate problems. Extension Training aims at providing timely education needed both to extension personnel specially to encourage immediate action.

Extension Training is an important aspect of the work of any extension organization. It has two important dimensions, viz. (1) To develop the required professional competency of the extension staff, and (2) To train voluntary leaders in rural areas to accelerate agricultural development with their assistance.

Who are to be trained?

(i) *Extension Personnel*-There are several categories of extension staff in an extension organization from the State level to the village level. For example the various category of extension personnel to be trained in the Department of Agriculture are as follows:

State level – Directors/Joint Directors Divisional level – Joint Directors District level – Principal Agril. Officers/Deputy Directors District level Specialists Sub-divisional level – Specialists Taluk level – Asst.Directors Extension Officers

Village level – Agricultural Assistants Similar lists of the personnel to be trained are requested to be prepared for development departments like Animal Husbandry, Veterinary, Horticulture, Sericulture etc.

Extension training is necessary for all the above mentioned staff through induction and inservice programmes. In case of village level workers even pre-service training is given by the department of Agriculture through its training institutes.

> Farmers: Training is necessary for two categories of farmers viz., 1) Farm Leaders and/or Voluntary rural leaders, and, 2) Farmers. Training of voluntary rural leaders is more important.

Types of Training

There are two broad types of training, viz.

1. Induction or orientation training
2. In-service training

Induction Training

It is that training given immediately upon employment to introduce the new staff member to his position. It begins the first day the new employee is on the job.

Purpose of Induction Training

1. To acquaint the new employee with the organization and its personnel.
2. To make him feel that he is a part of the organization.
3. To provide him with opportunity to learn to perform the job for which he was employed.

Other Desirable Effects of Induction Training

1. Provide a realistic picture of the terms under which a person is employed.
2. Indicates the types of activities in which he will be expected to engage.
3. Points out the level of performance expected.

Who Should Provide Induction Training?

Induction training is a cooperative enterprise involving the supervisor, the specialists, the new employees and other experienced employees. The supervisor is, however, the key person in providing the new employee with a satisfying induction training experience.

Guides for providing induction training:

1. Give information, emphasizing its use and application to the job.
2. Stir the learner to activity by getting him to participate.
3. Give the employee time to digest what he is learning.
4. Help the employee to develop the discernment necessary to separate the trivial from the important.

5. Help the employee achieve a real understanding of what he is learning.

Inservice training

In-service training is the job training that continues throughout the employees career.

No employee gets adequate training before he is employed which is suitable for his job for all time. Hence in-service training is a must for every employee in each organization.

The need for continuous in-service training is felt more in extension organizations where the technical employees have to be up-to-date in their subject matter competency. Research has indicated that deficiency is pre-service training of field extension workers is made good by in-service training.

Principles of Inservice Training

1. In-service training programme should be confirmed, i.e. supported by written administrative policy and administrative proceedings.
2. In-service training programme should be purposeful, i.e. directed towards definite purposes and objectives and provide for systematic evaluation.
3. In-service training programme should be co-operated, i.e. planned cooperation by the trainees and the trainer.
4. In-service training programme shall be need oriented, i.e. based on individual needs with allowances for individual differences.
5. In-service training programmes should be dynamic i.e. direted towards improvement of the on going educational programmes engaged in by the individual worker and the agency.
6. In-service training programme shall be flexible adjusted to the various experiences of personnel, changes in subject matter, methods and proceedings, changing emphasis in programme context.
7. In-service training programmes should be comprehensive i.e. it should be stimulated intellectual

curiosity and add to the enthusiasm of life as well as develop sound production personnel for the programme.

8. In-service training should be long time, continuous in character, i.e. available throughout the professional life of personnels.
9. In-service training programmes should be Developmental – Directed towards answering the maturing needs of individual extension workers.
10. In-service training programmes should be well organized, i.e. planned to achieve continuity, sequence and integration into the experience of the learning.
11. In-service training programmes should be imaginative – i.e. forward looking, making use of the more advanced thinking.
12. In-service training programmes should be efficiently designed to effect change and to use the hand available resources, including human resources.
13. In-service training programmes should be scientific, i.e. based upon scientific information.

Areas of Training in Extension for Extension Personnel

A. General Areas

1. State Extension Service – its aims, objectives, policies, job responsibilities of personnel etc.
2. Human Development
3. Programme Development
4. Educational Process
5. Social Systems
6. Communications
7. Philosophy and Values
8. Technology

B. Areas of Training for special groups

1. For Administrators
2. For Supervisors
3. For Specialists
4. For Field Workers

For Rural People

A. For Voluntary rural leaders for farmers

Behaviour sought as outcomes of Extension Training

1. Understanding of important facts immediately
2. Ability to interpret data
3. Ability to apply
4. Familiarity with dependable sources of information
5. Social attitudes of stalls
6. Ability to study and report results of study.
7. Broad and mature interests.

These outcomes are not achieved automatically through presentation of information to learners. If they are to be achieved, learning experiences having characteristics appropriate to the outcome are necessary. A list of required learning experiences will be made available.

In-service Training Situations

The in-service training of extension workers is accomplished through providing a variety of training situations as detailed below.

1. Short courses
2. Workshops
3. Conferences
4. Clinics
5. Field trips
6. Committees to study specific problems
7. Exchange of work responsibilities
8. Studies
9. Leader training meetings
10. Professional associations
11. Summer schools

Planning Inservice Training Programmes of Extension Workers

In-service training of extension workers must be planned to fit the needs of individual extension workers whose background, previous training, knowledge, interests and capabilities vary considerably. New scientific findings, recent developments in the communication media and the changing situational factors make it essential that extension workers participate in a wide range of In-service training activities each tailor made to accomplish a specific purpose. Extension supervisors have a very important role to play in the field.

The in-service training just cannot be fully accomplished by sending employees to some training institutes where some institutional in-service courses are being conducted. The Supervisor has to develop his own plan to create a variety of In-service training situations in consultation with extension workers, specialists and administrators.

Learning Experiences Appropriate to Certain Types of Objectives

1. Learning experience is helpful in acquiring information.
   - Give learners an opportunity to consult various sources of information.
   - Provide practice in analyzing these sources to see where they are adequate and where they are unsatisfactory.
   - Have learners develop criteria by which to judge the dependability of a particular source of information.
   - Provide for acquiring information as a part of the total process of problem solving rather than requiring memorization as a thing in itself.
   - Bring up important items of information in various ways, in varied context and with a considerable degree of intensity.
   - Suggest re-organization of information in varied ways appropriate to various situations in which it can be used.
2. Learning experiences is helpful to develop skill in thinking.
   - Utilize real problems usually arising in life situations
   - Allow the learner to follow the steps in problem solving.

- Show learners a number of solutions or a number of possible facts and conditions and have them practice suggesting various possibilities when attacking problems.
- Give learners an opportunity to come in contact with data that is new to him and some practice in trying to interpret them without over generalization and other common errors.

3. Learning experiences are helpful in developing social attitudes and skills
   - Provide learners with an opportunity to behave in the way desired and to get satisfaction from it.

Study on the Quality of Training Sessions

While it is easy to keep quantitative track of the fortnightly training sessions, project management usually has difficulty in monitoring their quality. A small group of participant observers, attending a reasonable number of sessions, could gain useful insight into possible defects in the training and possible ways of improving it.

It is not feasible in such a qualitative study to have each observer complete a questionnaire. Instead, he should be given a general outline of the aspects of the training session and be asked to make notes on each of them during the sessioned to write a narrative report on each of them immediately after the session. The aspects should include, but not necessarily be limited to, the following:

- Appropriateness of the physical environment;
- Effectiveness of the instructor, in terms of his knowledge and clarity of presentation;
- Reaction of the trainees in terms of attentiveness, questions asked, clarifications requested, objections raised etc.;
- Discussion of good and bad extension methods;
- Evidence of feedback from farmers to SMS and to agricultural research; and
- Amount of time and attention given to matters not relevant to the current extension messages.

Particular attention should be given to the ways in which the training sessions fulfilled two basic functions within the extension organization: (a) to ensure a two-way vertical communication flow between agricultural research and the farming system i.e. not limiting themselves to a top-bottom transmission of technologies but promoting permanent bottom-up circulation of field information, farmers' queries, local results, etc.; (b) to ensure the horizontal diffusion of good experience from one view to another by encouraging them to report on their most relevant achievements, problems and difficulties.

The reports of the participant observers of these training sessions should be submitted to a group discussion to distil the principal conclusions only then, a report should be prepared for transmission to the management of the extension project.

The sample size for each study need not be large. Each observations should cover several training sessions in a single fortnight, thus giving a sample of about 20 sessions for the whole group. The sample should be selected from strata defined by sets of AEOs within extension subdivisions. This will help to ensure that the range of quality of training is represented in the sample.

This case study may be carried out by a small team of extension specialists from the Department of Agricultural Extension of the State University. Alternatively, the group of Junior Research Officers in the State Evaluation Unit, with proper instruction, may also be an appropriate team for making the participant observations.

Another simple option for evaluating the quality of training is to question the VEWs about their perception of the training sessions. The VEWs are the immediate "Users" of training sessions possibly at the end of the session, their evaluation and criticism. They are in the best position to say whether what they hear and discuss at the session is sufficiently helpful for their work in the field.

10.3 EXTENSION STRATEGY IN DEVELOPMENT OF CHANGE AGENT SYSTEM AND IMPROVING COMPETENCE OF VILLAGE EXTENSION WORKERS

Human resource development is a prerequisite and often a necessary condition for the success of any development programme. This is because by human resource development we ensure leaders involvement and peoples' participation in development work. Experience, however, has indicated that HRD to enlist peoples' participation is often lacking in our country as revealed by large number of research and evaluation studies. Human resource development is rightly being given prominence in our new education policy. Extension education is very closely linked with the human resource development programme. Extension education's basic philosophy is 'development of the people'.

Extension education has to be taken to the people by specially appointed village extension workers or change agents working under a state level extension system. Such extension systems are in operation in most of the democratic countries of the world since several years. During the last 30 years, attempts are made to overcome these limitations by reorganizing extension systems in the developing countries. An important development in this regard was the starting of the Training and Visit (T&V) system with the support of the World Bank. The T&V system was designed to tackle the human resource development especially of the extension system, viz. to improve the competence of village level extension workers. According to Bennor, Harrison and Baxter (1984), "A professional system of Extension based on frequently updated training extension workers and regular field visits (and, therefore, called the Training and Visit – T&V system) is one approach to agricultural extension that has proved to be particularly effective." The work of extension education should be focused on supporting the field level agent, since he is the only extension worker who is in regular direct contact with farmers."

Extension Strategies in Human Resource Development

Extension strategies in human resource development have different facets. These are :

1. Development of change agent system and improving competence of village extension workers from time-to-time.
2. Identification training and use of local leaders in development programme.
3. Educating rural people so as to enable them to:

(i) identify important farm problems as their needs which could be solved by the use of scientific knowledge.
(ii) get motivated to apply the scientific knowledge.
(iii) develop desirable changes in behaviour.
(iv) get acquainted with various kinds of services available from different agencies dealing supplies, services, credit, inputs, market facilities and other agri-support activities.

4. Educate rural youth and women.

Extension Strategy in Identification and Use of Local Leaders in Development Programme

In spite of the crucial role to be played by the village level extension worker as a friend, philosopher and guide for local people, he can never play the role of natural group leader. He can be effective in his role of change agent only if he knows who the local leaders are and works with local groups through them. Extension education has an important role to play in identifying, developing and using these human resources. This idea is nothing new in India's rural development work. Right from the beginning of Community Development Programme in the early 50s, focus was given to identify, train and use local leaders. However, in recent years sufficient focus is not given on this aspect of human resource development in the extension system.

It is, however, seen that there is no systematic approach in using contact farmers as the local leaders, except that village extension worker in T & V system of Extension was instructed to visit the contact farmers regularly once in fortnight. This method alone does not deliver the goods in developing and using these local leaders. Systematic efforts are, therefore, necessary on the part of every village extension worker to identify, train and use a band of local leaders, in his extension work. There must also be a continuous support to be given by the administrators for this work to be undertaken by the village extension worker.

Extension Strategy in Educating People so as to Enable Them to Identify Important Farm Problems as their Needs

Efforts to promote planned change under village conditions in a democratic country are successful only to the extent that they focus on the important needs of people and are effective in helping people meeting these needs. Needs which influence local level change projects can be sub-divided into four categories as indicated below:

1. **Demonstrated felt need**: A need which has been demonstrated to the people in their prior attempts to solve the problems on their own.
2. **Solicited felt need:** The need, which the rural people are aware of, to the extent that they solicit assistance from the village extension worker or local authorities for its solution.
3. **Ascertained felt need:** A need which although already existing is only latent in the awareness of the people and requires to be clarified through consultation with the extension worker.
4. **Generated felt need:** A need which is created through deliberate efforts of the village extension worker and his extension system.

One of the basic approaches in carrying out extension education is to help rural people to identify their needs. It is important to harmonize what rural people feel they need and what village extension workers think they ought to have. What people want, may not be what they need most. What village extension workers think people need may not be what they want. It is the function of the extension system and especially the village extension worker to teach people to determine accurately their own problems, help them to acquire knowledge and to inspire them for action. But it must be their own action out of their own knowledge and convictions. This is accepted as one of fundamental objectives of carrying out extension work which is closely related to "human resources development" or "development of people".

Extension Strategy in Getting People Motivated for Action

Motivation explains how men are moved without being pushed. A very important aspect of human resource development in rural work is to motivate people for action once they have recognized the needs. People are motivated to act when they are convinced about the practical feasibility of a new practice to be adopted. Extension education requires to use the demonstration method to create confidence in the people about the advantage and suitability of a new practice. Although this method is the basic method in extension education, with the advent of T & V system, less focus is given in organizing demonstrations in a systematic way. This needs to be looked into.

A recent development in inspiring people for action is to educate them in a special way to inculcate high achievement motivation (N-Ach). High achievement motivation or the desire to act to achieve high standards, develops from the basic psychological phenomenon that high aspirations and low realizations will have strong needs to change the situation, while one whose aspirations are quite similar to realizations will be satisfied with things as they are.

The extension system should, therefore, initiate new focus in its educational work to promote achievement motivation in the rural people, which will ensure their involvement and quick action by them in rural development programme.

Extension Strategies in Educating Rural People to Develop Desirable Changes in their Behaviour

The basic premise for instituting an extension education system for a rural society is based on a belief that desirable changes in the agricultural enterprise can be achieved only through behavioural changes in the rural people, who are the ultimate decision makers in implementing rural development programmes. Human resources development is, therefore, a more realistic and reliable indicator of modernization or development than any other single measure.

The human resources development aspect of extension education therefore, requires that village extension worker conducts extension education in such a way that desirable changes in the behaviour of rural people is brought about. There are three kinds of behaviour changes, which are to be promoted, viz.:

1. Developing desirable attitudes towards new practice;
2. Learn the new knowledge relating to the scientific practices; and

3. Practice new skills which are essential for the success of new practice.

The village extension worker must carry out his extension educational work in a systematic way in order to enable the rural people to change their behaviour whether relating to attitude, knowledge or skill.

Another critical point in the process of teaching and learning in extension education related to human resources development is to enable the learners, i.e. rural people to have exposure to effective learning experiences.

Observations, however, indicate that extension teaching in T & V system of Extension through fortnightly visits by the village level worker was more or less converted into a mechanical process of meeting villagers and contact farmers and talking to them in a casual way instead of paying attention in setting up conditions in which learners will have effective learning experiences.

Extension Strategy in HRD Concerning with Rural Youth and Women

In HRD youth in extension must find a prominent place. That is why, in all countries where extension educational programmes have succeeded, youth work was considered as an important component. The book *"Extension Education in Community Development"* published by Government of India in 1961 provided special chapters on extension's role in youth activities. However, the new guide books of Agricultural Extension under T & V system have not included youth work as component of Agricultural Extension. It is time that youth work is included as integral part of T & V system. This is necessary as an important step to improve HRD relating to the countries rural youth.

In many countries extension work with rural women has been entrusted to extension service along with agricultural extension providing separate cadre of women extension workers in home sciences. The T & V system has also recognized the need for agricultural extension work for rural women. Women have an important role in agriculture. Their involvement in agriculture varies between cultures, but in most there are a few major agricultural operations in which women do not participate. To be truly effective, an agricultural extension service must deal with the activities handled by women. This is not often done, however, because of sociological constraints and inadequate focus on women's agricultural activities. An agricultural extension service can adopt a number of strategies to improve its support for farm women, among others by developing with research suitable production recommendations for activities solely or largely performed by women, orienting staff to the activities and needs of farm women, having some subject matter specialists concentrated on women's activities and employing women in areas in the extension service for which they are qualified. These steps are important, but by themselves achieve little unless extension staff regularly meet women. Wages to ensure this contact include the selection in each farmers' group of some female contact farmers. Whatever approach is adopted to have extension service for women, local agricultural, sociological and administrative considerations should be taken into account and involvement of extension, research and training staff at all levels is required.

In Karnataka and also in some other states, a special project has been launched with DANIDA assistance to take up women and youth training extension programme (WYTEP) at Farmers Training Institute. Under this programme, special work in agriculture for rural women. More thinking is needed in the country regarding extension's role in training women in agriculture so as to assist in HRD with particular reference to rural women in the field of agriculture.

Extension Strategies in Educating Rural People to Acquaint them with the Various Kinds of Services Available from Different Agencies

Extension Education alone is not going to deliver goods with the rural people when adoption of new scientific practices by farmers is expected. Rural development of which extension education is an important component also requires the other supporting services for rural people like supplies, services, credit, inputs, market facilities and other agri-support activities. There are various agencies and organizations specially set up to provide these services. However, it is the village extension worker who is required to educate people about the various kinds of services available from these agencies.

10.4 ROLE OF EXTENSION SUPERVISORS IN THE TRAINING OF EXTENSION PERSONNEL

Training is an important function of supervisors. Out of seven functions suggested for supervisors, training is one of them. These functions of supervisors can be stated as:

(i) Training function
(ii) Function of programme development and execution
(iii) Counselling function
(iv) Personnel management function
(v) Maintenance of an effective two-way communication system
(vi) Development and maintenance of adequate budgets and facilities
(vii) Development and maintenance of good relations.

Job of Supervisors relating to training functions: It is the supervisor's job to arrange the needed training to his subordinates. This does not mean that the supervisor alone should train the workers. Specialists have to be involved in these training programmes.

Supervisors should recognize that training is a continuous process, which begins at the time of implementation and continues throughout the workers' career. Through out the individual workers' career it is the supervisors' responsibility to continually apprise the training needs of the workers and to make arrangements for the training necessary to maximize the effectiveness of performance of individual workers. This training may be in technical subject matter, extension policies, administrative procedures or extension methods.

Some Guidelines for Organizing Effective Training of Extension Workers :

1. In-service training of extension workers in order to be effective must be wide spread and imparted near the work spot. It is in this light that the supervisors have got important responsibility regarding training workers.
2. Training to become effective must be given at the appropriate time. If extension workers have to be trained

for the work to be carried out during the next season, training must be over before one month of start of the season, so that extension workers will be able to use the benefit of the training in implementing their programme and to develop suitable methods and strategies based upon the training.

3. Training has to be given in continuous, phased manner in order to make it simple for implementation. Recently recommended Benor model tries to focus attention on this aspect of training. Benor actually is recommending training of extension workers every two weeks and only on those items which they are required to implement in the next two weeks.
4. The precise nature of the training needs of individual workers can be determined through the use of annual performance of evaluation and long-term professional improvement plan. The professional improvement plan provides the means for the workers with the assistance of the supervisors to set a long-term professional goals through planning step by step professional improvements. Many individual workers and their supervisors are not availing themselves of this opportunity usually pleading that they do not have time.
5. The annual inspection or evaluation of field workers should provide means for planning training programmes for individuals. Some suggestions for annual evaluation which should help in developing training programme would include:
   (a) A standardized evaluation sheet should be prepared.
   (b) Evaluation should be done in terms of programme and worker performance. The annual evaluation should not only be designed to rate the worker as a person.
   (c) Evaluation is successful only when those being evaluated are willing to participate in setting up an evaluation programme and in using its findings as a check on their work.
   (d) Results of the evaluation should be discussed with each worker individually and plans made to bring about improvement.

Ways of Identifying Individual Worker's Needs for Training

(a) Through use of personnel appraisal form:
   (i) For self-analysis by the worker
   (ii) By the worker and supervisors in a counselling situation.

(b) Through use of the following available materials
   (i) Plan of work
   (ii) The reports of field workers
   (iii) State staff reports
   (iv) Letters, circulars, teaching outlines and other written materials prepared by workers;

(c) Through observation of the worker's performance on the job by supervisors, specialists and other state staff members;

(d) Through an analysis of the programme made jointly by workers and supervisors;

(e) Through programme emphasis evolving from State and National levels;

(f) Through group discussions by workers and staff members to pin point specific training needs;

(g) Through the use of some form for maintaining a continuing record of such items as;
   (i) Training needs and progress to be made towards improvement in performance;
   (ii) In-service training in which the worker has participated;

(h) By an attitude survey of personnel;

(i) Through an examination of general socio-economic and technological trends in projecting future training needs;

(j) Through the use of Anecdotal records.

Some Requirements for Good Training Programmes for Workers

1. The supervisors demonstrate the importance attached to workers training through policies, budget and staffing.
2. Workers as well as supervisors and specialists are involved in determining training needs and plans for meeting them.

3. Supervisors provide opportunities for workers to apply the teaching under actual conditions and through problem approach.
4. Training is based on job requirements and clearly defined job descriptions.
5. Training is based on a clear understanding of the policies, procedures outlined by the administration.
6. Supervisors relate training to programme needs.
7. Training is planned systematically.
8. Training programme combines group training with an individual on-the-job approach.

10.5 THE ORGANIZATION FOR EXTENSION TRAINING

1. All State level extension personnel have a training function and should be involved:
   (a) To assist in determining needs for training.
   (b) To assist in developing a training programme for extension workers.
2. Training is a line responsibility. Supervisor should be responsible for training because:
   (a) He should know the worker best – motives, attitude, work habits, problems.
   (b) He is the person who hires and fires the worker.
   (c) He should not be able to "pass the buck" to the training officer.
   (d) He must be in sympathy with training if a good employee attitude towards training is to be maintained.
3. The Training Officer (or Personnel Officer) should serve a staff function. His duties might include work with supervisors and specialists to:
   (a) Plan training programme.
   (b) Assemble or prepare materials to be used in training.
   (c) Evaluate results.
   (d) Adapt training programme to needs of youth, home economics, and agriculture phases of the programme, but the responsibility for the training traces back to supervision. How well the worker does, and how well he knows his job is up to supervisor.

4. The functions of the Training Officer, specialists and supervisors should be clearly defined in written job descriptions.

Carrying Out Training Functions

1. A job description is the basis for determining training needs. Just writing out a job description is not enough to be sure that the person whose job is covered by that job description knows and comprehends what the statement say, nor that they understand how to go about applying these talents in carrying out the job.
2. The people performing the job must be involved in deciding the specific functions of the job and the training needed.
   (a) They should help in writing the job description.
   (b) They should be given an opportunity to express their feelings about training needs.
   (c) A statewide committee to advice on training is suggested.
      (i) Across the board representation to decide upon overall training needs youth, agriculture, home economics, special field workers, specialists, resident staff, and experiment station personnel.
      (ii) Additional sub-committees might deal with specific training needs in special interest fields.
      (iii) Training should be planned in advance.
3. Annual plans for the training programme should be made, based on:
   (a) The needs for training expressed by field workers, supervisors, and specialists through their representatives on the committee.
   (b) An analysis of the changes in job requirements. (*Example*: New methods in farm and home development, TV techniques)
4. In thinking of training needs of workers, attention should be given to:
   (a) Those who are new workers.
   (b) Those being considered for promotions – a worker doing one job well might very profitably use training for the increased responsibilities of another job.

(c) Those who are transferring from field to specialist status or supervisory positions.
(d) Those experienced agents needing subject matter refresher courses.
(e) Those whose programmes are undergoing major shifts.
(f) Those whose work fails to meet acceptable standards.

5. Major phases of in-service training are concerned with:
   (a) Orientation of entry training, including :
      (i) Employment conditions – what the job is – probably best done on job by supervisors.
      (ii) Philosophy, objectives, and programme of extension and the methods of work – probably best done in group conferences.
   (b) There is a need to re-examine the role of extension specialists and to give training to help them fulfil their teaching role.
   (c) There is a need for more specific training for supervisors. Supervisory training should include training in:
      (i) Functions of supervisors
      (ii) Human relations
      (iii) Principles of leadership
      (iv) Group methods
      (v) Communication skills
6. Results of training should be evaluated. This is not easy to do in extension as results, particularly in supervisory training, may be long and in showing up. Individual performance review should be the method used to evaluate training and determine future needs.
7. Training costs and time must be kept reasonable. The final decision is one for the Extension Director.
   (a) Pressure for certain training may become excessive.
   (b) The extension director will determine how much and what kind of training for effectively carrying out the extension programme will be given during the year.
8. Methods used in training should be purposeful.
   (a) Use as many varied techniques as possible, planned in advance, to meet the indicated needs.

(b) Use the best resources available. The good resources right at hand is often overlooked. Examples:
   (i) Other subject matter departments in University,
   (ii) General extension,
   (iii) Resource persons from other Development Departments.

REFERENCES

Anonymous (1956), The organization to do Extension Training and How it functions. An excerpt from the report of the Personnel Management Group at the *Fifth National Administrative Workshop,* University of Wisconsin, Madison, USA.

Anonymous (1958), A recommended In-service training programme for the co-operative extension service. The Task Force on Co-operative Extension Service Training, Federal Extension Service, USDA, USA.

Nadler, L. (1984) Handbook of *Human Resource Development.* John S. Wiley and Sons, New Delhi.

Rogers, F.E. and Olmsted, A.G. (1957), In-service Training of Extension Workers. *Supervision in the co-operative extension service.* National Agricultural Extension Centre for Advanced Study, University of Wisconsin, Madison, USA.

11

Implementing Public Programmes in Agriculture

11.1 CONCEPT OF IMPLEMENTING PUBLIC PROGRAMMES IN AGRICULTURE

At present the common method used in implementing public programmes in agriculture mostly depends on training the extension workers about the new technology and leaving them to implement the programme on their own. In this connection, the subject of implementing agricultural programmes comprises nine important activities which are part of that implementation process. This concept envisages the following activities. According to this concept, the concerned areas involved include (1) establishing operating objectives and targets, with some effort of setting standards, (2) formulating operating policies for an action organization, budgeting, accounting etc., (3) defining technical practices to be followed in the operating units and sub-units (4) determining and appraising the systems needed to do the job (5) coordinating internally with various sub-systems and externally with and to other systems, (6) directing the work of subordinates; reporting to superior, (7) monitoring and appraising performance (8) modifying and adjusting internal systems; and (9) Organizing the facilities and equipment needed to do the job.

11.2 APPROACH REQUIRED IN IMPLEMENTING AGRICULTURAL PROGRAMMES

In the approach to be used in implementing the programme with the help of above mentioned activities should be a cyclical one and not linear approach generally followed in most of the areas. In linear approach, the methods followed from year to year will be the same. It will not be taken into consideration the experience obtained in the previous year. In the cyclical approach, all activities carried out in the previous year are reviewed before the new programme for the next year is finalized. It will take into account the shortcomings and the highlights of each kind of activity carried out and based on that next year's programme is redesigned. The advantages of the cyclical model can be further stated as follows:

1. Continuous monitoring and evaluation of the acceptance of the innovations by the project beneficiaries and analyzing this in combination with current policy, technical knowledge and resource availability.
2. Activating the implementing agency as recently attempted in the new Agricultural Extension Project of the Karnataka State Department of Agriculture.
3. The initial need appraisal and analysis of policy, technical knowledge and resource availability be documented for purpose of continuous comparison with new data.
4. The initial work plan is thought of as a projection of goals, which can be used for comparison purposes, rather than a fixed operational sequence of specified activities.
5. The work plan should provide a provision for continuous monitoring of both the acceptance of change by the project beneficiaries and the performance of the implementing agency.
6. The work plan should include distinct periodic reviews of acceptance of change by the project beneficiaries; analysis of current policies, technical knowledge and resource availability; modifying the plan and making new projections and development of a strategy for implementing the revised plan.
7. There must be the commitment by the people who plan and implement the programme to be receptive to the needs and desires of the project beneficiaries and of the people at various levels in the implementing agency.

11.3 MANAGEMENT APPROACHES TO OPERATING PROBLEMS FOR IMPLEMENTING PUBLIC PROGRAMMES IN AGRICULTURE

Organizations concerned will face several operational problems in implementing public programmes in agriculture. These problems have to be tackled by following suitable approaches in management. A list of 84 operating problems has been identified for extension administrators in programme implementation. These problems along with approaches recommended have been tabulated. The implementing agencies will be benefited by going through this list, which is given in Annexure I.

11.4 ORGANIZATIONAL CONSTRAINTS FOR IMPLEMENTING AGRICULTURAL PROGRAMMES

In the task of implementing public programmes in agriculture there are generally few details given beyond the general explanation of the Government unit, which is responsible for implementing the project. This is rather important because some of the important problems in implementing development project revolve around organizational constraints rather than technology, resource availability or even getting developed messages to be communicated to the intended beneficiaries. The project managers based on their major drawbacks in implementing the programmes revolve around getting the various organizational units to provide support to the project. Similarly some other project managers often complain about not getting adequate quasi-level support for their programmes and cooperation from some other departments and also lack of capability of their field staff. Further, there are complaints about duplication of efforts being made by different departments and their unwillingness to cooperate and the absence of technical inputs from various agencies such as Universities. While doing the social system analysis of agricultural project it was discovered that the primary blockage to the success of a soil testing laboratory project was the store keeper's unwillingness to provide sufficient amount of chemicals and test tubes. In almost any agricultural project there are many organizational units which in one way or the other can block the progress of project implementation.

In order to overcome such organizational constraints four kinds of activities must be carried out.

1. Identify all the organizational units, which have important roles to play in the project implementation.
2. Analyze each organization's role in terms of how it might help or block the implementation of the project.
3. Study the linkages between all of the units and find out their present location on the relationship continuum in implementing the project.
4. Think of the problems that may come about in the process of linkage development among all of the sub units during implementation of the project. Study these possible problems to determine if they are structural (should the organizational structure be charged; political (can anything be done about this?); technical (Is the right type of technology being recommended from the proper source?); Communication method (Is there need for more formal and informal communication channels?); compatibility of the staff (Is there a need for staff training and orientation to remedy the problems?) etc.

The following information gives example of a social system analysis of the agricultural project to be implemented giving an idea at least of some of the organizational units. In many cases even one of these organizational units can block the progress of the project. Most of the units involved can be classified in one of the six following categories:

1. **Primary Implementation Unit**: This includes the project head and his staff. It is unit's present capabilities, resources, role etc.
2. **Policy Level Support**: Most developed projects will not succeed without a firm commitment by policy level administrators within the ministry. In some cases, there may be a need for general public support to the project which in turn encourages political and administrative support.
3. **Administrative Support**: The Public Service Commission had a key role in recruiting the staff for the project implementation. Similarly cooperation from

treasury and other ministries are required. Within the implementing ministry important support units include (a) Providing supplies, (b) Transportation services, (c) Technical services etc. Special attention should be given to get cooperation from these administrative support units for success of the project.

4. **Technology Support**: There must be a continuing flow of technical subject matter being fed to the project. To achieve this close linkages are necessary to establish with other agencies such as Universities.
5. **Intermediaries**: The implementing unit generally is not direct contact with the intended beneficiaries. Generally sufficient attention is not given to intermediary personnel infrastructure in the planning and implementing development projects. In many cases, the field staffs are not adequately motivated nor are they capable of performing services required. These graphs require being motivated and provided professional inservice training, and be given practical teaching aids to carry out the job properly. It is also necessary to coordinate effectively with other channels of communication such as mass media, school systems, voluntary TVGO activities and private sector. Each of these graphs must be thought of as a target audience in their own sense.
6. **Intended Beneficiaries:** Many times adequate attention is not given to the intended beneficiaries. In most cases, very little information is given in terms of location, current practices, size attitudes etc. However, in order to bring about change in practices by the intended beneficiaries, considerable amount of benchmark information should be collected before planning and implementing the project. An important point to be considered is to find out whether the intended beneficiaries are capable or willing to make the changes being recommended by the project.

Potential Problems

Problems concerning organizational constraints in implementing agricultural projects generally revolve around (1) coordination;

(2) communication; and (3) commitment. Some detailed information about these are as under:

1. Lack of communication between the Units: The problem can be a lack of communication or too much communication causing information overload.
2. There are 3 types of communication with other organization – downward, horizontal and upward. In almost organizations, the primary flow of functional communication is downward. The other two flows are not generally functional effective remedies have to be found out for these deficiencies.
3. Many information flows from within the organization require two-step flow or multi-step flow. The further away the primary implementing unit is from the cooperating unit, the more deficient it is to control. One example is motivating the village level workers to carryout the programmes which involve workers through several intermediaries and completing with number of other implementing units requesting the same workers to also carryout their programmes.
4. Many times Government implementing units tend to be closed systems looking inward for new ideas and all the supporting services required. It is especially true in Government Organizations. They wrongly believe that "it's much easier to do it ourselves rather than rely on other units which have not been too cooperative with us in the past. This belief has several basic flaws (i) It is impossible for any one Government unit to provide all other services required in implementing the project. (ii) The success of the programme is generally hampered by lack of new ideas coming from outside. (iii) The unit will gradually lose the broad base of the support for the programme. (iv) It is impossible to reach the intended beneficiaries without utilizing outside groups in implementing the development projects.

11.5 CO-ORDINATION METHODOLOGY FOR IMPLEMENTING AGRICULTURAL PROGRAMMES

The term co-ordination has been used rather loosely in project management, when people call for co-ordination, they usually mean that they need support which they cannot command.

According to Newman (1963) co-ordination involves the synchronizing or dove tailing of interdependent activities and demands harmonized programmes and policies.

In administration, co-ordination is of two types viz. (1) Intra-institutional, and (2) Inter-institutional. In project management, it is the Inter-Institutional Co-ordination which assumes importance.

Factors of Inter-Institutional Co-ordination

There is no systematic reference in the administration literature regarding factors of Inter-Institutional Co-ordination with special reference to implementation of agricultural projects at the operational level.

A Ph.D. study by Sawant (1978) has delineated these factors which are :

1. Each institution to have a clear programme with objectives which need co-ordination from other institutions.
2. To have knowledge and complete understanding of working of each other's institutions.
3. To develop a strategy/plan of work including work procedure, responsibilities of each institution etc. i.e. pattern of relationship.
4. Delegation of appropriate authority to the technical personnel to facilitate joint decision making at the operation level.
5. To recognize co-ordinated action as official by all participating institutions.
6. Formation of a co-ordination committee of participating institutions with adequate authority.
7. To prepare a plan for co-ordination committees according to plan.
8. To conduct meetings of co-ordination committees according to plan.
9. To have a common orientation training programme for workers of different institutions.
10. To make arrangements for adequate and timely supply of funds and input requirements.

11. Physical proximity of participating institutions.
12. To develop an agreed programme of reporting and interpretation to give all institutions their due credit for the progress and accomplishment of the co-ordinated endeavour.

A Scale to Measure Inter-Institutional Co-ordination

Based on the above factors, an objective scale to measure Inter-Institution has been developed by Sawant (1978) which is enclosed.

Evaluation of a Co-ordinated Programme Using this Scale

The Block Demonstration programme conducted by the Department of Agriculture in collaboration with other agencies was evaluated using this Inter-Institutional Co-ordination scale and the results are summarized below:

1. Classification of Block Demonstrations according to nature of Inter-Institutional Co-ordination

Nature of Co-ordination	*Percentage of Block Demonstration*
1. High	36.59
2. Medium	36.59
3. Low	26.82

2. Inter-Institutional Co-ordination and involvement of small farmers

	Co-ordination		
	High	*Medium*	*Low*
	(Percentage of Block Demonstrations)		
High involvement of Small farmers	66.67	46.67	18.18
Low involvement of Small farmers	33.33	53.33	81.82

3. Inter-Institutional Co-ordination and number of farmers financed in Block Demonstrations.

	Co-ordination		
	High	*Medium*	*Low*
	(Percentage of Block Demonstrations)		
Above 50% farmers financed	86.67	40.00	—
Less than 50% farmers financed	13.33	46.67	36.36
No farmers financed	—	13.33	53.64

4. Classification of activities under the co-ordination scale

I—Highly Satisfactory

(a) Furnishing subject-matter information in advance.
(b) Preparing list of input requirements in advance.
(c) Ensuring full and mutual understanding of objectives of each organizations work.
(d) Ensuring that materials (inputs) are received at the village level in advance.
(e) Estimate total credit requirements in advance.

II—Satisfactory

(a) Training leaders in time,
(b) Conducting periodic visits to remind the people about technical information.

III—Fair

(a) Taking steps to ensure co-ordinated action as official.
(b) Seeing that materials (inputs) are supplied to farmers in time.
(c) Ensuring that credit is made available at the village level in advance.
(d) Training workers of agencies in advance.
(e) Have clearly written objectives and programmes.
(f) Naming representatives of each agency at the operational level.
(g) Forming local committees with local leaders.
(h) Providing adequate authority to facilitate joint decision making.

IV—Poor

(a) Developing clear plan for linkage with reference to co-ordination.
(b) Constituting co-ordination committee.
(c) Planning schedule of co-ordination committees meetings.
(d) Conducting co-ordination committees meetings according to schedule.
(e) Ensuring attendance of agencies' representatives in meetings.
(f) Developing agreed programme of reporting to give all institutions their due credit.

Inter-Institutional Co-ordination Scale
(Developed by the University of Agricultural Sciences, Bangalore)

Sl. No.	*Scale item and sub-items*	*Maximum scores*	*Weightage*
1.	**To have clearly written statement of objectives and programme which need co-ordinated work** (a) Objectives and programme of all agencies written in a clear form (b) Objectives and programme of some agencies written in a clear form (c) Objectives and programme of none of the agencies written in a clear form.	2	4
2.	**To train workers of different agencies well before start of the season** (a) Staff of all agencies trained (b) Staff of some agencies trained (c) Staff of none of the agencies trained.	2	4
3.	**To ensure full and mutual understanding of the objectives of each organization's work in respect of the programme to be co-ordinated** (a) Staff of all agencies had such understanding (b) Staff of some agencies had such understanding (c) Staff of none of the agencies had such understanding	2	4
4.	**To develop a clear plan for inter-institutional linkage (pattern of relationship) with reference to co-ordinated programme** (a) A clear plan for inter-institutional linkage was drawn	2	3

(*Contd.*)

Sl. No.	Scale item and sub-items	Maximum scores	Weightage
	(b) Some plan for inter-institutional linkage was drawn (c) No plan for inter-institutional linkage was drawn.		
5.	**To ensure that materials (inputs) are received at the village level in advance** (a) Materials received at the village level in advance (b) Materials received at the village level at the nick of time (c) Materials were not received at the village level.	2	3
6.	**To ensure that credit is made available at the village level through some agency in advance** (a) Credit was made available to more than 50 per cent farmers. (b) Credit was made available for 25 to 50 per cent farmers. (c) Credit was made available to less than 25 per cent farmers.	2	3
7.	**To name the representatives of each agency at the operational level, who will co-ordinate the activities** (a) All agencies had named their representatives. (b) Some agencies had named their representatives (c) None of the agencies had named their representatives.	2	3
8.	**To provide adequate authority to facilitate joint decision making at operational level** (a) All agencies had provided adequate authority. (b) Some agencies had provided adequate agencies. (c) None of the agencies had provided adequate authority.	2	3
9.	**To constitute co-ordination committee with representatives of all participating agencies** (a) Committee constituted with representatives of all participating agencies. (b) Committee constituted with representatives of some of the participating agencies. (c) Committee was not constituted.	2	3
10.	**To see that materials are supplied to farmers in advance** (a) Materials supplied to more than 50 per cent farmers. (b) Materials supplied from 25 to 50 per cent farmers. (c) Materials supplied to less than 25 per cent farmers.	2	3
11.	**To estimate total credit requirement in advance (2-3 months)** (a) Estimation was made in advance (b) Estimation was made at the nick of time (c) Estimation was not made.	2	3
12.	**To prepare list of inputs requirement in advance (2-3 months)** (a) List of inputs was prepared in advance.	2	2

(*Contd.*)

Sl. No.	*Scale item and sub-items*	*Maximum scores*	*Weightage*
	(b) List of inputs was prepared at the nick of the time. (c) List of inputs was not prepared.		
13.	**To develop agreed programme of reporting to give all institutions their due credit for the progress and accomplishment of the co-ordinated work** (a) An agreed programme of reporting for the Agricultural programme was developed. (b) Some agreed programme of reporting for the Agricultural Programme was developed. (c) No agreed programme of reporting for the Agricultural Programme was developed.	2	2
14.	**To conduct co-ordination committee meeting according to the planned schedule to review the up-to-date progress** (a) Above 75 per cent of the meetings conducted according to the schedule (b) 25 to 75 per cent of the meetings conducted according to the schedule (c) Less than 25 per cent of the meetings conducted according to the planned schedule.	2	2
15.	**To train leaders in time** (a) Leaders were trained in time (b) Leaders were trained at the nick of the time (c) Leaders were not trained.	2	2
16.	**To conduct periodic visits to remind people about technical information which should be used in phases** (a) Necessary periodic visits made by staff of participating agencies (b) Some periodic visits made by staff of participating agencies (c) Staff of none of the agencies made periodic visits.	2	2
17.	**To take steps to ensure co-ordinated action as official by all concerned agencies** (a) All agencies had issued instructions (b) Some agencies had issued instructions (c) None of the agencies had issued instructions.	2	2
18.	**To form local committees, with local leaders, with specific responsibilities, related to the programme** (a) More than one committee was formed locally (b) One committee was formed locally (c) No committee was formed locally.	2	2
19.	**To furnish subject matter information to the people in advance, atleast 2 to 3 months** (a) Subject matter information was given in advance (b) Subject matter information was given at the nick of the time (c) Subject matter information was not given.	2	2

(*Contd.*)

Sl. No.	*Scale item and sub-items*	*Maximum scores*	*Weightage*
20.	**To ensure that representatives of all agencies regularly attend the co-ordination meetings** (a) Representatives of all agencies attended most of the meetings (b) Representatives of some agencies attended some of the meetings (c) Representatives of all agencies did not attend any meeting.	2	2
21.	**To develop a plan of schedule of co-ordination committee meetings** (a) Schedule of meetings was worked out throughout the period (b) Schedule of meetings was worked out for part of the period (c) No schedule was worked out.	2	2

11.6 EFFECTIVE COMMUNICATION FOR IMPLEMENTING AGRICULTURAL PROGRAMMES

Development Communication is described as the art and science of human communication applied to the speedy transformation of a country and the mass of its people from poverty to a dynamic state of economic growth that makes possible greater social equality and the large fulfilment of the human potential. Thus, development communication indicates its orientation to goals and not only to means as generally implicit in the terms mass communication or inter-personal communication or the newly developing tele communication. Governments and international agencies have invested large sums of money in creating communication resources to facilitate the transfer of technology. With the communication and information explosion that is now taking place in the country, these investments are likely to be further strengthened.

There have been primarily two generations of communication technical assistance programme. The first one concentrates primarily on supplying equipment and building physical facilities for individual communication channels such as Radio Station, T.V. networks, News Papers, Audio-visual production centres etc. These are bound to get further strengthened and modernized with the communication revolution that is now taking place in the country. For example, in recent years, we have seen large number of Television stations being set up in the country, including many private satellite communication channels. Presently, the second generation of communication technical assistance programmes have sought to train professional communicators and improve the information delivery capacity of these communication channels.

Experience through the world especially in the Third World countries has, however, shown that these investments in communications have had only limited impact on development programmes, due to two reasons:

(i) Development workers have not utilized communication resources properly in the planning and implementation of their development programmes. As a result, most of the communication efforts in the development field tend to focus on public relations aspect of the programme rather than being an integral element of the transfer of technology. Similarly there has been practically very little co-ordination of the information flowing through the various channels of communication. For example, it is very common to have a farm radio broadcast giving recommendations even before the agricultural extension workers in the villages are aware of them.

(ii) Communication workers do not understand the development process and therefore, the information flowing through the various channels is not suitable to support development programmes. Handling and educational development message is much different than news, public relations, advertising and entertainment in which most channels of communication specialize. The manager of the communication resources not be private to support a country's development process and their staff be trained to handle development messages correctly.

Third Generation Communication Assistance Needed

There is, therefore, an urgent need of a new third generation communication technical assistance, one which concentrates on assisting governments, build a linkage between development programmes and communications resources. The activities required to be carried out as a part of the third generation communications technical assistance are enumerated below:

Communication should be used as an integral part of the development process. For example, if a new information is communicated through a radio broadcast in a particular week, it should also be communicated during the same week through other mass media like TV, Newspapers and Posters. Without losing time, workers in the rural areas must take up this same message communicated through these media and use inter-personal methods for further communication of these messages especially to key communicators of local areas. Wherever needed, demonstration methods to convince key communicators about the advantages of these messages transmitted should also be organized before the key communicators forget these new messages. When this is done, the key communicators themselves start communicating these ideas to other local people and also start adopting these techniques. Thus the two-step flow of communication gets in to action. This would also ensure the systematic utilization of all appropriate communication methods starting at the earliest stages of development planning and continuing throughout the programme implementation. Recently a beginning in this direction has been made in the country by organizing state-level seminars in collaboration with the UNICEF to promote health practices for mothers and children. Every development agency should start taking action on these lines and establish a close linkage between communications resources and development activities.

This linkage system should also take into consideration, the three basic information flows involved in the development process:

1. From Beneficiaries to Planners

Information on the needs of beneficiaries, their attitudes, current practices and many other characteristics should be one of the inputs for designing relevant development programmes. A continuous monitoring of "feedback" of the reaction of the beneficiaries to the programme is also important. Communication methods to be used for this information flow include pre-project social survey research, certain types of field reporting and management information systems, some media such as Video-tape and photographs to document field conditions etc.

2. Within the Implementation Organizational Framework

There is a need for good communication and co-ordination between many agencies that must be involved. These include subject matter researchers, administrative support units, field level workers, non-governmental cooperating agencies, administrators and political leaders, training institutions etc. There is a constant need for a flow of relevant information related to programme policies, technology, field conditions etc., within the organizational framework. Communication methods for this information flow include many administrative communication techniques such as reports, newsletters, conference, management information systems, staff development training programmes, information clearing houses etc.

3. To the Intended Beneficiaries

Systematic information flow is needed to the intended beneficiaries, which should involve both motivational and educational. For the programme to be successful, the beneficiaries must understand, accept and be able to properly use the new technologies, which are recommended and communicated. Different communications methods are required to be used starting from mass media such as Radio, TV, Posters, Publications and all forms of non-formal education methods including personal contact methods and demonstration techniques.

11.7 PROJECT DEVELOPMENT INCLUDING THE CALENDAR OF OPERATIONS FOR A SPECIFIC AGRICULTURAL PROJECT

1. Project Development at Local Level – A Research Study

One of the cardinal principles of agricultural project development is that the planning must be done at the local level involving local leaders and organizations. In the re-organized set up of Agricultural Extension System, the local field worker must actively participate in the project development work with the assistance of village organizations and local leaders. Although it is generally known that this approach is seldom followed in agricultural project development, very few empirical studies are reported. A study by

Radhakrishna Setty (1973) as a part of his M.Sc. research work at the University as a part of his M.Sc. research work at the University of Agricultural Sciences, Bangalore has thrown some light on this aspect. A summary from this research is given below:

1. Where are Agricultural Extension Programmes Were Developed?

Programme	*Gramasevaks reporting*	
Where developed	*Number*	*Per cent*
At the Gramasevak circle level	—	—
At the Block or District level	55	100.00

2. How programmes developed elsewhere were made known to local people? Only 16 per cent of Gramasevaks had conducted village meetings to discuss and familiarize the programme with local people. In majority of cases, only individual discussions were held with few farmers.

How programme was informed	*Gramasevaks reporting*	
	Number	*Per cent*
1. Meetings conducted	9	16.36
2. Individual discussion	42	76.37
3. Nothing done	4	7.27

In order to ensure that the programmes are discussed with the farmers and local leaders, it is essential to conduct special programme committee meetings to inform the content of the programme well in advance of the season.

3. To what extent the programmes had taken care of the local problems. Two programmes; viz. (i) Demonstration programme, and (ii) Seed supply programme were studied on this aspect.
   (a) Coverage of demonstration programme: In only 3 per cent of the Gramasevaks' circles there were demonstration programmes for all the important crops. In majority of the circles, there were demonstration programmes for only 50 per cent of the important crops.

(b) Coverage of seed supply programme: There were no seed supply programme for all important crops even in one Gramasevak circle. Programme for seed supply for 50 per cent of important crops were taken up in 43 per cent of Gramasevak circles.

	How programme was informed	*Gramasevaks reporting*	
		Number	*Per cent*
1.	For all important crops	–	–
2.	For 50% of important crops	24	43.64
3.	For 25% of important crops	21	38.18
4.	For none of the important crops	10	18.18

To ensure sustainability in farming, it is necessary to see that every year seed supply programmes are developed for each village to ensure seed supply to all farmers who need the same. This will enable the village to become self-supporting.

2. Project Development Including Calendar of Operation for a Specific Agricultural Project

Suggested Procedure for Kharif Project

First Year

January February	1. Organize a project committee involving developmental staff, local leaders of local organizations, representatives of agencies dealing with input supply, finances, marketing, processing etc, depending upon the need of the project.
February March	2. Study the local situation to find out the needs regarding the project.
March	3. Have a meeting of the project committee and develop a long range programme statement. Consider the programme statement for the ensuing year and select priority programme objectives for emphasis.
April	4. Have a village meeting to explain the project objectives for the current year and enlist names of farmers who volunteer to participate in

demonstration/adoption programme for the current year.

5. Conduct benchmark survey of farmers who have come forward to participate in the demonstration/adoption programme.
6. Formulate sub-committees one for input supply and the other for credit supply and involve representatives of the concerned agencies and village leaders on these committees. These committees should keep in touch with the sources of input supply and administrators of credit supply organizations and ensure their participation for the agricultural project.
7. Conduct a pre-seasonal training programme for participating farmers.
8. The sub-committees should work out the requirements of inputs, credit etc., needed by participating farmers and provide management services particularly for small farmers and arrange for the supply of inputs and credit in time.
9. Continue activities by the input supply and credit supply committees to provide management services to ensure timely supply of inputs and credit.
10. Start fortnightly visits and method demonstration programmes for participating farmers. Use contact farmers as project leaders. Focus on technologies to be practiced in the next fortnight.
11. Repeat fortnightly training, visits and method demonstration programme.
12. Review the working of the sub-committees on input supply and credit supply to ensure timely supply of inputs and credit to farmers.

July

13. Repeat fortnightly trainings, visits and method demonstrations.
14. Review the seasonal factors if the project is on rainfed crops and find out the need for contingency plan. Take steps for input supply if needed.

August

15. Consider the possibility of implementing the contingency plan where needed.

16. Repeat fortnightly trainings, visits and method demonstrations.

September 17. Repeat fortnightly trainings, visits and method demonstrations.

18. With the help of the project committee, organize field days and field trips including sample harvest.

October 19. Repeat fortnightly trainings, visits and method demonstrations.

20. With the help of the project committee, organize field days and field trips including sample harvests.

November 21. Repeat fortnightly trainings, visits and method demonstrations.

22. With the help of the project committee organize field days and field trips including sample harvests.
23. Collect yield data from participating farmers and compare it with benchmark information. Prepare a brief report.
24. Call a meeting of the project committee and appraise the results. Evaluate the project.
25. Request farmers who have participated in the programme to return loans.

Second Year and Onwards

Repeat the 25 above steps with suitable modifications.

11.8 PLANNING EXTENSION PROGRAMMES AND GETTING THEM INTO ACTION

A. Why Have a Local Extension Programme?

1. Effective extension teaching is a result of design and planning.
2. The local extension staff and village leaders must have a picture of the total programme before they decide on priorities to be given for various activities included in the programme.
3. A prepared extension programme assists to develop useful extension activities.

4. Programme development gives confidence to local extension staff on getting people's participation.
5. Developed extension programme provides scope for all interests, a rallying point.
6. Extension programme provides extension supervisors an instrument for being helpful and for objective evaluation of the programme implementation.
7. A local extension programme helps to develop understanding by the local people which is necessary in supporting the extension work.

B. It is necessary to have a co-ordination and integration of various development organizations in implementing extension programmes

1. By co-ordination we mean the activities and objectives are compatible and consistent, not competitive or conflicting. By integration we refer to the process of unifying all aspects into a single programme.

It envisages: separate activities towards common objectives, combined activities towards separate objectives, separate activities towards multiple objectives, combined activities towards common objectives.

Integration includes relationships between separate agricultural projects, between any two as well as between all aspects of extension work to be taken up in the field of various agricultural sciences like agriculture, animal husbandry, horticulture, sericulture, co-operation and marketing, youth work etc.

C. General procedure for planning and executing a overall extension programme at the local level

A long range local extension programme is required for every local area at *taluk, hobli* or village. It is an activity in which all extension organizations working in that local area are involved. The following general steps should be considered to develop a long range local extension programme.

1. Get understanding, acceptance and commitment by all the field extension staff to develop an extension programme for the taluk, hobli or village.

2. The local extension staff with the assistance of their supervisors should analyze the situation in relation to development of a long range extension programme planning including the ongoing planning procedures, previous experiences, categories of local people involved in annual and long range programme planning, status of present programme developed in relation to needs and opportunities as seen by extension staff and influences of various local groups in this extension programme.
3. The field extension staff with advice of supervisors and existing advisory committees of local people prepare a specific plan for developing a long range field extension programme. These plans will include who will be involved, committees required, schedule of meetings to be held and a detailed plan for conducting meetings and developing report.
4. Select local people who will be required to participate. The number of people to be involved should represent all segments and interests of the *taluk, hobli* or village as the case may be. The actual number of persons can be decided by discussing with the representatives of local people including the basic institutes other local organizations and informal local leaders. The group finally selected should slowly represent all segments and interests in the *taluk, hobli* or village.
5. Various approaches can be used in developing the extension programme at the local level. The important point, however, is the idea and objective of the programme. The exact procedures can be tailored to the local conditions and extension workers desires personalities and capabilities. In developing a good local extension programme considerable factual information on local situations and opportunities is needed. All of these may not be available at the beginning of the process. Local facts can be collected as and when they are needed. However, there should be sufficient minimum factual data available to start with which is required to stimulate thought and provide a starting point for discussion.
6. Assist the planning group or groups through the

decision making or problem solving approach which are part of an effective programme planning procedure including Programme Development and Programme Implementation.

Thus, entire process should not be hurried through. It might be necessary to have series of meetings to be held over several months if needed.

7. The programme developed should result in a written statement which sets forth the details in simple and understandable terms. The developed extension programme should include the general idea of providing priority among the several goals. In establishing priorities the programme should be related to the size of the local extension staff to do the job.
8. Inform as many local people and local organizations as possible in the *taluk, hobli* or village about the programme, specific techniques for carrying out this, a copy of the programme printed in posters, local news papers where available, sending copies of programme to all the farm families of local areas and explaining the same at meetings organized by various institutions and or committees.
9. Develop annual plan of work as an instrument for implementing the long range programme into action. This plan of work should clearly indicate the specific objectives which are probably sub-objectives of those included in the long-range programme which the local extension staff expects to accomplish in a year's time even though the local advisory groups and committees may and perhaps should be consulted about the content of the plan of work. It is primarily the responsibility of the local extension staff. In this way it is slightly different from the long-range programme, which is the joint responsibility and understanding of the local extension staff and village leaders.
10. It is necessary to review and evaluate the programme regularly preferably at the end of the year and completely revise the long range programme periodically at the end of every five years to synchronize with the five year plan.

11.9 THE PROCEDURE TO BE FOLLOWED IN EFFECTING A BREAKTHROUGH FROM DEMONSTRATION STAGE TO ADOPTION STAGE IN THE DIFFUSION OF AGRICULTURAL INNOVATIONS

In extension education, it is an accepted principle that demonstration work should be developed stage by stage until a continuous growth of educational efforts result in adoption of improved practices by farmers in that area. To be specific, the demonstration work requires to be developed in three stages:

1. **Test or Trial Demonstration:** It is also possibly called district or farm trials. This is a part of applied research. The responsibility for conducting these farm trials rests with agricultural universities or other non-departmental research agencies usually coordinated by National Agricultural Research Organizations. The purpose of these farm trials, which are generally few in number, may be one or two per block, is to confirm research findings under various agro-climatic zones, which is wholly based on the findings of these trials as the research results are to be recommended to farmers of the concerned agro-climatic zones. These trials provide the necessary confidence to research workers who are testing their research results under field conditions. They should compare only two to three research recommendations including one alternative reflecting the present local practice. There is no need for replications. The number of trials conducted themselves become replications. The primary responsibility of conducting these farm trials should rest with the concerned research organizations with the support of field extension staff of the University as well as concerned Departments of the Government. Village Extension Workers with the help of Agricultural Officers and field extension staff of the Agricultural University should select the farmers on whose fields farm trials should be conducted.

   Since the farm trials are testing the results of research for the first time in the local area, it may be justified to meet the additional cost involved in conducting these trials by the State Government or the Universities or Zilla Panchayat organizations. It is better to provide some specific budget to the concerned Research Stations by these organizations for conducting these farm trials so as to avoid possible conflicts in co-odination.

2. **Early Demonstration:** It is also called as first line or frontline demonstration. This stage will commence only after the concerned research practice is recommended. These early demonstrations are required to provide the necessary confidence to local field extension workers and the local leaders about economic feasibility of the new practice. Concomitantly these demonstrations should also provide confidence to the farmers in whose fields these early demonstrations are to be conducted. Ten to twenty early demonstrations may be required per block and these demonstrations may have to be repeated for one to three years depending upon the type of technology and need. Particularly in dry farming areas, there is a need for conducting the early demonstrations even for a period of 5 years to test under varying conditions of rainfall.

Since farmers have to develop confidence in the results of early demonstrations, it is desirable that the farmers themselves should meet the additional cost involved in the new practices to be tested through early demonstrations. It has been established several years ago that farmers are not convinced in India or anywhere else with what they see on the Government Demonstration Farm operated with public money not intimately connected with the farmer and not on a self-sustaining basis but they are impressed by what they do themselves. This procedure will also fix the required responsibilities on the field extension staff of the Universities or the development departments to be more careful to carry out this demonstration work properly. There is no need to provide any budget for meeting the additional cost on conducting the demonstrations. The money thus saved may be earmarked for budget items required to popularize results of demonstrations to the neighbouring farmers of these villages.

People may argue that conducting early demonstrations may become easy and simple if the Government itself spends money on additional cost required in conducting these demonstrations. We have also the tradition of following this method all these years since independence. But it is not the right way as indicated by the experience of extension work in other countries like USA and Japan. Japan followed this method of farming demonstrations under what was known as Nogyokai system. This system failed because the Government tried to encourage farmers to try new practices by giving subsidies for the additional cost, which the farmers would have been able to finance themselves. What is required however in conducting early demonstrations at farmer's cost is to follow a systematic educational procedure to discuss and educate farmers on the advantage of the new practice to be demonstrated.

Educational Procedure Recommended for Conducting Early or First Stage Demonstrations at Farmer's Cost.

1. Publicizing the results of farm trials through the use of mass media like Posters, TV, Radio and Newspapers, Village meetings should also be conducted using photographs and charts to highlight the results of farm trials.
2. The economics of the newly recommended practice showing the advantage to farmers should be worked out using the partial budget technique and presented to the farmers attending the meetings.
3. The meetings organized to discuss the early demonstration programme should be held for $1\frac{1}{2}$ to 2 hours to provide adequate time for thorough discussion.
4. Appealing to conduct demonstrations at farmer's cost: At the end of each meeting an appeal should be made to the farmers to come forward and conduct the demonstrations at their own cost. Farmers may be requested to conduct the demonstration on a small scale to find out for themselves the advantage of the new practice.
5. Assisting farmers to conduct demonstrations properly: A simple leaflet in local language giving the details of

the practice to be demonstrated should be prepared and each volunteer farmer who is desirous of conducting the demonstration at his own cost should be supplied a copy. At each of the important stages of conducting demonstrations, field extension worker should visit the farmer's demonstration plot and provide technical guidance needed on the spot.

6. Conducting educational field days: Organized simple educational field days are required to be conducted at each of the demonstration plot during the cropping season, show to the demonstrator farmer and other farmers of the village/neighbouring villages the progress of the practice demonstrated. These field days are a must to show a visual evidence of the practice during its various growth stages to enable discussion by farmers about the advantage of the demonstration practice.
7. Harvesting the demonstration plot in presence of the demonstrator farmer and other farmers: The sample of plots both demonstrated and that of the existing practices shown as the check plot should be harvested in the presence of the demonstrator farmer and the other farmers. At the same time, sample plot yields should be recorded in the presence of farmers and farmers should be encouraged to work out the economics of the practice being demonstrated to stimulate their thinking regarding the net profit possible by following the demonstrated practice. A visual picture of the heaps of the harvested sample should also be obtained by using photographs and closed circuit TV where it would be possible to develop audio-visual material from local facts for subsequent use.
8. Developing teaching aids like charts, flash cards to summarize the results of the demonstration conducted at farmer's cost: This step is necessary to develop teaching aids from the local facts for further use in developing the third stage of the demonstration work, viz. late demonstrations or large scale demonstrations required to be organized in each of the villages by the field extension workers.

Late Demonstration or Large Scale Demonstration Stage: After developing the confidence on the part of demonstrator farmer and local field extension workers in the early or first stage demonstration phase, the next step in the programme of conducting demonstrations is to organize a systematic large scale demonstration work at farmers' own cost in all the villages which are to be covered under the programme. In this work, the same series of eight steps as mentioned under the first stage or early demonstration programme above should be repeated in each village by the field extension worker. The only difference will be to involve a demonstrator farmer/farmers to present their experiences in conducting the first stage or early demonstrations for explaining to other farmers in the village meetings and field days. Their photographs and the results of the performance of the demonstrations conducted by them at their own cost should be highlighted by developing suitable audio-visual materials like pamphlets, charts, graphs and video cassettes.

The taluk/block extension officers should themselves participate in few of the educational programmes to be conducted in the local area to provide field oriented action training to local extension workers to assist them in organizing the large scale demonstration programmes later in their villages.

If the above mentioned procedure is followed in conducting the three stages of demonstration work, there should not be much difficulty in effecting a break through from demonstration stage to large scale adoption stage of any recommended new technology in any area.

11.10 BLOCK DEMONSTRATION

The Block Demonstration is a recent innovation in Extension Strategy in implementing agricultural programmes. This was initiated for the first time during summer 1974 in Karnataka State of India. Block Demonstration is actually a mini-village adoption programme where both big and small farmers in contiguous areas are to be involved. The unique feature of this strategy consists of a special organizational mechanism built at the village level to integrate the efforts of various agencies responsible for the success of implementing agricultural programmes.

Organizations Involved

Each Block Demonstration has to be established with the integrated efforts of the (1) Technical agency, (2) Input supplying agencies, (3) Credit supplying agency, and (4) Village organizations.

Criteria for Selecting Villages

Only such villages are selected where one or two successful demonstrations are conducted in the previous year (s) and the superiority of the technology to be adopted in the Block Demonstration is already established.

Main Purpose of the Block-Demonstration

The main purpose of the Block-Demonstration is to promote village adoption of an improved technology by setting up a special organizational mechanism in the village to integrate the efforts of various agencies and to provide timely and continuous technical assistance, make available credit needed by farmers and arrange for the required supply of agricultural inputs like seeds, chemicals and fertilizers in time.

Modus Operandi

1. The work starts two months in advance of the crop season by holding a night meeting at the village. In this meeting farmers are motivated about the advantage of the new technology and are motivated to volunteer for participating in the adoption of the same. The representative of the credit agency also attends the meeting and assures all farmers in need of credit that it will be made available without any difficulty. The fertilizer and other input supplying agencies also promise in the meeting that these inputs will be made available at the village level.

2. A second village meeting is again held within 15-20 days of the first meeting. In this meeting, a list of village farmers who are interested to participate in the programme is prepared and the requirements of seed, fertilizer, credit, chemicals needed by each farmer is worked out and different committees are constituted taking advantage of the local leadership to take responsibility for making available the various kinds of inputs.
3. The representatives of the technical agencies involved like the Agricultural University, the State Department of Agriculture, and the credit and input agencies determine their individual responsibilities relating to soil testing, farmers' training, method demonstrations and technical supervision of field operations. For each village the village level worker, the Agricultural Extension Officer and/or the University Extension Worker and a representative of input agency constitute the team of representatives and they start visiting the village regularly at least once a week.
4. Soil testing is done in all fields of farmers who have volunteered and the fertilizer scheduled worked out. Technical information is made available to each participating farmer and the farm plan and calendar of operation are worked out for each farmer.

The farmers are educated on each aspect of new technology by some more night meetings and with the start of the season, method demonstrations are conducted to show important field operations. Each operation of every farmer is supervised in the field by the technical representatives or a trained local leader. Arrangements for delivery of inputs, on time, like seed, chemicals, fertilizers and credit are made at the village by the different committees.

The agricultural production was considerably increased in the Block-Demonstration areas.

Some of the results of Block demonstrations conducted in 1975 in Karnataka are given in the following Table.

Some Results of Block-Demonstrations in Karnataka (Summer 1975)

Village	*Crop*	*Number of Farmers*	*Area in Acres*	*Average yield/acre (kg.)*		*Percent increase over Benchmark*
				Benchmark year	*Year of Demonstration*	
1.	Paddy	45	43.13	2172	2897	33.3
2.	Paddy	87	110.00	1550	2830	82.0
3.	Paddy	49	57.11	1296	2015	56.0
4.	Paddy	50	92.20	2262	2549	12.7
5.	Paddy	52	85.00	2110	2660	26.0
6.	Paddy	58	61.00	1750	2790	59.0
7.	Paddy	30	51.20	692	1520	119.0
8.	Paddy	30	30.06	669	1126	73.5
9.	Paddy	31	33.21	1440	2400	66.0
10.	Hybrid Jowar	28	29.00	584	770	31.8

11.11 INTEGRATED FARMING SYSTEM DEMONSTRATION (WHOLE FARM DEMONSTRATION)

It is an innovative and unique approach to promote integrated land use and animal management technologies as well as resource management capabilities among the farmers, more particularly small and marginal farmers of rural populace. It is a micro approach and the entire farm of an individual farmer is considered as a unit. This approach calls for concerted educational efforts with farmers with primary focus on maximizing the net income of farmers over a period of time. This is closely related to realistic planning of farms of selected farmers in order to help to generate maximum family employment and to get sustained stable net income. Such planning and implementation require identification of potential for development, needs, interests and capabilities of farmers, availability of resources and also to train them in farm management techniques. The different enterprises not only compete for scarce resources such as land, labour and capital on the farm but also they exhibit inter-dependence due to supplementary or complementary relationship. This also helps in recycling of farm wastes and residues without polluting the environment and degrading the resource base. In short, the main purpose of this approach is to assist the farmers to develop their entire farm over a period of three years and to educate them to become real farm entrepreneurs.

The specific objectives of this approach are :

1. To encourage farmers to take up improvement of all the crops grown by them in different seasons by demonstrating new agricultural technologies.
2. To assist farmers in introducing other subsidiary enterprises, like dairy, poultry, fisheries, sericulture, piggery etc., to utilize all the available resources more efficiently.
3. To educate farmers to make them account conscious.
4. To help farmers improve their standard of living by working with them over a period of time.
5. To develop Integrated Farming System Units as centres of agricultural development in the local areas so that other farmers will be able to use them as sources of new agricultural information leading to rapid spread of farm innovations.

Important Steps

1. Collection of benchmark information on the existing cropping pattern and other enterprises, farm resources and potentialities and also the socio-economic condition of the family.
2. Preparation of appropriate and feasible complete farm plan based on the type of land, irrigation facilities and other such physical as well as financial resources at their command.
3. Farm plans includes introduction of new crop varieties/ hybrids, practices, methods, technologies along with related enterprises.
4. Farm plans guide tile demonstrators to follow dry farming practices for soil and water conservation.
5. Helping farmers to secure required financial assistance from financial institutions for purchase of inputs, animals, farm machinery and equipment, etc.
6. Working with farmers for a period of three or four years to achieve stable net income at regular periodic intervals.

7. Involvement of selected farmers in planning, implementation and evaluation of the programme.
8. Using IFSD as centres to educate other farmers through educational activities like field visits, field days and interaction sessions, etc.
9. Non-provision of subsidies to farmers for conducting of demonstrations.

Advantages

1. Consequent to adoption of Integrated Farming System approach, there would be a considerable increase in the net farm income in the demonstration farms due to adoption of technologies in various enterprises. By using both high and low cost technologies, the farmers would able to increase productivity and production of crops.
2. Farmers can use organic manures, crop residues, animal waste which help to improve son health and conservation of son moisture thereby reducing environmental pollution and would result in sustained agricultural production. Balanced combination of crop and livestock enterprises to take advantage of complementary and supplementary relationship between them help in providing more family employment opportunities.
3. Integrated Farming System demonstration farm serves as a centre for dissemination of new farm information to other farmers in the village and around.
4. The other advantages of Integrated Farming System demonstration are changes in food habits, health care, nutritional status, clothing, material possession (agricultural and non-agricultural), saving pattern and shift in borrowing from non-institutional to institution.

11.12 ACTION TRAINING REQUIRED IN IMPLEMENTING AGRICULTURAL PROGRAMMES

A. Concept

Action training is first and foremost a combination of the three very important elements of training, to wit; research, training and consultation. It is in a sense departure from conventional training approaches and methods in that it requires a longer, greater and more dynamic involvement of the training agency in the very process of development of the chosen target area. The programme is continuous in nature and thus it is also called an open-ended training programme.

The second feature of this programme is that it is based on a block-method. In its so-called "vertical approach" an area (an administration unit, or a department etc.) is identified as a target area/unit. Within this unit personnel from all levels and from all sections or divisions will be involved in the programme. This down-to-earth and Integrated approach to training through seems laborious, compares much more favourably with the conventional "critical mass" approach, which now seems too slow and ineffective.

The "horizontal approach" which is part and parcel of this programme, is the second stage of the activity. The target unit is functionally identified, that is more specific and specialized training is made available to persons performing common and related tasks. (E.S. training for staffs of the agriculture department).

B. Objectives

1. To train participants to view a problem in its totality. After the training it is expected that participants will be able to see their tasks as parts of a greater total system.
2. To emphasize that their roles are closely interdependent and therefore they must perform their functions in an orchestrated manner.
3. To emphasize the fact that to planning and project implementation, the people's problems, interests and needs must be given due consideration. The nation's progress and development must ultimately mean the progress and development of every one of its citizens.

C. Rationale

Action Training is designed to cater for the training needs of busy politicians, executives, department heads, local leaders as well as ordinary farmers and peasants. This class of people cannot be spared for more than two or three days at a stretch. Long courses and seminars are not suitable for them. Thus, action training, which is run on two or three days basis at any time, generally during weekends, can be expected to give them the maximum benefits in the shortest possible time.

In recognition of the fact that a true process of development partakes both the policy makers and the executives on the one hand and the local leaders and ordinary peasants on the other. Action training provides for the first time an equal training opportunity for all these groups. More important still, action training provides a real opportunity for these groups to indulge in meaningful dialogues in the various workshop sessions within which it is expected that a greater degree of understanding and even tolerance could be achieved. Only when people understand each other there can be effective communication. And only then can true and genuine effort at development begin.

D. Methodology

(a) Identification and selection of the target area/unit.
(b) Preliminary research with the intention of identifying key problems. Analysis of the problems and identifying alternative solutions to the problems. (Trainer's view of the problems and probable solutions).
(c) Fixing the dates of training and informing the participants. Number of participants not more than 40.
(d) Conducting the training programme in the form of workshop sessions. Participants are divided into three groups.
(e) The first and second days are devoted to workshop discussions of problems attended to resource persons. Workshops are not to make resolutions but mainly to discuss and analyze problems and to attempt at finding ways to solve those problems. Problems, which are beyond the scope of the participants to resolve, shall be noted for the attention of the authority concerned. It is the responsibility of the training agency to bring the matter up.
(f) The third and final day is scheduled for the plenary session. Workshop Chairman present their workshop proceedings – open to comments and criticism of the house.
(g) Following operations are the initiative of both the training agency and the participants. For the former, it is its

responsibility to bring up the problems, which were not previously solved at the workshop sessions (e.g. policy matters) to the notice of the various responsible authorities concerned. As for the latter, it is their responsibility to bring to the attention of the training agency any new problems that may arise from time to time. At this stage the training agency is performing a consultant role.

(h) Further research, training (at both the "vertical" level and the "horizontal" level) and consultation may be carried out as and when necessary. The ultimate objective is only arrived at when there is an improvement of the system and the fruits of progress and development reach the final target, i.e., the ordinary masses.

ANNEXURE I

Management Approaches to Operating Problems

Operating Problems	*Approaches*
1. Punctuality in attending offices.	1. The head office should be the first to come and the last to leave, so as to set example and not to check.
2. Understand the philosophy of teaching and research (project base and field oriented).	2. Periodic disciplinewise workshops and seminar; review of research accomplishment at quarterly intervals by the head of the institution. Interchange of ideas between the head and the middle and lower level staff.
3. Dissemination of research findings for the benefit of farmer through the extension agency.	3. Identify the items of value from the bulk of research findings; prepare extension literature for the use of extension agencies; arrange group meetings to explain the research findings.
4. Collaboration with the extension agencies in the state.	4. Arrange periodical meetings; discuss the progress and problems in agriculture in the state; review the research findings and accomplishments in extension works, formulate new programmes.
5. Insufficient fund	5. Try to get more fund.
6. Insufficient trained staff.	6. Recruit more trained staff.
7. Lack of training facilities—for both staff and small farmer.	7. Set up training centres for both staff and small farmers.
8. Lack of reliable applied research of more relevance to the small farmer situation.	8. Set up more local demonstrations or trial plots.
9. Lack of two-way communication between agencies and small farmers.	9. Organise the establishment of local small farmer organization.

(Contd.)

Operating Problems	*Approaches*
10. Ineffective implementation.	10. Existing district, state and national actions (development committees), through quite effective, require some forms of catalyst to realize and identify the course of grassroots level implementation.
11. Lack of coordination/ cooperation between the agencies, the implementers, the local politicians and the clientele.	11. Break the ice regarding rapport between those elements of grassroots level implementation i.e. through "open-ended action training". When all the three elements are made aware of national organization and clientele objectives.
12. Imposition of programmes.	12. Programmes should be chalked out in consultation with the agency concerned.
13. Lack of coordination among related agencies.	13. Question of coordination is likely to be lighter,with the frequent communication with the related agencies.
14. Paucity of resources.	14. Resources are likely to be expanded with the cooperation of government.
15. To ameliorate the core interlocking problems of the small holders – uneconomic holdings, low productivity and the marketing situation.	15. As provided by order, through the constitution of the corporation; the finances of the corporation; the repayment of loans to the corporation, the accounts to be kept by the corporation and the audit of the accounts.
16. To ensure the continuous source of income to the small holders during rubber crop gestation period through activities of planting short term cash crops.	16. Under the purview of the Minister responsible: through an administration by a Board and the rubber industry who are responsible in formulating policies and coordinating operations; providing grant and credit facilities replanting less of 4½ cents per pound of rubber exported to the country and

(*Contd.*)

Operating Problems	*Approaches*
	extra government replanting grants and income from investments, and undertaking projects in land development programmes, modernization, extension/advisory and marketing programmes.
17. To obtain "feedbacks" from the small holders on its implementation programmes through evaluation and socio-economic research activities.	17. To obtain and keep the necessary statistics relating to the small holder sector and collect such information to be available to the government.
18. Insufficient budger.	18. Keep asking with better justification facts.
19. Insufficient trained staff.	19. Improve specific training activities.
20. Insufficient guidelines from headquarters.	20. Prepare draft of proposed guidelines for headquarters approval.
21. Poor internal operating procedures.	21. Employ one or more systems or procedures specialized to work with key people in improving procedures set up a task force.
22. Too little advice from farmers.	22. Set up a farmer's advisory group; travel more around the country.
23. Too much review by the media.	23. Relax and "tell it like it is."
24. Not enough help from Politicians.	24. Relax and "tell it like it is."
25. Too much limitation on consultation with other agencies.	25. Seek approval from headquarters for broader consultation authority.
26. Coordination/cooperation among agencies.	26. Cooperate closely among department of Agriculture, University and Department of Agriculture Extension.
27. Transfer of technology to farmers.	27. Rural Community and farmers' associations be promoted; carry out demonstration plots keep both extension officers and leader farmers well informed.

(*Contd.*)

Operating Problems	*Approaches*
28. The bad debts from year to year become increase.	28. Obtain an evaluation in: bad debt, disbursement, marketing of the production supplies of fertilizer and using new technology.
29. The realization of credit never reach the target.	29. Report result to the head office and bring to the meeting in the province. Make a special training in procedure; the training for branch managers by the head office and for the employees by the regional office, and more control/supervision.
30. National office (headquarters) tends to request report on the progress of the project too often from local office.	30. Promulgate standard operating procedure on reporting system.
31. National programmes often formulated uniformly irrespective of provincial situations and conditions result in frequent change of the programmes.	31. It is encouraged to hold meetings and workshops as often as possible with provincial staff prior to make a decision of projected programme.
32. Local offices submit exaggerated and sometimes false progress report to the national office thus causing many problems.	32. Strengthen the inspection and evaluation system.
33. Reluctancy of full coordination among the concerned bureaus and divisions delays programme formulations and hurts effectiveness of the programme.	33. It would take time to cancel this bureaucratic behavior inherent to government officials in developing countries. Coordination is also largely affected by the personality of the heads and directors.
34. Lack of management skills and direction.	34. Intensive management service workshops for regional heads.
35. Lack of incentive – hence the implementing or working staff is not sufficiently motivated.	35. Regular performance audit conducted by separate agency; such audit has a built-in rating system and salary scale.

(*Contd.*)

Operating Problems	*Approaches*
36. Overlap of functions.	36. Multi-sectoral planning involving the client population or its representative, other agencies in the area, the private sector.
37. Not enough support or backing from higher management after the programme is launched.	37. An independent feedback and data-gathering system.
38. Middle level managers/ supervisors are not granted flexibility of decision and judgment.	38. Management audit by an independent agency.
39. Predetermined guidelines (handed down by the higher or highest government level) restrict or limit the spheres of action/decision of staff.	39. Management audit by an independent agency.
40. Staff is not knowledgeable enough.	40. Management audit by an independent agency.
41. Lack of information of national stock of fertilizer and insecticides.	41. Better coordination with central bureau of statistics and department of agriculture for the data of fertilizer and insecticides.
42. Lack of stock and distribution of fertilizer and insecticides in a planting period.	42. Programming national and regional stock for fertilizer and insecticides with other departments for better distribution, decide the sea and land transportation and communication, survey the supply and demand of fertilizer and insecticides in certain central production area; and decide to build fertilizer godowns in the central production area.
43. Price policy and implementation of income distribution activities.	43. Department of trade together with national logistic agency should fix the floor price of rice.

(*Contd.*)

Operating Problems	*Approaches*
44. Selection and approval of projects by higher bodies to suit the needs of national, regional and local areas.	44. Include experienced agricultural personnel on the highest planning committee. This is being done "gradually".
45. Approving projects without providing adequate funds to meet the expenses.	45. Provide adequate funds for all purposes regarding implementation of projects.
46. Staff – inadequate in number and experience; lack of dedication in some.	46. Implement projects only if enough experienced staff are available. Revise whole salary structure – incentives or disincentives; promotion to be on merit.
47. Official red-tape affecting speed of implementation.	47. Greater authority to and trust in heads of departments.
48. More organizations (government and semi-government) than necessary to do the same functions.	48. Instead of establishing new agencies (government and semi-government) to do certain functions because of numerous constraints (lack of staff, finance, etc.) it would be better to strengthen existing organizations by revitalizing, increasing staff, facilities, etc.
49. Greater decentralization and delegation of authority.	49. Decentralization is to be case in a number of organizations.
50. Evaluation of targets and goals from time-to-time.	50. Evaluation – the system is being streamlined. A unit for this task will be set up at the federal and state level.
51. Extension staff given too many tasks.	51. Extension staff – increase in staff with specialization. Considerable increase in subject matter specialists on state and federal levels is necessary. Orientate and train farmers in monitoring data (recording data) with respect to that of own farm holdings.
52. Coordination within and between organizations as well as among programmes or projects.	52. Development of team work for programme implementation and the integration of planning and implementation.

(*Contd.*)

Operating Problems	*Approaches*
53. Lack of well trained programme manager.	53. Training of programme/project implementer.
54. Communication problem.	54. Decentralization of programme/ project planning.
55. Delay in formulation and processing of projects for approval.	55. Streamlining of procedures for project formulation and processing.
56. Annual fund allocations not according to approved phasing of the projects, therefore short falls in physical achievements – late release of funds.	56. Allocate funds as far as possible, according to approved phasing or revise the project. Revise procedures for prompt release of funds.
57. Poor coordination of concerned departments.	57. Streamline coordination.
58. Inadequate trained staff.	58. Increase availability of trained staff.
59. Inadequate facilities for mobility of staff.	59. Provide adequate transportation facilities.
60. Land titles not in order to receive grants.	60. Grants are approved only after a thorough processing of applications to identify correct ownership. Growers are also allowed to participate after fulfilling all other requirements such as declaration form, indemnity forms and such other forms that are required. This process is slow and can only be made fast by close cooperation and coordination with the district land officer.
61. The small holder termed as the "hard core" depends solely from the income of the little piece of land they own. For this reason they have not participated in the "Replanting programmes".	61. Incentive given to them in the form of credit to plant short-term cash crops to supplement their income while waiting for the rubber trees to produce adequate income and sit years after planting.

(Contd.)

Operating Problems	*Approaches*
62. Lack of participation by small holders.	62. Many holdings give poor yield due to poor up keep. RISDA group replanting project has helped to improve this situation by giving them better supervision, correct technique and technical support.
63. Poor yield due to poor supply of planting materials in the early part of the programme.	63. Better planting materials are not available at decentralized nurseries and close by to their holdings.
64. Wrong use of fertilizer. Supply did not reach the trees.	64. This cause has been partly solved by eliminating the stockist and RISDA now supplies fertilizer direct to the small holder. More courses are now held at village level to educate the small holder the benefits of applying fertilizer to the plants.
65. Poor quality of rubber produced.	65. Formation of "Group Processing Centres" to enable RISDA staff to teach the techniques of producing good sheet rubber in order to fetch better price.
66. Poor marketing facilities.	66. The small holders were exploited by middlemen, RISDA set up "Rubber Buying Unit" to counter exploitation.
67. Extension makes difficult due to the scattered nature of the small holdings and poor infrastructure in the inland areas.	67. Formation of development centres and treating them as means for future development.
68. Lack of experienced extension staff and also in quality.	68. Most of the field staff were originally from the Rubber Industry Board who had little experience in extension except inspectorate job. Inservice training has been formulated and carried out.

(*Contd.*)

Operating Problems	*Approaches*
69. The village level workers (VLWs) who are under the administrative control of the Community Development Department are now required to carry out 100 per cent agricultural work. The technical staff of Agriculture Department find difficult in getting the work done by VLWs since the VLWs are also asked to do non-agricultural work by the Community Development Block.	69. VLWs are now borne under the establishment of the Agriculture Department and their appointments and transfers are being made by the Department of Agriculture.
70. The government target prescribes that all the village area to be covered by high yielding varieties of crops however, it is observed that most of the small farmers are not participating in the programme.	70. Special agencies like small farmers service cooperative societies are established to help in this regard.
71. Farmers in an area who are advised by the community development staff apply for a bank loan for starting a poultry. The bank manager refuses their request on a plea that there is no assured veterinary assistance in that area.	71. The banks advise the technical departments to concentrate their poultry work in few pockets where veterinary assistance is assured.
72. In a new inspection project area the Government has notified the area under inspection for Kharif season. At the end of season it is observed that only 30 per cent of the notified area is irrigated by farmers. The Government asks the explanation of the Agricultural Department for the slow progress. The	72. The government has set up coordination bodies at the village, taluk, district and the state levels to solve this problem.

(Contd.)

Operating Problems	*Approaches*
Agricultural Department reports that water was not made available to farmers in time and also that field channels were not available to take water from the main channel.	
73. In spite of several years of work on promotion of fertilizer use on dry land crops in dry-farming areas, farmers are still reluctant to use fertilizer. It is said that they are afraid of the drought year, which however may come only once in 4-5 years.	73. The government departments are continuously demonstrating the use of fertilizers to dry-land crops in selected farmers' fields.
74. Synchronizing and coordinating various agencies as needed by the programme.	74. Establishing systems of active consultation in formulating programme, monitoring of day-to-day progress, taking coordinated action to solve problems. A standing team consisting of representative of different departments and agencies has been put into action since 1970. The chairman of this team is the Secretary of the Directing Boards of Bimas who is responsible for day-to-day activities in implementing intensification programme.
75. Lack of extension staff qualitatively as well as quantitatively – now necessitates field extension agents need some time to gain competence.	75. Recruitment of about 6400 field extension agents and about 300 subject matter specialist since 1970. Improving extension methods being used and strengthened extension organization by giving more adequate facilities (transport, action, budget and equipment).

(Contd.)

Operating Problems	*Approaches*
76. Farmers' ability to act in group/organization, leadership and mechanism.	76. Develop farmers' group to adopt new technology and facilitate group actions in water management, plant protection, etc.
77. Infrastructure in rural areas, roads, irrigation, drainage, institution.	77. National, provincial and local budget are directed to the development of production infrastructure, such as irrigation, roads, terminals, etc. Stimulating cooperative development to perform service activities for the farmers – availability of inputs marketing of produce. Establishing village units of rural banks.
78. Specific technological recommendations for wide variety of local conditions.	78. Carrying out experiments and trials more extensively covering various local conditions.
79. Flow of feedback information.	79. Improving reporting systems to collect, store and process data by using computer.
80. Lack of commercial incentives for agricultural support agencies (inputs, distributors, bank/credit agencies, etc.).	80. Giving financial support (special credit) and price subsidy for inputs, but it seems as there is still lack of commercial incentives for the company involved.
81. Poor agricultural administrative system.	81. Training in administration that is training with the purpose of imparting knowledge, skills and capabilities in the various aspects of administration. All top managers, middle and lower managers have to be trained on general administration, management techniques and development administration.
82. Planning activities hampered by the lack of reliable data as well as by a limited number of technically competent intermediate staff.	82. Training in management tools and functions of the middle level managers in agricultural programmes.

(*Contd.*)

Operating Problems	*Approaches*
83. Uneven distribution of population. The pressure is particularly great in certain areas (e.g. Java).	83. Transmigration.
84. Coordination vertically and horizontally.	84. In order to reach the agricultural development objective the functions of coordination, integration and synchronization must be carried out. These functions could be applied through the pressure planning, implementing and evaluating of the project strengthening of the institution and consultative and coordination meetings.

REFERENCES

Anonymous, (1970), A Note on Whole Farm Demonstration Work. A Mimeo prepared by the University of Agricultural Sciences, Bangalore.

Anonymous, (1976), Definitions – A mimeo distributed to participants of International Workshop on implementing public programmes in agriculture. East-West Food Institute. Hawaii – U.S.A.

Anonymous, (1976), A summary prepared on Management approaches to operating problems of the workshop by the participants. East-West Food Institute. Hawaii – U.S.A.

Creec, L. Gleenwood (1959), A Report of the Proceedings of the Seminar in Extension Supervision for the Western Region. National Agricultural Centre for Advanced Study, University of Wisconsin, Madison, Wisconsin, U.S.A.

Ferguson, C.M. (1964), Reflections of an Extension Executive – "Who decided that"? The National Agricultural Extension Centre for Advanced Study, University of Wisconsin, Madison, Wisconsin (Chap V, pp.: 69-78)

Green Donald, (1976), A Systems Perspective of the Agricultural Programme Management Process. A mimeo, *op. cit.*

Gilbertson, H.W. and Gallup, G. (1957) Result Demonstration Manual for Extension Workers. Agriculture Handbook 123, Federal Extension Service, USDA, USA.

Hooja, B. (1979), Peoples' participation in Agricultural Development. Some comments in Ramesh K. Arora (Ed), *Peoples' Participation in Development Process*. The Home State Institute of Public Administration, Jaipur, India.

Schaefer, K.W. (1977), Approaches to the decision of Agricultural Projects 1932. International Development Institute, Indiana University, Bloomington, Indiana, USA.

Sawant, A.G. (1978) Development of a Scale for measuring Inter-Institutional Co-ordination in Agricultural Programmes with application. Unpub. Ph.D thesis in Agricultural Extension, University of Agricultural Sciences, Bangalore.

Woods, John L. (1976) "Organizational constraints in implementing developing projects." Working paper prepared on behalf of Development Support Communication Service UNDP/DSCS Bangkok – Thailand and distributed to participants of International-Workshop on implementing-public programmes in agriculture held at East-West Food Institute. Hawaii – U.S.A.

Woods, John L. (1976) Programme planning and work plans working paper distributed to participants of International – Workshop on implementing – public programmes in agriculture held at East-West Food Institute. Hawaii – U.S.A.

Woods John L. (1976), Utilizing Communication Support to Development. Working paper prepared for the Development Support Communication Services, UNDP, Bangkok, Thailand.

Index